Who Are We—And Should It Matter in the 21st Century?

Who Are We—
And Should It Matter
in the 21st Century?

GARY YOUNGE

NATION
BOOKS
New York

For Tara and Osceola with love

Copyright © 2011 by Gary Younge

Published in the United States by Nation Books, A Member of the Perseus Books Group
116 East 16th Street, 8th Floor
New York, NY 10003

Published in Great Britain by Penguin Group

Nation Books is a co-publishing venture of the Nation Institute and
the Perseus Books Group

Books published by Nation Books are available at special discounts for bulk purchases in the United States by corporations, institutions, and other organizations. For more information, please contact the Special Markets Department at the Perseus Books Group, 2300 Chestnut Street, Suite 200, Philadelphia, PA 19103, or call (800) 810-4145, ext. 5000, or e-mail special.markets@perseusbooks.com.

A CIP catalog record for this book is available from the Library of Congress.
LCCN: 2011925041
ISBN: 978-1-56858-660-1
E-book ISNB 978-1-56858-663-2

10 9 8 7 6 5 4 3 2 1

No man is an Island,
Entire of itself;
Each is a piece of the Continent,
A part of the main;
If a clod be washed away by the sea,
Europe is the less,
As well as if a promontory were,
As well as if a manor of thy friends
Or of thine own were.
Any man's death diminishes me,
Because I am involved in Mankind.
Therefore, send not to know
For whom the bell tolls;
It tolls for thee.

—John Donne

Contents

Contents

INTRODUCTION

Over a breakfast of pancakes, bacon and scrambled eggs in a backroom in the Nuggett Casino in Pahrump, rural Nevada, the conversation among around forty men turned to the most auspicious moment for armed insurrection.

"The last thing we want to see is to break out our arms," said one. "But we need to have 'em in hand, and the government needs to know that we will use [our arms] if they continue down the path they're on. I'm not promoting arms against our government. But the government needs to know if they go past a certain line in the sand that will take place. That's why we have the second amendment. That's why it says we should have a well-regulated militia. Do we have a well-regulated militia? No, we don't. We're not even ready. We need to get ready."

Another, fearing such talk could give a visiting journalist the wrong impression, insisted few in the room would agree with such a ridiculous view.

"This talk about taking up arms against the government is ridiculous, and I don't think many people in this room believe that. We have a lot of legal avenues to exhaust before we ever get to that."

But it turned out quite a few did. "Look how much damage Barack Obama and his socialist congress did in eighteen months," bellowed another. "It could take us ten years to undo this crap. And you say we can't consider using weapons."

They call it the "old farts' club": a gathering of elderly, conservative men (all but two of them are white) that has been meeting every Friday morning for the last five years at the Nugget for breakfast and a bull session. On the day I was there (just a few days before the 2010 mid-term elections), they discussed topics that ranged from judges— one calls for Sonia Sotomayor and Elena Kagan to be removed from the Supreme Court—to the fate of a local park. The discussions are spirited, but it is a warm, convivial, garrulous bunch.

For all that, however, one cannot escape a pervasive sense of anger and fear in the room that portends some encroaching, escalating and all-encompassing calamity. The list of sources for this fear seems endless: the media, illegal immigrants, gays, civil rights leadership, the judiciary, Democrats, liberals, establishment Republicans, China, government, schools, the coastal states in general, California in particular. Each place setting comes with a copy of the constitution: a sacred document being violated by the government. When I ask how many believe they are living in tyranny, they all raise their hands. When I ask how many believe President Obama was born in the United States, only one arm goes up.

Being a white man in America is not what it used to be. True, wherever power is exercised that demographic group is overrepresented and has been for centuries. They also earn more than women of any race, more than men of any other race (except Asians) and more than most people in most countries. And yet the sense of fragility as a cohort is palpable. Before a single vote had been cast for the 2008 Democratic presidential nomination that saw Obama face off against Hillary Clinton, *Esquire* ran a cover asking: "Can a white man still be elected president?" and a book had been released entitled: *The Neglected Voter: White Men and the Democratic Dilemma*.

But while the nature of the crisis might be miscast the notion that there is a crisis is difficult to deny.

For working and middle-class white men—the overwhelming majority—their race, gender and nationality had done little to shield them from the economic ravages of the new global economy. Over the last generation median income for white American men has stalled, as has social mobility, taking with it the very American notion that each year will be better than the next and each successive generation more prosperous.

This sense of regression has been particularly acute for men. Women are now more likely to apply to and graduate from a university than men, and in some metropolitan centers women under 25 earn more than their male peers. Even if things have been getting tougher because of the recession, most women born in or before 1980 had more options (economic, social, sexual and academic) than their mothers.

But the problems went beyond race and gender. Many blamed their problems, in part or in whole, on the outside world. The United States may have been one of the principal motors of neoliberal globalization, but its citizens are also its victims. From 47 countries polled by Pew in 2007, Americans showed the sharpest decline in their support for foreign trade and had the least positive view of it. By at the latest 2030 China's GDP will overtake America.

To the sting of economic vulnerability has been added the indignity of geopolitical decline and the erosion of the myth of invincibility that lay at the heart of America's post–World War II national identity. As the sole global superpower since the end of the Cold War, the United States was once able to rig the competition with carrots, sticks and, if need be, B52s. Now it must accept that Indians, Chinese, Brazilians and others can also change the rules.

"Owing to the relative decline of its economic and, to a lesser extent, military power, the US will no longer have the same flexibility in choosing among as many policy options," concluded the National Intelligence Council (which coordinates analysis from all US intelligence agencies) shortly after Obama's election. The report acknowledged that, while the United States would remain the single most powerful force in the world, its relative strength and potential leverage are waning.

This downward trajectory was, in no small part, aggravated by failed wars against predominantly Muslim countries that followed terrorist attacks by Islamic fundamentalists and that also sparked something close to a moral panic among the Right at home. A national furor was sparked by plans to build an Islamic community center in Lower Manhattan. There were protests against the "9/11 mosque." But this was not about either 9/11, which had taken place almost a decade earlier and several blocks away, or a mosque, given that no such thing was being built. It was a crude attempt to invent the kind of enemy that could rally popular prejudice around an increasingly narrow nationalist agenda. And it worked. At the height of the controversy one in three Americans said a Muslim should not be allowed to stand for president. In a referendum in 2010 more than 70 percent of Oklahomans voted to ban the introduction of

Sharia law in a state where muslims comprise less than .2 percent of the population.

A few months later, in the same room where Senator Joseph McCarthy sought to target communist sympathizers, congressman Peter King held the "Extent of Radicalization in the American Muslim Community's Response," hearings, arguably placing an entire community under suspicion of links with terrorism.

Finally came a portentous, generational demographic shift at home where almost half the children born the year Obama was elected were nonwhite and by 2042 whites will be a minority in the country as a whole. Put all this together and it's not difficult to divine the root causes of American white male anxiety. When activists from the tea party, which is overwhelmingly white, insist "We want our country back," this is partly what they are referring to, albeit usually implicitly. It was in this period that the country elected a black president, with an African name and a foreign father who was a nonpracticing Muslim. Those who claim opposition to Obama is fueled by race are looking through far too narrow a lens. Racism not only does not explain all of the opposition; it isn't even the half of it.

Back at the Nugget the participants in the Old Fart's Club understood this only too well. So sick were they of being accused of racism that they raised the question of the accusation themselves only so that they could deny it. Meanwhile Nevada boasted the highest rates of unemployment and home foreclosures in the country, and the proportion of Latinos in the state is set to double in just a generation. It was just a few days before the midterm elections, and the "Old Farts" were ready to turn the tide. Across the country the Republican Right was resurgent and nowhere more so than here. The governor's race was all but sewn up for Republican Brian Sandoval. And the old farts didn't think there was a chance tea party candidate Sharron Angle could lose to Democratic Senate leader Harry Reid unless Reid cheated by registering "illegal aliens." And so it was that this loyal and enthusiastic band of conservative white men dispersed to do everything in their power to secure the election of the first female senator and Latino governor in the state's history.

Identity is like fire, both an essential component of daily life and yet so elemental that its existence and influence are often overlooked. It can create warmth and comfort or burn badly and destroy. It is at the forefront of some of the most inspiring achievements in world political history, whether it be women's suffrage, the end of apartheid or advances in gay rights. But it has also taken center stage in the most lurid moments of global affairs—the Holocaust, and the wars in Rwanda, Bosnia, Darfur and the Democratic Republic of Congo.

Identity can make connections over oceans, languages, generations and cultures. On the day the United States went to the polls in 2008 to elect a new president, Obama Sorin Ilie Scoica was born in the tiny Romanian village of Rusciori. "When I saw Obama on TV, my heart swelled with joy. I thought he was one of us Roma because of his skin color," said Maria Savu, the boy's grandmother, who hoped his name would bring him luck. But identity can also sow division among those who live side by side. On the day that Obama Scoica was born, 94 percent of black Californians voted for Barack Obama and around 55 percent voted against gay marriage. Black churches were the focal point for both efforts. In January 2011 a fruit stall holder in Tunis who set himself on fire in protest against a petty slight sparked an uprising that spread throughout the Arab world from Libya to Iran, prompting the overthrow of Egyptian despot, Hosni Mubarak. The next month demonstrators against an anti-union law in Wisconsin marched through Madison with banners stating: Walk Like an Egyptian. The largest democracy in the world (India) and the newest electorates (Iraq and Afghanistan) have political cultures underpinned by allegiance to sects, castes, religion, warlords or ethnic groups. No one is immune from these contradictions. None of us comes to politics from a vacuum—we arrive with affiliations that mold our worldview. It was no coincidence that women led the charge for female suffrage or that Ghanaians spearheaded the battle for Ghanaian independence. Had they waited for men or the British occupier to come around to these ideas, they might still be waiting.

On the one hand, we are all more alike than we are unalike. Whether it's the Manchester United–supporting, fish-and-chip–eating bombers of the London transport system, the homophobic Colorado preacher who paid for sex with a male prostitute or the Bush family and its long history of connections with the bin Ladens, the "other" is rarely as foreign or as threatening as we are led to believe. Growing numbers of us watch the same shows, eat the same food and wear the same brands. Never have we traveled as much, interbred as much or conversed as much. In their own gnarly, voluble, cantankerous, genial way, the participants of the Old Farts Club were familiar to anyone who has ever encountered a gathering of old men anywhere in the world.

On the other hand, the ways in which we are unalike matter. For all that is common in the human experience, the differences are stark and, in some respects, getting starker, and it is these differences that are increasingly creating the framework for political activity, public anxiety and, at times, moral panic.

In Britain the English Defence League, an extreme right-wing party with a history of violence, had a gay chapter whose members wore pink triangles. "This is the symbol gay people were made to wear under Hitler," explained one. "Islam poses the same threat, and we are here to express our opposition to that." Within half an hour's train ride from Brussels, the polyglot home to both the North Atlantic Treaty Organization and the European Commission, children in Flemish schools are not allowed to speak French on the playground. In China, they have banned Buddhist monks in Tibet from reincarnating without government permission in the hope of crushing nationalist dissent. As familiar as the characters at the Old Farts Club are, their particular obsessions with guns, God and Obama would shock many not only globally but also in the United States. Obvious as it may seem, it bears emphasizing—if only because so many well-meaning people are in denial about it—that, in all sorts of ways, our differences make a difference.

This is the vexed terrain this book seeks to explore: to what extent can our various identities be mobilized to accentuate our universal humanity as opposed to separating us off into various, antagonistic camps? At what point does refusing to acknowledge the importance of difference become a callous denial of human diversity, and when does stressing it become an indulgent and insidious obstruction to what could potentially unite us? When can identity inspire, how can it inflame, what drives it, who does it empower and what does it enable them to do? These are questions that go beyond philosophy to the central issue of power—who has it, how do they wield it and in whose interests do they use it?

That identity stands at the core of political activity is not a new idea. But until relatively recently, in the West, it was tempered by the understanding that the interests of various groups could be filtered through democratic activity and should be underpinned by human rights. Elected majorities would rule while minorities would have protection. That, at least, was the promise and the model. But the escalation of neo-liberal globalization has eroded the relevance of the basic unit of democracy—the nation state—and in so doing disabled the levers previously available to assert our collective will on the world. In the absence of any meaningful way to advance their interests as citizens, many retreat into their laagers of place, race, religion—to name but a few—as a means of self-defense.

But while identity is a crucial place to start in politics, it is a terrible place to finish. As a prism, it is both crucial and deeply flawed. None of the identities we generally work with are even remotely as definite as commonly believed. The dividing lines of who is what and why shift and blur. The French government's efforts to combat Islamic extremism by banning headscarves in schools were triggered by two sisters who converted to Islam, whose father is a Sephardic Jew. Despite America's self-image as the primary twenty-first-century civilizing force, the overwhelming majority of Americans believe in angels and miracles and, among countries where people believe religion to be very important, America is closer to Pakistan and Nigeria than to France or Germany. The world champion in the women's 800 meters, South African Caster Semenya, had to undergo gender-verification tests in 2009 to prove she was really a woman.

It is in no small part because the borders of our identities are so porous and fluid that some seek to police them so rigorously. Appeals to the innate, fixed, pure and essential nature of any identity are the stock-in-trade of any fundamentalist and generally have the same effect—to isolate one particular group from the rest of the human race.

But it doesn't have to be like this. "To be attached to the subdivision, to love the little platoon we belong to in society, is the first principle (the germ, as it were) of public affections," wrote Edmund Burke in *Reflections on the French Revolution*. "It is the first link in the series by which we proceed towards a love to our country and to mankind. The interest of that portion of social arrangement is a trust in the hands of all those who compose it; and as none but bad men would justify it in abuse, none but traitors would barter it away for their own personal advantage."

On the face of it, to underline our common and universal humanity seems obvious to the point of being trite: a "Kumbayah" for all seasons; the weak, inadequate balm applied to minimum effect by the vicar, stoner or diplomat; an agenda for those who espouse global citizenship, Esperanto and a whole litany of other worthy utopian projects that are never going to happen. And yet, at the root of all of this lies the deeply radical notion that those various ways in which we are distinct are dwarfed by the essential facts of our commonality: facts that have simultaneously been brought to the fore by global issues—from climate change to various epidemics— that pose a potential threat to us as a species, even as they have been diminished by efforts to dismantle the post–World War II consensus that human rights are universal.

The United Nations charter on asylum is routinely ignored, while the Geneva Convention on torture has been declared obsolete. Meanwhile, freedom of movement is now only supported in the most abstract terms. The world's poor quite simply do not have the right to travel in an effort to improve their lives, while many governments have assumed the right to snatch people off the street and transport them across the world to be tortured. For the hundreds of thousands, if not millions, who roam the globe without papers, rights or citizenship, the crucial issue is not to have their particular identity recognized but to have their essential humanity acknowledged and respected. In 2009, more than a hundred immigrants, roughly a quarter of them children, were found living in a sewer system under Rome's railway stations. Above ground, an anti-Gypsy pogrom took place in Naples while prime minister Silvio Berlusconi (who would later become embroiled in a sex-scandal with a teenage Moroccan bellydancer) branded undocumented workers "an army of evil" and voiced his opposition to a multiethnic society. It was just one graphic metaphor in a world of many illustrating global economic inequality, local racial fragility and general political anomie.

But to evoke universal humanism also throws down a gauntlet to the Pan-Africanist, Islamist, Zionist, patriot, radical feminist and others, to reach beyond their immediate term of reference and make common cause on the basis of a common bond—our humanity. Women may have led the charge for suffrage, but there were many men who supported them, and many women who did not. Ghanaians may have led the campaign for independence, but there were Britons who supported them and Ghanaians who did not. Ghanaian independence and feminism, in turn, had their ideological roots in aspirations of liberation and equality that go beyond either anticolonialism or gender equality. People are not hostage to their identities—we have free will, imagination, morality and principle.

"The acorn becomes an oak by means of automatic growth," writes psychologist Rollo May in *Man's Search for Himself.* "No commitment is necessary. The kitten similarly becomes a cat on the basis of instinct. Nature and being are identical in creatures like them. But a man or woman becomes fully human only by his or her choices and his or her commitment to them. People attain worth and dignity by the multitude of decisions they make from day to day. These decisions require courage."

Easy decisions take no courage at all. Most of us grow into our identities as easily as acorns do into oaks—rarely questioning, resisting or protesting those events that do not appear to affect us directly. It is the difficult decisions, the ones that have consequences, challenge orthodoxies, bear risk and threaten status, that take real courage.

One would think such courage would easily find a political home. The Left, after all, made great strides through the sixties and early seventies thanks to the advances of civil rights, gay rights, feminism and anticolonialism, and still nominally supports its historical contributions. But by the early nineties, much of the Left had come to regard the politics of identity as an obstacle to further progress rather than an opportunity for it.

For others on the Left, the journey into the more vague area of identity marks so great a departure from the hallowed class struggle that they are simply unable to take it seriously. Orthodox Marxists believe anyone who has been distracted by the fickle matters of gender, region, ethnicity, race, religion—anything that cannot be reduced to the relations of production—has essentially been duped.

They have half a point. To the extent to which class is about the distribution of resources, there is very little in politics that makes sense unless one understands its class dimension; but, similarly, there is very little that makes sense when viewed only through the prism of class. So while it may be true that the powerful exploit difference in order to divide the powerless and thereby strengthen their grip, it is no less true that the powerful did not invent difference and oftentimes need do little to keep it alive. Otherwise, the only way to explain poor white Republicans or Hindu nationalists is as people who don't understand what's best for them. "The anguish and disorientation which finds expression in this hunger to belong, and hence 'the politics of identity' is no more a moving force of history than the hunger for 'law and order' which is an equally understandable response to another aspect of social disorganization," writes Eric Hobsbawm in *Nations and Nationalism*. "Both are symptoms of sickness rather than diagnoses, let alone therapy." This would be news to Zimbabwe's Shona, Serbian nationalists and British jihadis—to mention but a few—who have "moved history" through their identities in ways that have little connection to the therapeutic.

While liberals occasionally pay lip service to an agenda of social equality that they no longer believe in, conservatives have done the opposite. In principle, the Right has long been opposed to the very idea that identity has any relation to politics at all.

In practice, however, it was always only particular identities the

Right had a problem with. Appealing to white, male and national identities has been a central part of conservative politics for more than a century. Indeed, over the last couple of decades, the most full-throated claims of powerlessness and discrimination have come from conservatives in their defense of the most powerful groups in society. When Barack Obama nominated Sonia Sotomayor, a Latina of Puerto Rican parentage, to the Supreme Court, the Right behaved as if the sky would fall in. Even though the court contained six white men—and one black man and one white woman—the threat to white men was, apparently, palpable. "God help you if you're a white male coming before her bench," said Republican leader Michael Steele (who, incidentally, is black).

Shortly after the far-right British National Party won two seats in the European elections in 2009, its leader, Nick Griffin, conceded there was a "huge amount of racism in this country," before going on to explain that "overwhelmingly, it's directed against the indigenous British majority [by which he means white people]. . . . It's the indigenous majority who are the second-class citizens in every possible sphere, not as a consequence of themselves but because our ruling elite has made us second-class citizens." The BNP's magazine is called *Identity*.

Oftentimes the Right will appropriate the symbols of the Left, to hilarious effect. Back in 2003, Roy Moore, the former Republican chief justice of Alabama, led a failed bid to keep a monument to the Ten Commandments in his courthouse. "If the 'rule of law' means to do everything a judge tells you to do," he said, "we would still have slavery in this country." I remember standing in amazement on the steps of the courthouse watching people in T-shirts that proclaimed "Islam is a lie, homosexuality is a sin, abortion is murder," as they sang the civil rights anthem "We Shall Overcome" and waved the Confederate flag—the emblem of the slave-holding South.

The absurdity is not the Right's use of identity per se. There is nothing inherent in any identity, or the politics that emerge from it, that makes it necessarily either reactionary or progressive. The rights of white people, Christians or men are no less important than those of black people, Muslims or women. The issue is whether those who seek to rally those groups are campaigning for rights that should be exclusive or universal.

The only arena in which identity has been explicitly and consciously embraced in recent years has been marketing. At the Republican convention that nominated George Bush as its presidential candidate in 2000, the leadership felt the need to transform the party's image, which many Americans regarded as backward-looking, narrow and elitist. To counter that impression, the three cochairs for the convention were an African-American, a Latino and a white single mother. The headline speaker on the first day was Colin Powell. The primetime news slot the next day went to Condoleezza Rice. On the opening night, the pledge of allegiance was delivered by a blind mountaineer while a black woman sang "The Star-Spangled Banner." On one later night of the convention, the entertainment featured Harold Melvin (black) and Jon Secada (Cuban). The convention was closed by Chaka Khan.

But while the emphasis in presentation was on race and ethnicity, the message was not directed at minority voters (whom the Republican party would effectively disenfranchise in order eventually to "win" the election). "What the Republicans are doing is aimed more at white Americans," said David Bositis, a political analyst at the Joint Center for Political and Economic Studies in Washington. "Moderates do not want someone who's negative on race. It says something very significant about America as a whole." Race had simply become a signifier of the Republican desire not to appear mean-spirited.

Similarly, in 2002, the British newspaper *The Daily Mail* printed a picture of a range of non-white Metropolitan police staff with a caption stating: "It is a picture that reflects changing times and attitudes within the police service . . . this exclusive picture of Yard employees shows forces are beginning to reflect the racial mix of the community they serve." The reality couldn't have been further from the truth. At the time, ethnic minorities made up 25 percent of the capital's population but only 4.5 percent of Met staff. Just a month earlier, Sir John Stevens, the Metropolitan police commissioner, had conceded he might look abroad for black and Asian recruits because he could not attract them in the UK.

They call this "diversity." A decent idea—that an institution should look like the people it serves and the world in which it operates—has spawned an industry of consultants, advisers and departments that, between them, have corporatized identity beyond all meaning. Having eviscerated from the issue of representation all notions of fairness, equality and justice, "equal opportunities" morph effortlessly into photo opportunities—a way of making things look different but act the same. It is what radical Angela Davis once described to me as "the difference that brings no difference, the change that brings no change."

So identity lay abandoned—publicly derided and hypocritically exploited by the Right; willfully neglected or carelessly promoted by the Left; shamelessly embraced and marketized by the corporate world. The notion is vulnerable to cynicism but can also act as the lynchpin to great acts of solidarity. It has the potential to be both source and pollutant: the starting point for some of the most inspirational moments in politics; the endpoint for some of the most insidious.

"At a market, a Hutu can spot a Tutsi at 50 meters, and vice versa," Innocent Rwililiza, a Tutsi survivor of the Rwandan genocide, told Jean Hatzfeld in *Into the Quick of Life*. "But to admit to any difference is a taboo subject, even among ourselves. . . . We have never been comfortable with these nuances which exist between us. In certain ways, ethnicity is like AIDS, the less you dare talk of it the more ravages it causes." But the way you talk about it matters. So let's talk about it properly.

1. Me, Myself, I

A political identity in ten parts

Every human being at every stage of history is born into a society and from his earliest years is moulded by that society. Both language and environment help to determine the character of his thought; his earliest ideas come to him from others. The individual apart from society would be both speechless and mindless.

— E. H. Carr, *Society and Individual*

Everybody has a story. Not, for most of us, a grand overarching narrative that draws together the various strands of our life into one neat, consistent thread but a collection of unique, discrete and occasionally contradictory chapters that come together only in the telling. Few of these tales belong to us entirely. We arrive in the middle of a random variety of stories and then set about weaving some together and discarding others in a bid to write our own. "I inherit from the past of my family, my city, my tribe, my nation a variety of debts, inheritances, rightful expectations and obligations," writes Alasdair MacIntyre in *After Virtue*. "I am born with a past; and to try to cut myself off from that past is to deform my present relationships. The possession of an historical identity and the possession of a social identity coincide."

Either way, it is through the prism of these vignettes that we frame our take on the world. "Facts speak only when the historian calls on them," wrote E. H. Carr in his landmark work, *What is History?* "It is he who decides which facts to give the floor and in what order or context. It is the historian who has decided for his own reasons that Caesar's crossing of that petty stream, the Rubicon, is a fact of history, whereas the crossing of the Rubicon by millions of other people before or since interests nobody at all." What is true for the historian is true for all writers. We have a decision about which events will influence us and how, but we rarely get to choose the events themselves. Refusing to recognize your influences is not the same as not having them. It simply disables you from interrogating them to find out why and how they have had the effect they have. The facts are there. But these are stories. And while I didn't write them all myself, I do own them.

i. 1968–9: Hitchin

Like everybody, I am a product of my time and place. The time was turbulent. In the period between when I was conceived and when I was born, Martin Luther King was assassinated; US president Lyndon Johnson signed the Civil Rights Act; Enoch Powell delivered his "Rivers of Blood" speech; French students took over the streets and almost took down the government; Robert Kennedy was assassinated; the Kremlin sent troops into Prague; Rupert Murdoch bought the most popular Sunday newspaper in Britain, the *News of the World*; police clashed with anti-war protesters at the Democratic party convention in Chicago; 150 women protested at the Miss America pageant in Atlantic City; the Marylebone Cricket Club cancelled its tour to South Africa because the apartheid regime refused to accept Basil D'Oliveira, a Cape Colored, as part of the team; France exploded its first H-bomb; the Mexican government massacred more than a hundred students in Mexico City; the Royal Ulster Constabulary batoned civil rights protesters in Derry seeking better housing and ran amok on the city's Bogside; Tommy Smith and John Carlos delivered a Black Power salute from the Olympic podium in Mexico City; students and Black Power activists rioted in Jamaica over the banning of lecturer Walter Rodney from the island; Swaziland and Equatorial Guinea declared their independence; Richard Nixon was elected president; Britain passed a new race relations act; and Yale University announced it would accept women.

The place was sedate. I was born in Hitchin, thirty-five miles north of London, and raised in nearby Stevenage. More of a satellite town than a suburb, it was created primarily to house Londoners bombed out of their slums during the war. A new town in an old country. A working-class town in a class-ridden society. A black family in a white town. Nominally Christian and effectively godless. An immigrant family in a town where almost no one was native.

My parents were teenage sweethearts who arrived separately in London from Barbados in the early sixties, at the tail end of post-war migration. Britain sent for labor, but people arrived. They came to work and ended up living. My parents already had two boys by the time they got to Stevenage, which, if not a great place to raise a family, was then, at the very least, not a bad one. And for my immediate family, these were good times. Probably the best. Two parents, both working, two boys aged three and four (I was the third) and a three-bedroomed council house with a garden front and back.

"You do not choose to be a son or a daughter," argues philosopher and cultural theorist Kwame Anthony Appiah in *The Ethics of Identity*, "a Serb or a Bosnian; a Korean or an Mbuti . . . In all sorts of ways, our identities are neither wholly scripted for us nor wholly scripted by us."

Many struggle with the idea that they belong to groups they never asked to join. Their reticence, in this regard, is both understandable and unsustainable. For some, these evasions are easier than for others. But whether we claim them selectively or not, our identities have a habit of sticking with us. I was named after Gary Sobers—a Barbadian and one of the most famous cricketers of his era. Only history could make sense of how I came to be born in that place, in that time, with that name. Only I can make sense of the rest.

ii. 1973–4: Barbados

The glare of sunlight from the runway; the night crickets' chorus after nightfall; a wave that was bigger than my mother; strangers who called themselves family. The memories of my first visit to Barbados are patchy. I was four years old, with an eye for detail but no sense of sequence or logic. I returned with an impressionistic patchwork of isolated moments rather than the continuous narrative of a six-week trip. I remember arriving but not leaving; the scent of my grandmother but not her face; the sun but not the heat.

My strongest and most reliable recollection is of getting up early and following my gran around the yard. She had some animals—turkeys, chickens and guinea birds, a goat or two and a cow. Before she put on her wellies, took up her cutlass and went to work cutting cane for the day, she would feed them. I would walk behind her as she did so, delighting her with my imitations of each animal.

The episode my extended family remembers best involves me showing off outside my granny's church. The way my grandmother told it—and she would tell it whenever I saw her—as soon as the service was over, I ran out on to the front steps and delivered my very own rendition of that year's calypso hit, to the indulgent delight of the starched, suited and booted of the congregation. "I am a pure-bred Barbadian/ Me don' fuss 'pon Otis Redding," I sang, and wiggled without much care for rhythm. I had been in the country for less than a fortnight, and already I had claimed it as my own.

In *Gender and Nation*, Nira Yuval Davis describes how Palestinian children in Lebanese refugee camps would call home a village that may not have even existed for several decades but from which their parents were exiled. Such is their sense of displacement that their geographical identity is rooted in the last place their families felt safely and happily at ease—even if they never lived there. We had never been through a war, lived under occupation or been forcibly removed. My parents had migrated of their own free will. Indeed, in some ways, the move from periphery to metropole was not much of a move at all. My mother arrived with a British passport and three A levels, in English literature, European history and the British constitution. Still, the first time she saw hailstones she picked up my brother and ran for their lives. Her journey to England was only supposed to be temporary. "In his imagination every migrant worker is in transit," wrote John Berger in *A Seventh Man*. "He remembers the past: he anticipates the future: his aims and recollections make his thoughts a train between the two."

Looking back on it, it is obvious that I ingested an affinity to Barbados with my mother's milk. I grew up with an understanding that there was a distinction between where I had always lived (Stevenage) and where I was from (Barbados).

Where we lived had become hostile territory. Just as I don't recall a time in my childhood when I didn't think of Barbados as home, I also don't recall a time when we didn't feel in some way embattled in England. When we visited Barbados, my father had left already. The good times were over. For some, we no longer existed as a family but as a black single-parent archetype. Before we'd left for Barbados a neighbor had already called social services to suggest that we be put into foster care because my mother couldn't look after us. My mother was a nurse. We had relatively little money. And racism was on the rise.

While I have no distinct memories to support this, I'm sure that my affinity to Barbados was linked in no small way to my sense of alienation from England. I was from "there" because I couldn't be from "here"—even if "here" was the only place I had ever really known. Clearly my mother was having misgivings too. The main point of the trip to Barbados was to see whether we should return home. She later claimed that we couldn't go back because, as children, we couldn't hack the schooling. I remember that, in the Infants, they didn't play with clay and draw pictures but sat in rows, recited their times tables and got whacked with a ruler. Every breaktime I would run away to find my brothers or my mother in the next-door school.

But I can't help feeling this was not the whole truth. Children are adaptable, and we were rarely indulged. In retrospect, I think my mother was not ready. She was just thirty. And for all the burdens of single-parenthood in a foreign country, my guess is that she enjoyed the independence and relative anonymity. Barbados is a small place. She could have fallen out with everybody within the first few months. In myriad ways, each of us had to deal with the fact that we weren't going "back" and that, in time, there would be no "back" to go to. The next time my mother actually returned to Barbados was more than a decade later, in a box. She had always said she wanted to be buried at "home."

iii. 1979: Stevenage

When I was about ten years old, my mother made me stay up to watch television. We had no bedtime in our house, and I had crashed on the floor, as usual. But rather than being shaken awake and ushered upstairs as she turned off the lights behind her, Mum prodded me to life in the TV glow of late evening. "You need to watch this," she said. "It's part of your history too."

It looked to me like a war movie, and since I had no interest in war movies I dozed off a couple of times, only to be nudged awake again. Within a short while I was both horrified and hooked. For the next few weeks, this series became compulsive, as opposed to compulsory, family viewing.

It was called *The Holocaust*—a made-for-TV movie that distilled the entirety of the systematic and systemic attempt to eliminate Jewry in Europe into the experiences of one family living in Berlin. The storyline was straightforward to a fault. By the time the Weiss family had decided they should get out of Berlin, it was too late. As the Nazis entrenched their power, the Weisses were split up. Some were deported to Warsaw, one joined the Resistance, another was placed in Buchenwald. One way or another, most ended up perishing in concentration camps. I have never seen it again, and my guess is that it is probably a terrible, simplistic film with important historical omissions and unforgivably schmaltzy trivializations. But it had an immense impact on me, in the same way that *Roots* had a huge impact on many white people who knew little or nothing about slavery.

Quite why my mum was so insistent in making this connection has never been clear. We were a very political household. But until then, Jews, anti-Semitism and the Holocaust had never really come up, and it was rarely mentioned afterwards either. There were very few Jews in Stevenage as far as I was aware, even if there was a fair amount of anti-Semitism.

But by the time the show was over and almost everyone was dead, it had created its own connection in my mind and in my world. True, we were not Jews, Stevenage was not Berlin, and 1979 was not 1933.

But we had had neighbors attack us, verbally and, occasionally, physically. We had had the police do nothing about it. And there were politicians who scapegoated us. People we knew had reported us to the authorities. So the notion that the veneer of civilization and conviviality that stretches over our daily lives might be just a mirage; that reasonable-seeming people could do completely unreasonable things to each other; that lies could rally mobs . . . in short, the idea that you could be "othered" to death was entirely believable.

The extremity, violence and depravity struck me as confirmation that the world was far more brittle than it appeared. With that came a realization that politics was about power and that, among other things, it had the power to kill; and when it came down to it, all the arguments, constitutional procedure and legislative process came to naught—if they wanted to murder you, they would. I had no idea who "they" were. But I knew "they" were out there. I can't remember if I thought it could actually happen to us—although it did give me nightmares—but I definitely thought it could happen.

I became obsessed. Whenever I visited the library, I would linger over the pictures in a book on the Holocaust with a ghoulish fascination. Two in particular stick in my mind. The first was of a good-looking young woman, maybe in her late teens, standing at a train station, waiting to be deported. She's looking off into the distance, with her hands clasped in front of her and her coat folded over them. It looks like summer, and she's wearing a star, without which the photo could have been a candid holiday snap. A few pages further on was a picture of naked bodies piled on top of each other—emaciated and boggle-eyed. I would keep flicking from one page to another, between life and death, the pretty individual and the anonymous mass, before realizing I had been standing in the same spot for half an hour.

One can overstate the influence of these lessons. While my interest was intense, it was not particularly broad. I was fascinated by the Holocaust, but I was not much interested in issues relating to anti-Semitism or Jews—whom I had never, to my knowledge, met. Given that my own experiences of discrimination had been limited to race, I couldn't understand how people knew they were Jews or why they didn't just lie and say they weren't. If they had to put stars on them so that everyone could tell they were Jews, then why, I wondered, did they just not wear them? An awareness of how social control functions and of the various ways, both subtle and blatant, in which people create, sustain and distinguish identities had yet to enter my pre-teen world. Nor had some of the more straightforward lessons one might draw from this obsession sunk home either. A few years later in class, I called my classmate (whose parents were Irish Catholic) a Jew when he refused to lend me his pencil. My history teacher called me on it. "What has the fact that he did not give you a pencil got to do with his religion?" he asked. "What has me calling him a Jew got to do with religion?" I replied.

iv. 1984–5: Clapham

Between my first kiss and my first A level, there was Trotsky. I am sure I would have met him sooner or later, plastered against the wall in a Student Union bar, or on a street corner hiding behind a petition. But he came to me on a sunny day in Hyde Park. It was 1984; the year of the miners' strike, the IRA bombing of the Grand Hotel in Brighton and Ronald Reagan's second victory in the US presidential elections. I was fifteen, a self-important teenage vegetarian who felt that all was not quite right with the world.

I had spent most of the day wandering around London alone, protesting against the visit of the South African president, P. W. Botha, when a young man with acne caught me unawares and offered me a copy of *Young Socialist*. I bought it, read it in less than five minutes—all the articles were basically the same: "Thatcher is horrible"; "Miners are great"; "Socialism is even better"—and thought little more about it.

A few weeks later, I pulled it from the bottom of my bag, wrote to the editor and asked if I could join the revolution, with much the same degree of forethought as others in my peer group applied to join fan clubs. I was bored. It was something to do.

Given the range of antisocial behavior available to a hormonally besieged adolescent, there were worse things I could have turned my attentions to than the overthrow of capitalism. I would be lying if I said that I was aware of precisely what I was getting into. I knew I was getting involved in some kind of socialist outfit. I suspected it was the younger section of the Labour Party—as it happened, it was the youth wing of the Workers Revolutionary Party. This was not a problem for me. After all, if you're going to go into politics at that age, you might as well get some cred and join something nobody's ever heard of.

My ideological affiliation had been established at an early age, even if its ties to an actual party were weak. When I was five—a year of two elections, many strikes, and power cuts—I asked my mother what the difference was between Labour and Conservative. My mother explained: "Labour take from the rich and give to the poor. The Conservatives take from the poor and give to the rich." With no political morality to make sense of this, I used the one follow-up question she would usually tolerate in such situations wisely. "What are we?" I asked. "Labour," said Mum.

Her response was logical. We were poor and black, and voting Labour was by and large what poor, black people did. But it was tribal too. Labour was our team. Supporting another team was unthinkable. In the years to come, I would be perplexed at how people could shift their votes from one party to another as though changing ice-cream brands. Like switching from, say, Protestant to Catholic, these were, in my mind, changes of fundamental worldview.

In any case, I loved the idea of being a revolutionary. To me it meant being uncompromising, and even unreasonable, in the single-minded pursuit of what you wanted. At the age of fifteen, that pretty much summed me up. I got a book out of the library called *Revolution* and coveted a picture of Che Guevara and Fidel Castro sitting on camp beds in the jungle smoking and joking in their fatigues. That, I thought, was the life.

The WRP credo was fairly straightforward. Britain in 1984, they believed, was more or less at the same stage as Russia in 1916—a nation on the brink of revolution. All that was needed to push it over the edge was a general strike. If we could get everyone out together we could bring the nation to a standstill, form some workers' councils, replace the police with a workers' militia and then Bingo!—capitalism would be dead before you could say "Fourth International."

This did not seem ridiculous to me at the time. Where class conflict is concerned, 1984 was a spectacular year. With bloody pitched battles between the police and pickets at Orgreave, courts sequestrating union assets, bailiffs removing Greenham Common protesters, and showdowns brewing between left-wing councils and the government over rate-capping, the idea that parliamentary democracy was in crisis and preferred foul means rather than fair to crush dissent seemed astute.

The simplicity of the thesis was a great source of comfort. The party provided such a comprehensive and unwavering worldview that I felt I would never have to work anything out again. It provided a reason for everything that was bad—from the famine in Ethiopia to racist policing. And for every problem, there was only one solution: revolution. Concerns about details of policy, from taxation to nuclear disarmament, became little more than micromanaging. This sense of self-confidence, bolstered by an equal lack of self-knowledge, lent a distinctly cult-like air to the entire enterprise which, as is the way with cults, I only really became aware of once I'd left. It was a fundamentalist venture and, like all fundamentalist ventures, what it lacked in intellectual coherence, it more than made up for in consistency, community and an abundance of feckless, faithless enemies.

The fact that nobody else wanted a general strike simply gave us a messianic edge. Our detractors were either capitalist lackeys (the TUC) or just plain chicken—the Communist Party, which did actually want a general strike, but only for twenty-four hours. Thanks to our superior analysis, we were in the possession of a valuable and exclusive truth—the world, as we knew it, was about to end. I actually pitied those who missed the big picture. I lamented the wasted lives of all the adults who tried to work out their views on individual issues on a case-by-case basis. They were playing dot-to-dot; I had the huge, broad brush.

For a while it was a lot of fun. I had a purpose in my life that went beyond school and home and was surrounded not just by like-minds but identical points of view. With no national identity worthy of the name, I welcomed my first dalliance with a flag (red) and an anthem ("The Internationale") that I might be proud of.

Commitment to the party was total. If Britain was about to explode into revolution then it followed that revolutionaries had to be ready and waiting. And if the party was to be prepared then its members had to be at battle stations at all times, with no excuses and definitely no time off for good behavior. It meant that everything— births, deaths, marriages, exams, you name it—took second place. "The needs of the individual must be subordinated to the needs of the party," chimed the mantra. You simply did not blow out workers' power for a disco or a date. That made a lot of sense in Russia in 1916. The problem with this was twofold: it was not Russia and it was not 1916.

Reality gradually intervened. It turned out that I had wedded myself ideologically to the fortunes of the British working class as it was poised to nosedive into inexorable political decline. The following year saw not revolutionary upheaval but their biggest defeat in over half a century, when the miners went back to work empty-handed. And yet they would keep trying to tell us that a nurses' strike in Hull, or the withdrawal of Israeli troops from Lebanon, marked a massive escalation in the global class struggle. But like Samuel Beckett's Godot, while the revolution was long anticipated, it simply never showed up—and I doubt we would have known what it looked like even if it had.

The final rift came when I asked for time off party work so that I could study for an A level. They said no. I knew that if I didn't do something myself, my mother would, and I would rather have taken on the self-appointed representatives of the international proletariat than her any day. I called when I knew the local organizer would be out and told his flatmate I was leaving the party. I didn't sleep that night, so tortured was I by the portentousness of my actions. The next day, he came round and lectured me again on party discipline. Revolutions don't come without hard work, and hard work needed sacrifice, he said. He sounded like a clergyman trying to save a marriage. But he might as well have been talking to the stack of pamphlets that was always sitting in his car. My mind was made up.

"Nobody leaves this party, Gary," he said. "They either get kicked out or they die."

v. 1986: Sudan

With no television, no alcohol, no phones, relatively few books and searing heat, there was nothing much else to do in Sudan but talk. We were there for a year. We were seventeen. And we had a lot to talk about. Family, books, girls, boys, politics, plans, ambitions, films, jokes—a life we hadn't lived yet. We didn't know much. But that didn't stop us talking.

The route that had taken me to Sudan at seventeen was strictly personal and completely random. I finished school a year early but felt burnt out. During my final year, chunks of my hair had fallen out and I had fainted once or twice. I needed to get off the conveyor belt and do something else. There was an organization—Project Trust—that sent kids between school and university all over the developing world. I applied hoping I'd be sent to Zimbabwe. They shortlisted me for Zimbabwe, Honduras or Sudan. Along with fifteen others, I was sent to Sudan—a country and culture in which I had not the remotest interest—where I would teach Eritrean refugees English.

Notwithstanding a vicious bout of amoebic dysentery and a mild dose of malaria it was a tremendous year. I traveled through the desert on a camel and across the country on trucks full of onions, climbed Jebel Marra in Darfur with a black cabbie from Harlem and learned how to relax in a country where nothing happens fast. I left speaking just about enough Arabic to get me around a souk and understanding just enough about Islam to know that it wasn't only Christianity that turned me off religion. But for all the incredible things I was introduced to that year—the poverty, the plight of my refugee students, the challenge of teaching a class of forty students all older than me, the rise of the Muslim brotherhood—the thing I learned most in that year was not about Sudan but about Britain, in general, and the British class system, in particular.

For while, during my time as a Trotskyist, I had talked a lot about class struggle, I had never actually encountered class privilege. Now here it was. Of the sixteen of us who went to Sudan, eleven had been to private school, one to grammar school (which, until that point, I hadn't realized still existed) and four (including me) to comprehensives. It was only on meeting the rest of the group that I even became aware that I had been to a "comprehensive." In Stevenage, the word had never come up. When a fellow volunteer asked me what kind of school I attended I was bewildered. "It was just school," I said. "You know, normal school."

Insofar as I had thought about upper-class people at all up until then, I had really only imagined their wealth. But, up close, they didn't strike you as particularly rich—at least, they didn't have lots of cool stuff that I wanted and couldn't afford. What was apparent, however, was their confidence: a social, intellectual and sexual self-assuredness I had not seen before. There was a bearing about them—a sense of entitlement—that left me awestruck. On reflection, this is somewhat ironic. None of us—least of all my self-important self—was particularly inhibited. We wouldn't have been in Sudan if we were, and yet I felt their confidence was backed by the kind of resources and cultural investment I would never have. It seemed as though they had been trained to talk about art, recognize literature, ski and know the difference between formal and informal in dress and conduct.

This was far more about me than it could ever have been about them. No one was ever offhand and very few were at all snobby. I'm sure some of them had never even been skiing and, over a year of incessant chatter, we would all become close friends.

But being around them made me feel not just *less* sophisticated but positively *un*sophisticated. My school life had been quite utilitarian. I read for my exams. I read things that might be useful for my exams. And I read quite a lot of Marx, Engels and Lenin. But I never really read for pleasure. I played tuba in an orchestra, but I was never into classical music. As the year went on, I began to feel like an uneducated person who had mastered the art of passing exams. Feeling my ignorance keenly, I went through various emotional stages: respect, resentment, envy and self-loathing and, finally, indifference. By the end of the year, two things had occurred to me. The first was that these people were no smarter than me or indeed many of the people at my school. They had been better prepared for middle-class life and had more grace. But for everything I didn't know and they did, there were just as many things I knew and they didn't. The fact that it wasn't in their canon didn't mean it didn't count. And I didn't fancy their canon much anyway. Moreover, for all their culture and worldliness, they were, in many ways, quite parochial. Outside academia, some of the things they didn't know shocked me. I remember explaining to one of them that many British people could not afford to go on holiday every year. A few of them simply couldn't—or wouldn't—believe it.

I ended the year feeling that, despite the fact that my family had little money or status, I had a freedom that many of my fellow volunteers did not. Indeed it was precisely because of their status that they did not have the freedom I did. They seemed like prisoners of their own wealth and class. Some referred to this year abroad as though it were their one chance to do something exciting before knuckling down to a routine of predictable if privileged drudgery—as though this one opportunity to exert their own free will would soon be over and the return to conformity inescapable. I had no idea where I was going with my life.

During one conversation about what would most upset our parents, one of the girls said, without any sense of embarrassment, "I know that my mother would be really disappointed if I didn't marry someone who was a similar class, and the same religion and race. It would just be really tough on her and I wouldn't want to do that to her. I don't think it would be fair."

At first I was deeply offended and upset. I was not even remotely attracted to her but, as the only black and working-class male in the room, I felt weirdly invisible—as though my presence as an emotionally sentient being were insignificant. But I quickly realized how much sadder it was for her. Here she was, still in her teens, having this terrific foreign experience and yet, all the while, preparing herself for a life of refined confinement.

I would later realize that the notion that identity is a refuge for the poor and dispossessed—a means of guarding the special interests of those who cannot support themselves—is sorely misguided. Those most wedded to preserving their identity—indeed, handcuffed to it—are often powerful. When all is said and done, they have the most to lose. They just don't refer to it as identity. They call it tradition, heritage or, simply, history.

vi. Edinburgh: 1988

After a year at university, the train journey from Edinburgh to Stevenage was an all too familiar unit of time. To fill it, I needed one copy of the *Guardian*, 120 pages of fiction or 60 pages of non-fiction, a roll with anything but cheese, two Cokes and a window out of which to stare occasionally.

But this trip was different. The day before, out of the blue, I learned that my mother had died suddenly. Now I had to go home and deal with it. There were no known units to measure this trip. For nineteen years she had been an imposing presence. The possibility of her absence had never really occurred to me. The train was pulling out of Waverley station and heading towards King's Cross, yet I had no idea where I was going or what I would do when I got there. I was motherless, clueless, hopeless, helpless and emotionally homeless.

With the castle behind me and my girlfriend Zoe at my side, I felt it as a void. My mother was dead. In time, I would have enough practice in saying it, but on that first day it was like an incantation: I had to say it to believe it and I had to believe it to feel it. The glory of Berwick's coastline passed me by. This journey had nothing to do with geography. I drew in and out of emotions far more frequently than the train drew in and out of stations.

By Newcastle, I had made up my mind that, now this well of unconditional love had unexpectedly dried up, I would have to toughen up. I was on my own. I could no longer count on anyone to catch me if I fell. As we crossed the Tyne, I was warming to this new self-image. It would be me against the world—a steely-nerved warrior wandering silent, barefoot and resolute, like David Carradine, through an emotional desert.

By Durham, I was sobbing, being consoled by Zoe and stared at by other passengers. The banality of my surroundings and the raw pain of my trauma did not travel well together. I did not wail but sobbed, like a Brit too self-conscious to wear grief with style—one eye on a pit of despair and the other on my dignity.

By York, I had decided that my mother had had a good life. She had three sons who loved her and a keen sense of her own freedom even as she remained shackled to motherhood and hard times. She also had a sense of humor which, like much else in our family, swayed between the chaotic and the mildly inappropriate. A few days later, rummaging through the house, we would find a leaflet inviting her to join the Conservative party. In a space for comments she had written: "Please do not stick this shit in my letterbox."

By Doncaster, I had changed my mind: my mother had had a terrible life. By the age of twenty-six, she had found herself alone in a foreign country with no money and three children aged six and under. She spent little money on herself and waged constant battles with racism, her weight, sexism and her own disinterest in housework, which she had bequeathed to her three messy sons. She had had plans to revisit Barbados that summer for the first time in fifteen years.

By the time we left Peterborough, I knew the jig was up. My mother had been the first person close to me who had died and I imagined there may be some eternal truths that only this immediate aftermath of her death could bring. As we tore through Bedfordshire and into Hertfordshire, I understood that whatever lessons I would learn would have to come from me—not death, life, love or Mum.

I got out at Stevenage like an immigrant docking on Ellis Island; the end of my journey marked the beginning of a new and unknown reality. Only, with this arrival, there was no hope.

This was the most traumatic event of my life. It had no impact on my politics whatsoever. The personal is not necessarily political. Most of the time, it is just personal.

vii. 1990: Paris

I remember his face. I was on the Boulevard St Michel on a student demonstration. A posh-looking man in a checked cotton suit sitting near the restaurant window looked up from his lunch at the protesters with something like disgust. A young black kid standing next to me saw him, walked up to the window—a huge, sheer, clear pane—and kicked it in. It seemed to shatter in slow motion. And between the shards the face of the man at the table contorted in fear. The thin film that separated him from chaos and retribution had been erased. He was terrified. The kid walked off laughing. And I looked on in envy, wishing it had been me who had had the courage to put my foot through a window and scare the bourgeois.

My six months in Paris as an exchange student were not supposed to be like this. I had imagined my time here as a series of clichés: after enrolling at the Sorbonne I would find a nice one-room apartment in Belleville and spend my days reading, smoking and playing pinball. Instead, it was the most intensely racist experience of my life, and it left me sufficiently alienated to be able to savor the sight of fear in the face of this man I'd never met but who had somehow, in that moment, come to represent everything I loathed.

The ordeal started almost immediately, when I began looking for flats. Landlords and ladies would ask me on the phone where I was from. If I said Britain, that just cost me a futile trip. Too embarrassed to turn me away at the door, they would show me the room and I would ask questions—both of us knowing from the moment we locked eyes that it was never going to happen. So after a while I would just tell them I was from the Caribbean and wait to hear their excuses, evasions and complications. After several weeks of rejection, I was about to give up when a posh Englishman—the very kind that I had learned so much from and about in Sudan—heard of my plight and, unbeknownst to me, set about finding me digs. I ended up staying with a fantastic journalist in a plum location just by the Panthéon. This was less of a catch than it might have seemed. Few black people could afford to live there so whenever I went out I ran the risk of being stopped, searched and rifled for my papers. The assumption was that I was either an illegal immigrant, a thief or a burglar. Almost every day I would suffer this indignity at the hands of the state, and some days more than once.

The humiliations were routine. Color bars in nightclubs meant that I needed white people to vouch for me. Standing in line at a taxi rank, I would wait my turn only for the driver to say he wouldn't take me anywhere (my trip was from one part of central Paris to another). After some arguing, I would finally step back, watch a white woman take "my" cab then try the next one. I would generally have to try three cabs before I got a ride. One evening, as the subway pulled into the Arts et Métiers station, I was pulled off the train and beaten up by several policemen who claimed they were looking for drugs. After that, whenever I saw police, my stomach would tighten and my legs weaken. There was no saying what they might do. My French, while not fluent, was actually too convincing for them to believe I was English. As my hair was in plaits and I wore tracksuit trousers, they would not believe I was at the Sorbonne or that I lived in this area. I was simply not credible and therefore incredibly vulnerable. And so, each day, I would be forced to explain myself to armed men in broad daylight.

This in turn made me incredulous about the French establishment and its high regard for its "values" and system of government. I was sickened by the sight of smug politicians and philosophers referring in such grand terms to a society of which they clearly had no knowledge. "Do you have any idea what is going on in this godforsaken country of yours?" I would think to myself when I saw them on TV. "Do you know how vile this place can be?" Every evening, I would walk up the Rue Soufflot on the way to my apartment and look back to see the top of the Eiffel Tower lit up and poking over the Jardin du Luxembourg's silhouette. Each time, I would think: "That is beautiful and has nothing at all to do with me."

By the time my stay drew to a close, I was deeply embittered and completely alienated, so much so that the sight of a foot going through a window and the terror on the face of an unknown man seemed not just appropriate but enjoyable and just.

viii. 1991: Leningrad

I rose, in a state of deep excitement, to the sound of a rumbling trolley bus and flakes of snow that looked as big as my palm. When I told people that, after Paris, I was going to study in Leningrad, they would purse their lips and inhale deeply. All the news reports claimed that Mikhail Gorbachev's attempt to democratize and modernize the Soviet Union was causing mayhem; there were food shortages, rationing and chaos. I couldn't wait. While I had never been particularly interested in the politics of the Soviet Union, I had always been fascinated by the place, and now I felt I was in a race between me and events. I wanted to get there before the whole thing collapsed in a heap. I just made it.

Shortly after we arrived, the full extent of the Soviet Union's economic implosion became clear. We were given ration cards for things that didn't exist. Roubles stopped meaning anything, since you couldn't buy anything with them. The woman I was lodging with saw the value of her wages shrink until they were worth about £5 a month. It was dire. When my brother heard just how bad things were, he rushed to his corner shop in Northern Ireland, bought some packet food and stuck it in an envelope without a letter. "If I'd waited to write something, I would never have sent it, and it looked like you really might need it," he later told me.

Those who had expressed envy at my stay in Paris, where I had such a terrible time, now voiced pity that I would be in Russia. In truth, I was having the time of my life. Being Western made you rich. If you could find anything to buy for roubles, it was almost as if it were free. I remember finding a kiosk that sold good champagne for the equivalent of 75 pence and buying eight bottles, which my fellow students and I glugged like we were bumpkin billionaires. Once, standing near the Cosmos Hotel in Moscow, I took a fistful of roubles out of my pocket while looking for a pen. It must have been the equivalent of £30 or a few months of a good local wage. I heard a man behind me laugh and remark, "That money means nothing to him."

Under these circumstances, capitalism was immensely attractive to many Russians. My attempts to try to correct the fallacy that everything in the Soviet Union was terrible and everything in the West was fantastic crashed on the rocks of their daily lives. "You have free health care here," I told one friend. "Have you seen our hospitals?" she replied.

You can't tell people they're happy when they're not. And if you try, you should not expect to be taken seriously. But this moment in global politics, in this time and place, had major implications for me personally. For my black skin, plaited hair, Levi's jeans and Converse trainers and the absence of other examples made me the quintessential symbol of wealth and Western cool—in the eyes of Russians, at least.

This position of privilege rested on two assumptions. First, I couldn't possibly be Russian (though this was not strictly true it was statistically likely). That meant I had no connection with the shame and poverty of the times. Now, when we wanted to go any-where where only the wealthy were welcome, such as hotels or hard-currency bars, I would occasionally have to vouch for my white fellow students who could have been taken for Russian and therefore might have been poor. Second, apparently, neither could I be mistaken for an African. The African students I met had a terrible time. Racism had long been a problem. But with the Soviet demise, they were more easily scapegoated than ever. To some, they signified living proof of the deluded grandeur of a system that had sought to establish solidarity with poor nations even as it struggled to feed its own people.

Being neither Russian nor African meant I was, almost by default, Western. And that meant I was wealthy. Whereas in Paris I could not get a cab even at a rank, in Leningrad, people driving regular cars would stop and offer to turn themselves into cab-drivers—at a price. For the first and really only time in my life, my particular identity conveyed power and wealth.

ix. *San Juan: 2004*

While on holiday in San Juan, Puerto Rico's main city, with my friend Erich, we were stopped by the police for driving the wrong way up a one-way street. We told them we were lost. They asked us where we were trying to get to. Erich told me to ask for directions. But I didn't really want to. We were going to Eros, a gay nightclub. And for all the various ways in which I was completely relaxed about that, the idea that I would volunteer it to an armed policeman in the Caribbean was not one of them.

I don't think of myself as straight. I don't need to. While being gay is relentlessly interrogated, straightness—its privileges, assumptions and presumptions—is never up for discussion. Straightness is everywhere and shapes pretty much everything. We put up pictures of ourselves kissing our partners in our offices, talk about our weddings and hold hands in public as a matter of course. Nobody asks me when I first realized I was straight; I didn't have to come out to anybody.

Like being Christian, Western or able-bodied, straight is one of my many dormant identities which hold sufficient power that I don't have to think about it. And then, suddenly, going the wrong way down a one-way street in San Juan, there it is. Sitting in a car with another man and asking directions to a gay club suggests I am gay. From then until the police wave us on, I will be treated like a gay man. And the problem was not that I would be mistaken for something I was not— as a black man living in the US with a British accent and two university degrees, that happens to me all the time. The problem, if I am honest, was that I specifically did not want to be mistaken for being gay. Quite what I thought the consequences of that "mistake" would be in this particular moment I'm not sure. Maybe I feared for my safety. Who knows? Until that moment, I hadn't had to deal with being straight in a way that had ever bothered me.

Months later, this non-incident long forgotten, I was telling Erich about how I had discovered that a longstanding friend whom I had assumed was straight was, in fact, gay. I'd only found this out after I had quizzed him extensively about his "girlfriend." After we'd had a laugh at my expense, Erich shared a strategy to make sure I never made that mistake again.

"Just assume everyone is gay," he said. "Straight people will tell you they're straight in no time at all." They tell you about their relationships, families, predilections and pursuits, he continued. Before they've got to know you they'll share stories and pictures and public embraces that set out their stall, without even thinking about it. You just can't avoid it. And the ones who don't talk to you about being straight are probably gay.

It sounded like he was exaggerating for effect, indulging himself in an elaborate rhetorical flourish. It felt like a strange way to try and understand the world. Until, that is, I tried it and discovered something even stranger. It actually works.

x. Brooklyn: 2007

The day I brought my newborn son home to our Brooklyn apartment, an article in *The New York Times* pointed out that "a black male who drops out of high school [in the US] is 60 times more likely to find himself in prison than one with a bachelor's degree." Looking down at him as he snoozed in the brand-new car seat, my first thought was: "Those are not great odds. I'd better buy some more children's books."

My son, Osceola, is a product of his time and place. Quite what that time and place will mean for him is anybody's guess. Statistically, the chances of him going to prison are horribly high. But, born on the weekend that Barack Obama announced his candidacy, his chances of being president are a lot higher than they once were too.

Becoming a father did not introduce me to this reality, it just gave me a different relationship to it. Understanding these contradictions is one thing. Providing the equipment for someone else to deal with them is quite another. Such was the transition to fatherhood—an introduction to a whole new field of interaction.

The sight of me carrying Osceola around as a tiny infant made black women, in particular, coo. A few actually congratulated me, not on fatherhood per se so much as my acting like a father, stopping to tell me how nice it was to see a black man out with his child. That made me sad.

In Charleston airport in South Carolina, an elderly white lady tendered words of affection to my baby son. I smiled, but was thinking: "Wait fifteen years, lady, and you'll be crossing the road to avoid him." It's difficult to think of a less generous response to a warm gesture. That made me sad too.

Working out precisely what my responsibilities are in this new role feels elusive. It seems there was a time when being a father meant something more definite if emotionally disabling: to be the provider and disciplinarian. I don't mourn the loss of that narrow function but crave some pointers towards a new one. On the way to daycare, one parent tells me that he's already spent more time with his two-year-old son than his father spent with him in his first ten years.

But Osceola's arrival also forces me to wrestle with the likelihood that I will end up living in America—a place I'd never intended to stay—for good. Having a child means putting down roots. On some level, I had got used to being rootless. I don't crave Britain, but I cannot help but compare Osceola's life chances there to here. In America, he is far more likely to be killed, be a millionaire, go to prison or become a national leader than he would be if we moved to England. But then, when he comes of age, that comparison will probably be irrelevant to him. By then, my English upbringing may well seem like an erratic blip in my family trajectory from Africa to the Americas. In personal life, as in politics, we build the future from our history. The thing is, we do not live in the past. In the words of the ancient Greek philosopher Heraclitus: "You can't cross the same river twice. The river is different. And you are different." Osceola is a product of his time and space. He may not have written the prelude, but he too owns his own story.

But this is not about me. This is just a personal illustration to demonstrate that we do not cut our politics from cloth but weave it from the material we have at hand. Everybody has their own tics, affiliations, grudges and connections which, together, comprise their identity. The tension between who we are, what we make of it and what we might do with it is rarely resolved.

2. A Wise Latina

The question is not whether we all have identities, but whether we are all prepared to recognize them

St Augustine looked at history from the point of view of the early
Christian; Tillemont, from that of a seventeenth-century Frenchman;
Gibbon, from that of an eighteenth-century Englishman; Mommsen,
from that of a nineteenth-century German. There is no point in asking
which was the right point of view. Each was the only one possible
for the man who adopted it.

– Robin G. Collingwood, *The Ideas of History*

On 2 October 2001, Federal Appeals Court judge Sonia Sotomayor
delivered the Judge Mario G. Olmos Memorial Lecture at the University of California, Berkeley, School of Law. The speech, entitled
"Raising the Bar: Latino and Latina Presence in the Judiciary and the
Struggle for Representation," sought to make the case for what a
Latina judge might contribute to a system that draws from too shallow
a pool of experience and talent. Sotomayor herself clearly had a great
deal to offer. She graduated top of her class at Princeton before going
on to Yale, where she edited the *Law Journal*. After a brief stint in
private practice, she was nominated to the federal bench, where she
spent five years, before being nominated to the Court of Appeals.
She also had a compelling personal story—one of those tales of taut
bootstraps and meritocratic uplift that make America's heart beat just
that little bit faster. She was raised in housing projects in the Bronx
by Puerto Rican parents; her father, a factory worker, died when she
was nine; her mother was a nurse. As a child, Sotomayor was diagnosed with diabetes. Initially inspired by reading about the adventures
of the fictional sleuth Nancy Drew, she later had a shift in ambition

and decided to become a judge after watching fictional defense lawyer Perry Mason on television. Before she became a teenager her mind was made up. "I was going to college and I was going to become an attorney, and I knew that when I was ten," she once said. "Ten. That's no jest."

Statistically, it was a straightforward argument to make. At the time, women made up 13 percent of the federal judiciary while Latinos (who constituted around 13 percent of the population) comprised just 5 percent. For non-white women, it was even worse. In 1998, black women (6 percent of the population) made up 1.6 percent of the federal judiciary, and Latinas (also 6 percent of the population) just 1 percent. The higher up the hierarchy, the more scarce non-white women became, until you reached the Supreme Court, where there had never been any non-white women at all and white men had ruled exclusively for the first 178 of its 212 years.

But the philosophical and political case for what difference a Latina presence on the benches would make to the judicial system, beyond ethnic difference itself, was more complex. Sotomayor noted Judge Miriam Cedarbaum's contention that "judges must transcend their personal sympathies and prejudices and aspire to achieve a greater degree of fairness and integrity based on the reason of law." She also gave a nod to the claim of Yale Law School's Stephen Carter that, among any group of human beings, there is a diversity of opinion, because there is both a diversity of experiences and of thought—put bluntly, not all Latinas think alike. And she acknowledged Professor Judith Resnik's theory that feminism does not have one single voice but many.

Notwithstanding all of these caveats, Sotomayor deduced that her difference did make a difference. Quoting Martha Minnow of the Harvard Law School, she said, "There is no objective stance but only a series of perspectives—no neutrality, no escape from choice in judging." And those choices, insisted Sotomayor, are rooted in our life histories. "I further accept that our experiences as women and people of color affect our decisions," she argued. "The aspiration to impartiality is just that—it's an aspiration because it denies the fact that we are by our experiences making different choices than others.

Not all women or people of color, in all or some circumstances or indeed in any particular case or circumstance but enough people of color in enough cases, will make a difference in the process of judging."

Sandra Day O'Connor, the first woman ever to be nominated to the court, had long argued that there were limits to such a position. She was often quoted as saying that a wise old man and a wise old woman would reach the same conclusion when deciding cases. Sotomayor disagreed: "First . . . there can never be a universal definition of wise. Second, I would hope that a wise Latina woman with the richness of her experiences would more often than not reach a better conclusion than a white male who hasn't lived that life." She concluded: "Personal experiences affect the facts that judges choose to see. My hope is that I will take the good from my experiences and extrapolate them further into areas with which I am unfamiliar. I simply do not know exactly what that difference will be in my judging. But I accept there will be some based on my gender and my Latina heritage."

Sotomayor's speech attracted relatively little attention at the time. Delivered about a month after the terrorist attacks of 9/11, the nation's mind was on other things. But eight years later, when Barack Obama nominated her to the Supreme Court, conservatives returned to it with avid interest. From all the judgments, speeches and rulings she had made in her life, for the most part, they focused on just the one sentence about the relative merits of being a "wise Latina."

"If Lindsey Graham said that I will make a better senator than X because my experience as a Caucasian male makes me better able to represent the people of South Carolina, and my opponent was a minority, it would make national news, and it should," said Senator Lindsey Graham, who insisted, "If I had said anything remotely like that, my career would have been over."

Senator Jon Kyl was aggrieved on two issues: "a) you understand [your gender and ethnicity] will make a difference; and b) not only are you not saying anything negative about that, but you seem to embrace that difference in concluding that you'll make better decisions. That's the basis of concern that a lot of people have."

They had a point. There is nothing inherent in race or ethnicity that makes blacks or Latinos better judges. After all, just a month earlier, the only member of the Supreme Court to vote to overturn an important piece of the 1965 Voting Rights Act that forced areas with a history of racism to provide advance notice before changing their election rules was the only black judge—ultra-conservative Clarence Thomas. The measure was devised to ensure that there would be no slippage back to the period of black disenfranchisement of the segregation era. In his dissent, Thomas, who was raised in extreme poverty in the Deep South, argued that, "The extensive pattern of discrimination that led the Court to previously uphold [this law] . . . no longer exists." The eight other, white, judges, who were raised in relative affluence, disagreed. Given the trend of Sotomayor's previous rulings, it's fair to say she would have found Thomas's conclusion anything but "wise."

Moreover, there are courts in Latin America packed with Latinos and (to a far lesser extent) Latinas, some of whom make terrible decisions. Wisdom is not shaped by gender or ethnicity. A wise white man, almost by definition, would reach intelligent conclusions too. Forced to clarify that particular line in her speech during the Senate hearings, Sotomayor said her comment "was bad, because it left an impression that I believed that life experiences commanded a result in a case," but went on to insist that the aim of the speech was to inspire young Latino law students by showing them that their experiences were valuable. "Life experiences have to influence you," she explained. "We're not robots who listen to evidence and don't have feelings. We have to recognize those feelings, and put them aside. That's what my speech was saying."

For all the furor over that one line, this was an argument the committee had heard many times before. In 2006, during the hearings for the conservative Supreme Court nominee Samuel Alito, he confessed that being the son of Italian immigrants had an impact on his rulings: "When a case comes before me involving, let's say, someone who is an immigrant, I can't help but think of my own ancestors, because it wasn't that long ago when they were in that position."

Indeed, when Clarence Thomas's confirmation hearings in 1991 risked being derailed by accusations that he had sexually harassed a black woman, he intimated that his racial identity was the principal reason why he was undergoing such hostile questioning. "This is a circus," he said. "It's a national disgrace. And from my standpoint, as a black American, it is a high-tech lynching for uppity blacks who in any way deign to think for themselves, to do for themselves, to have different ideas, and it is a message that unless you kowtow to an old order, this is what will happen to you. You will be lynched, destroyed, caricatured by a committee of the US Senate rather than hung from a tree."

But when it came to Sotomayor, the committee's conservatives just couldn't let it go. She was evoking an identity with which they had little sympathy, towards ends with which they did not agree: "Isn't it true this statement suggests that you accept that there may be sympathies, prejudices and opinions that legitimately can influence a judge's decision?" asked Alabama senator Jeff Sessions. "And how can that further faith in the impartiality of the system?" Mr Sessions went on to insist that Sotomayor's statement went "against the American ideal and oath that a judge takes to be fair to every party. And every day when they put on that robe, that is a symbol that they're to put aside their personal biases and prejudices."

Sessions knew a thing or two about personal biases. When Ronald Reagan nominated him to be a judge on the District Court for the southern district of Alabama, four Department of Justice lawyers who had worked with him testified that he had made racist statements. As an assistant attorney, he had branded a white civil rights lawyer who concentrated on voting-rights cases a "disgrace to his race" and described the nation's oldest civil rights organization, the National Association for the Advancement of Colored People (NAACP) as "un-American" and a "Communist inspired" body that "forced civil rights down the throats of people." He also called a black fellow assistant attorney "boy" and told him he thought the Ku Klux Klan was "okay until I found out they were smoking pot." He was only the second nominee in forty-eight years to have their nomination rejected by the judiciary committee. Even some of his fellow Republican colleagues had reasonable doubt that his personal prejudices would get the better of him.

*

Everybody has an identity. Indeed, we all have many. "We know of no people without names, no languages or cultures in which some manner of distinctions between self and other, we and they are not made," writes Craig Calhoun in *Social Theory and the Politics of Identity*. "We are distinct from each other, and often strive to distinguish ourselves further. Yet each dimension of distinction is apt at least tacitly also to establish commonality with a set of others who are similarly distinguished." It takes a while for some people to figure this out.

While talking to a group of African-American children in Brooklyn some years back about my childhood, one of them asked me, "Was it strange growing up in England with an accent?" "Well, in England, everybody spoke like me," I said. Grappling with the notion that all things are relative, the boy opened his eyes wide as he suddenly realized that he too had an accent. But many go through life believing that everyone has an accent apart from them.

In general, the more power an identity carries, the less likely its carrier is to be aware of it as an identity at all. Those who have never been asked, "How do you balance childcare and work?" or "How can you prove that you will return home after this holiday?" are less likely to think that their masculinity or Western citizenship and the privileges that come with them are anything but the normal state of affairs. Because their identity is never interrogated, they are easily seduced by the idea that they do not have one. Strip them of their citizenship, recategorize their ethnicity or put them in a place where they become a minority, and see how quickly they will cling to attributes they have inherited. That section of the media in Britain that has long dismissed issues of race when it relates to black minorities in Europe was the most likely to overemphasize race when referring to white minorities in Africa. These contradictions are usually obvious to all but those who have them. Devoid of any awareness that they too possess a perspective rooted in their own experience, for them every food with which they are unfamiliar is "ethnic food" and every month is their history month.

Those who assume the primacy of their own experience expect the powerless to learn about the powerful—their language, history, culture—but never vice versa. "But for me I had just one question," says Gilbert, one of the Jamaican protagonists, who served in the British Army and arrived in Britain on SS *Windrush*, in Andrea Levy's novel *Small Island*. "How come England did not know me? . . . It was inconceivable that we Jamaicans, we West Indians, we members of the British Empire would not fly to the Mother Country's defense when there was threat. But tell me, if Jamaica was in trouble, is there any major, any general, any sergeant who would have been able to find that dear island? Give me a map, let me see if Tommy Atkins or Lady Havealot can point to Jamaica. Let us watch them turning the page round, screwing up their eyes to look, turning it over to see if perhaps the region was lost on the back before shrugging defeat."

Mistaking freedom of thought and action for abstraction and detachment, those who claim they are not influenced by perspectives inherited through their various identities essentially believe that by will alone they can declare unilateral independence from this world and create a new one in which their lives make sense only in complete isolation. Unshaped by time and unmoved by place, they insist that their thoughts, unfettered by background or circumstance, are theirs alone. They must assume that, had they been born a girl in India or a boy in the eighteenth century, their worldview would be exactly the same. But follow that logic, and you are left with a person who lives outside history, geography or civilization. And those people simply do not exist.

For most people, constant reminders of difference are ubiquitous. In times of crisis, they are inescapable. In 1994, in Rwanda, Tutsis had to think of themselves as Tutsis in order to know they had to flee. Similarly, in Saudi Arabia, a woman who does not think of herself as a woman will soon find herself flogged and ostracized for failing to behave accordingly. While to thrive they will have to reject the roles that have been assigned to them, to survive they still have to acknowledge that those roles persist.

"When you're my size and not being tormented by elevator buttons, water fountains and ATMs you spend your life accommodating the sensibilities of 'normal people,'" says Cady Roth, the protagonist of restricted growth from Armistead Maupin's novel *Maybe the Moon*.

"You learn to bury your own feelings and honor theirs in the hope that they'll meet you halfway. It becomes your job, and yours alone, to explain, to ignore, to forgive—over and over again. There's no way you can get around this. You do it if you want to have a life and not spend it being corroded by your own anger. You do it if you want to belong to the human race."

But those who feel they are without identity do not see the need to meet people halfway and thereby fail to recognize that everyone else is doing all the traveling. It's not that they deny that group identities exist, it's just that they don't believe that such identities apply to them. Referring to a controversial case over which Sotomayor had presided, Sessions chided her for not siding with another Puerto Rican judge: "You voted not to reconsider the prior case," he told her. "Had you voted with Judge Cabranes, himself of Puerto Rican ancestry, had you voted with him, you could've changed that case." Ultimately, it seems, Sessions' problem was not that Sotomayor had been guided by her ethnicity but that she had been guided in the wrong direction.

The underlying assumption of the conservatives on the judiciary committee was that, while Sotomayor had to negotiate her gender and ethnicity in order to reach an objective decision, being a Caucasian male is an objective position in itself: not an identity but an orthodoxy.

Common sense and empirical evidence suggest otherwise. The facts show that, where the American judiciary is concerned, not only do judges who have different identities make different kinds of decisions, but white male judges make different decisions when they are not surrounded solely by other white male judges. A 2005 *Yale Law Journal* study found not only that "female judges were significantly more likely than male judges to find for . . . plaintiffs in sexual harassment cases" but also that "the presence of a female judge significantly increased the probability that a male" on a three-judge panel "would find for the plaintiff."

The experiences of the only two female judges to have sat on the court at that point, Ruth Bader Ginsburg, a liberal Jew from Brooklyn appointed by Democrat Bill Clinton, and Sandra Day O'Connor, a conservative Protestant appointed by Republican Ronald Reagan, bear this out. "As often as Justice O'Connor and I have disagreed, because she is truly a Republican from Arizona, we were together in all the gender discrimination cases," said Ginsburg.

This is not just true for gender. A study in the *Columbia Law Review* in 2008 found a similar effect with race in voting-rights cases. "When a white judge sits on a panel with at least one African-American judge," the study, conducted by Adam B. Cox and Thomas J. Miles, concluded, "she becomes roughly 20 percentage points more likely to find" a voting-rights violation.

One of the most right-wing voices on the court, and a firm opponent of affirmative action, Antonin Scalia effectively confirmed this from his own experience. Referring to the presence of the first black justice, Thurgood Marshall, Scalia recalled: "[He] could be a persuasive force just by sitting there . . . He wouldn't have to open his mouth to affect the nature of the conference and how seriously the conference would take matters of race." Ginsburg recalls a case involving Savana Redding, a thirteen-year-old girl who had been strip-searched at school on suspicion of hiding some ibuprofen. Ginsburg believes the men on the court, several of whom had suggested, during oral argument, that they found little troubling about the search, were slow to grasp the stakes. "They have never been a 13-year-old girl," she told *The New York Times*. "It's a very sensitive age for a girl. I didn't think that my colleagues, some of them, quite understood." The court eventually ruled 8–1 in Redding's favor. The sole dissenting voice was Clarence Thomas. Justice, it turns out, is anything but blind. It depends on who's looking, what they are looking at and who they are looking with. In the words of Mr Bumble in Charles Dickens's *Oliver Twist*, who famously branded the law an "ass": "The worst I wish the law is that his eye may be opened by experience—by experience."

Although we all have several identities, not all those identities are political, even if most have the potential to become so. Take names. In Northern Ireland, one of the key ways of telling people's religion there is by their name. Those with first names such as Eoin, Sinéad, Niamh and Aoibheann or Irish surnames had a tougher time at the checkpoints. Those with Jewish and Muslim names will have encountered similar assumptions in different places at different times in history. In *Freakonomics*, Steven Levitt proved that people with names that were identifiably African-American had a worse life outcome than those with identifiably white names, although this was concluded to be an indicator of broader societal and historical issues rather than a cause of them.

The notion that the "personal is the political" gained currency during the sixties and became a mantra, particularly for the feminist movement. There was good reason for this. When cast as "personal," issues such as abortion, domestic violence, childcare responsibilities and housework were effectively excluded from broader political discussion, leaving women isolated in their attempts to seek equality, safety and greater freedom. By reframing them as political, feminists opened up fresh terrain, which would also prove particularly fertile for environmentalists. By the turn of the century, issues such as the use of condoms, the purchase of SUVs and fair trade produce and recycling your rubbish had become part of mainstream political conversation. But along the way, there were some who equated the "personal is political" with the "emotional is empirical." Personal decisions and psychological conditions were endowed with political import, and vice versa: black people who chose white partners were branded sell-outs, and anti-Zionist Jews were diagnosed as self-hating. Experience gained primacy over argument. A survivor of rape, concentration camps or homophobic or racist attack claimed the right not only to be heard but not to be argued with. People could silence any opposition simply by insisting, "I've been through it, I know." The idea that others who had been through it might have different interpretations or that those who hadn't might have valid things to contribute was brushed aside.

This is not just an issue with the Left. The Right is also extremely fond of promoting individual members of a community who will push the Right agenda, as though the fact of their identity is the argument itself: the African-American who is opposed to affirmative action; the woman who wants less stringent rape laws; the Muslim who will castigate political Islam. These are legitimate political positions but receive disproportionate attention primarily because the people who hold them do not represent the usual views of the group with which they are associated—as though the identity of the person who holds a particular idea makes the idea itself better or more valid.

In reality, the distinction between the personal and the political is blurred, fluid and important. Take height. There are plenty of people who are very tall and plenty who are very small. Being either is not just a matter of aesthetics, it can have a major impact on your life chances. Research has shown that taller people are regarded as being more persuasive, more attractive and to have greater leadership potential. Americans have not elected a president of below-average height since 1896. Various studies have shown that 78 percent of recruiters believe that taller salespeople are more impressive and that shorter police officers receive more complaints and are responsible for lower morale.

"Although it is tempting to dismiss this belief as a folk tale, research suggests that some elements of life are easier for taller people because height is a socially desirable asset," argue Timothy Judge and Daniel Cable in their paper "The Effect of Physical Height on Workplace Success and Income." There are substantial consequences to these prejudices. "An individual who is 6 feet tall would be predicted to earn almost $166,000 more across a 30 year period than an individual who is 5 feet 5," they concluded. They found this was true even when they allowed for gender difference. "Height has a more important effect on earnings than gender," they wrote.

So height matters. There is a clear pattern of discrimination against smaller people that appears to transcend culture. Like race, it is a physical phenomenon over which people have no control but which seems to have a disproportionate impact on their opportunities, be they professional, social or political. So why isn't it up there in the premier league with race, gender, sexual orientation, nationality and the like? Why don't people generally talk about height as being a political identity?

Well, first of all, in some contexts, we do. Little people (more commonly referred to as dwarves), for example, have to negotiate all the obstacles that come with having a physical disability and all the competition for resources that entails. And second, for those contexts to become political, they generally involve something discrete and definite. "Being a little person is inherently political but that's not how most of our members describe it," explains Gary Arnold, a spokesman for Little People of America. "They have a shared experience. The political side to it is latent. But when we lobby for ATMs that are lower or less deep or produce position papers in response to various developments, our members relate to that as being relevant to their lives."

Outside of such a specific experience, however, at any given time in any given place, we would not know where to find people of our own height and they would not know how to find us. And if we did find each other, it is not entirely clear what we would talk about. For while we clearly have a shared experience, that experience simply is not substantial enough to warrant a special meeting. Tall women and short men could talk about their trouble getting dates and clothes that fit. After that, the well would run pretty dry. They would have no shared history. There have, to my knowledge, been no riots, suffrage campaigns or marches over issues of height. People have not been violated, enslaved or massacred because they are small. (In Rwanda, tall people were often identified as Tutsis and therefore slaughtered but, in that case, height was understood not as an identity in itself but as a crude shorthand for an ethnic identity.) Smaller people are not a community in any meaningful sense of the word and neither are tall people. That doesn't mean they could not become one. Nor does it deny the fact that discrimination against shorter people exists. But what it does mean is that, for now, they do not represent any kind of group from which one could claim a viable social identity.

To have meaning, such an identity demands some sense of community: a societal connection that links what is personal and particular to what is collective and general. Such identities emerge organically, and messily, as a result of an experience that is sufficiently relevant and coherent as to be meaningful at a given moment.

The fact that we all have identities does not mean that all identities are interchangeable. The context matters. To try to understand what an identity means from outside its context is tantamount to misunderstanding it completely. When Senator Graham told Sotomayor that if he had said his experience as a white man would enable him to better represent South Carolinians he would get into serious trouble, he was being, at best, disingenuous. For most of the time that South Carolina has been electing senators, only Caucasian males have been allowed to vote and stand and only they have stood a serious chance of winning. So he wouldn't need to say that. Such a statement would make as little sense as a straight person talking about when they came out to their parents. And, unlike Sotomayor, if Graham did say such a thing it could not reasonably be understood as an attempt to redress the race and gender inequalities of this former slave-holding state.

Like Sotomayor, Frank Ricci has the kind of personal drive that makes America's heart race. In late 2003, the firefighter, from New Haven, Connecticut, studied eight to thirteen hours a day for exams that could lead to promotion to lieutenant and captain in the city's fire department. This was no small feat for Ricci. He gave up a second job so he could study and, because he is dyslexic, paid a friend to record the books on tape because he learns better by listening. All in all, his preparation cost him around $1,000. He not only passed, but passed well. Then he was told the results were invalid. While several black firefighters had passed the exam, too few of them had scored highly enough to be considered for the management positions available on the basis of the test alone. Fearing that to appoint only white firefighters would leave them in violation of civil rights legislation and open to a lawsuit over racial discrimination, the City of New Haven decided to annul the results and promote no one. They became the target of a lawsuit anyway; Ricci was the lead plaintiff. He claimed he had been discriminated against because he was white. He was joined by sixteen other white firefighters and one Latino.

The District Court found against them. They appealed. The case went to the Second Circuit Court of Appeals, where Sotomayor was a judge. The Circuit Court upheld the District Court's decision. Ricci appealed again. The case went to the Supreme Court, after Sotomayor had been nominated but before she had been confirmed, which found 5–4 in favor of Ricci. Sotomayor's role in the earlier decision was heavily scrutinized during the hearings.

It is not difficult to understand why Ricci felt aggrieved. He had worked hard and sacrificed a great deal to take the test. He aced it. There was no evidence that the tests in themselves were biased against black people or towards whites. To deny him the rewards of that effort violates a basic sense of fairness. In this particular case, the City of New Haven was clearly at fault. You cannot start a competition and then change the rules when it's over because you do not like the results.

Unfortunately, in a city such as New Haven there is plenty of unfairness to go around. Black men in the town are more than twice as likely to be unemployed than whites; black household income in the town is 84 percent of that of whites; the median value of black people's houses is 83 percent of whites. In Connecticut, where New Haven is situated, black people are twelve times more likely to be in prison than whites. As a whole, black families in the state are more than twice as likely to live in poverty and not have medical insurance as whites—probably in no small part the reason why black infant mortality is almost three times, and the rate of AIDS nine times, higher than among whites.

This state of affairs was, not surprisingly, reflected in the New Haven Fire Department, which was founded in 1862 but did not employ a black firefighter until 1957. There was one black man hired before him, according to Lieutenant Gary Tinney, president of the New Haven Firebirds, the city's black firefighters association, but he was a chauffeur who drove the chief around. In 1973, African-Americans constituted just 18 out of 502 firefighters (3.6 percent) even though they made up 30 percent of the town's population. The department employed no Latinos. Much like the judiciary, the further you went up the ladder, the worse it got. Of the 107 officers in the department at the time only one was black, and he held the lowest rank above private. By 2005, improvements were only marginal—three African-Americans and three Latinos out of thirty-two officers had reached the level of captain or higher.

"This significant shortfall is not due to a shortage of black entry-level firefighters," explained the NAACP in its amicus brief to the Supreme Court, "where—in contrast to the supervisory ranks—New Haven has made some progress in hiring people of color . . . in 2007, African Americans held 32 percent of entry-level positions in the fire department, but only 15 percent of supervisory positions."

The situation represented by these statistics does not come about by accident (unless, of course, you subscribe to the idea that black people are inherently incompetent and lazy and brought all these disparities on themselves). It is part of a historical process of discrimination stretching back to slavery that has left African-Americans falling foul not just of the law of the land but of the law of probabilities. So while the process by which the New Haven Fire Department attempted to engineer diversity was deeply flawed, its desire to do so is rooted in efforts to redress a deep-seated, longstanding racial imbalance and could and should have been attempted in some other way.

However, as another story about affirmative action—the move to redress gender, racial and ethnic inequality—illustrates, the target of grievance is rarely the source of the resentment. In 1995, Jennifer Gratz, a working-class girl who finished in the top 5 percent of her high school class, was rejected by the University of Michigan in Ann Arbor. Gratz assumed she had been denied the place because of something she could not help—her race. The university used a points system when selecting applicants, and those from under-represented minorities automatically received extra points. Concluding that affirmative action had handed her place to a less qualified black student, Gratz turned, crying, to her father, her rejection letter in her hand, and asked, "Dad, can we sue?" With the help of a well-funded right-wing lobbying group, they did, and the case went to the Supreme Court in 2003. In the meantime, Gratz, whose parents had never completed college, subsequently applied to Notre Dame University in Indiana, by whom she was also rejected.

Ann Arbor is a popular establishment, founded in 1817 with the motto "An uncommon education for the common man." Places at the university are finite: 25,081 students applied for just 5,186 places in 2002. Whichever way you cut it, around 20,000 people are going to be disappointed. The question for the university is not whether or not it takes applicants who are qualified, but which qualified applicants it wants to take. "It's an issue of math," Julie Peterson, a spokesperson for the university, explained before the Supreme Court case. "There is no way that all of the students qualified to come here are going to come here. No matter what system you use, there are going to be some students who feel, 'That's not fair.'"

The odds that Gratz was turned down because she is white are very low. The number of African-American, Native American and Hispanic students who apply to the university is very small, so they have a negligible effect on the chances of white students being accepted. In 1995, the year Gratz was turned down, minorities constituted just 11 percent of applicants. Even if all of them had been rejected, the percentage of white students accepted would only have risen from 25 to 30 percent. The truth, says the university, is that Gratz would not have got in anyway—not because she is white or because she's not smart but because, given the stiff competition and limited places available, she was simply not smart enough. "People don't get in for a lot of reasons," says Peterson. "It's a myth to say, 'But for that minority student, I would have got in.' It's mathematically ridiculous. Race is a very emotional subject in our country. People have very strong feelings about it, and they are not always grounded in fact."

In her narrow focus on race, however, Gratz had ignored a far more prevalent but accepted bias—class. In most American universities, applicants receive special treatment if they are "legacies"—if their parents or siblings have studied there. This is true of the University of Michigan, and even more so of Notre Dame, where between 21 and 24 percent of the freshman class are legacies—twice the number of blacks and Latinos admitted combined. The assistant provost for admissions at Notre Dame, Daniel Saracino, told *Wall Street Journal* writer Daniel Golden, "The poor schmuck who has to get in on his own has to walk on water." Those "schmucks" such as Gratz who cannot walk on water demand a place on the rickety life rafts that African-Americans and Latinos have been crafting for the best part of a generation. And they all drown together while the wealthy and well connected cruise off in their liners.

In the absence of any appreciation of race or class, attempts to address historical imbalances of this sort are at best meaningless and at worst the basis for considerable resentment. For while it is true that, by any account, from cradle to grave, being white carries considerable relative privilege, the emphasis should be on the relative. Just because whites are more privileged than blacks does not mean they are necessarily well off. Most black people in the US are not poor, and white people make up the largest proportion of those who do live in poverty. While it is true that only white men have ever been senators in South Carolina, it is no less true that most white men in South Carolina would never stand a chance of becoming senator.

In a world where whiteness is rarely discussed, interrogated or even acknowledged, a man such as Ricci is hard put to locate himself as a political, economic or social agent. Race for him, like accents for the boy in Brooklyn, is about other people. Like a filmgoer walking into a thriller halfway through, when it comes to being a white American, he has no idea what is happening to him or why. The villain is the person he sees pull the trigger; the narrative that led up to that moment has no meaning. So he could be forgiven for wondering what any of the nation's racial complexities has to do with him. He's doing everything he can to get ahead when he suddenly finds himself buffeted by the crosswinds of history. "If you work hard, you can succeed in America," Ricci himself told the media after the verdict. "I think we view discrimination as discrimination, plain and simple," said another plaintiff, Matthew Marcarelli. "We were discriminated based upon our race just like African-Americans were in the past in other issues. So it's just plain old discrimination." Whether the purpose of the discrimination is to challenge inequality or compound it is, apparently, irrelevant.

This man, never having considered his whiteness or—worse still— only ever having been introduced to it as a mark of power he does not feel and as a signifier for bigotry he may not harbor, cannot fathom what effect it could possibly have on his career prospects. Never having considered his class as a basis for solidarity, he sees no potential to improve his lot by joining forces with blacks and Latinos. He is on his own. With no knowledge of the ways in which powerful white people have exploited racial difference to make working-class whites poorer, nor understanding that relative privilege, while relative, remains a form of privilege that is unearned, he is bereft of meaningful alternatives. Caught in a pincer between the battle for scarce resources and the battle for equality, he does not argue for more resources but against others getting the cut he has "earned." He experiences race and class not as identities but as a besieged grievance which the Right is only too happy to exploit for political gain.

This refusal to acknowledge possession of identity is invariably partial and inevitably problematic. Those who, at certain moments, claim they had nothing to do with slavery, denying women the vote or invading other nations will at others be proud to attach themselves to events at which they were not present and hail achievements to which they contributed nothing. They will boast, "We haven't been invaded since 1066"; "We've had this land in our family for generations"; or "We won the Cold War." But they would never say, "We tortured Catholics"; "We stole the land from Indians"; or "We backed death squads." That is why the most gruesome periods in history take place in the passive tense: "Jews were gassed"; "Women were denied the vote'; and "Africans were sold into slavery." Power, it seems, has many parents, but the brutality it takes to acquire it is an orphan.

While interviewing Rwandan perpetrators of genocide, Jean Hatzfeld slowly realized that his interviewees would not admit to having done anything personally: "During the first meetings, the men deny everything with a placid obstinacy whenever they are questioned about their own participation: they have not personally done anything or seen anything, period," he writes in *A Time for Machetes, The Rwandan Genocide: The Killers Speak*. It turned out that whenever he shifts from asking in the informal, singular "*tu*" form to the formal, plural "*vous*," the answers become more specific. The interviewees can speak collectively but never take responsibility individually. "Although each one is willing to recount, on his own, his experience of the genocide, they all feel the need to hide behind a more diluted syntax."

The grammar matters. The objects of oppression are many, but the subjects are few. In removing the instigators, we remove the agency and, in the final reckoning, both the historical responsibility and contemporary consequences. Nobody actually did anything bad. Only, somehow, bad things were done to people. And once the bad things stop, their legacy is erased—since nobody "did" anything, nobody could possibly have benefited. "Action," wrote Hannah Arendt in *The Human Condition*, "without a name, a who attached to it, is meaningless."

"The essential characteristic of a nation is that all its individuals must have many things in common," wrote nineteenth-century French philosopher Ernest Renan in *Qu'est-ce qu'une nation?*, "and must have forgotten many things as well." What is true for nations is true for all identities. We remember Rosa Parks, the seamstress and activist who was thrown off the Montgomery bus because she refused to sit at the back. But who will claim James Blake, the bus driver who ejected her? Ricci discovered his whiteness at the precise moment when it became advantageous for him to do so, and saw in it only victimhood.

Sotomayor's rejection of Ricci's appeal, along with her "wise Latina" comment, rendered her a valuable target for conservatives. But as time went on, the extent to which they were driven not by a yearning for meritocracy but by the defense of entitlement became clear. As Pat Buchanan's accusation that Sotomayor was a beneficiary of affirmative action illustrates, the very identities they refuse to recognize—whiteness, class and masculinity—are the selfsame ones they so eagerly evoke.

The fact that Sotomayor had more judicial experience than anyone confirmed for the court in seventy years, and more federal judicial experience than anyone in a century, was clearly not enough for Buchanan. His case was, in truth, no more based on who was best qualified than the City of New Haven's had been. Buchanan had argued that, "Frank Ricci is to be denied a promotion he worked for and won, and be robbed of his American dream by the liberal bigots who run New Haven." Yet here he is disparaging Sotomayor despite her qualifications, as though her nomination represented a specific, deliberate and lethal blow to the aspirations of the generic white male—a group that constitutes 37 percent of the population and whose representation on the court would be reduced from 78 to 67 percent as a result of her nomination.

This assault on white masculinity was taken up a notch by right-wing radio host Rush Limbaugh: "Here you have a racist—you might want to soften that, and you might want to say a reverse racist," he said of Sotomayor. Liberals, "of course, say that minorities cannot be racists because they don't have the power to implement their racism," Limbaugh added. "Well, those days are gone, because reverse racists certainly do have the power . . . Obama is the greatest living example of a reverse racist, and now he's appointed one."

Such talk is part of a growing attempt by the Right, not just in the US but globally, to reclaim victimhood for the powerful through the worst methods of identity politics, which they so freely and routinely scorn. First they create a sense of siege. "We, as a people, and the government, must make strenuous efforts to promote and defend our culture, and especially the place of Christianity in it and the rights to self-expression by Christians," wrote Simon Heffer in the *Daily Mail* in 2004—as if there were a real threat to a Christian's freedom of speech in a country with an established church and in which 72 percent of people identify themselves as Christian.

Any siege needs something to defend, hence myths such as the alleged "war against Christmas" by secularists in the US or "the banning of 'Baa Baa Black Sheep'" by anti-racists in the UK. The aim, always, is to invent a scenario where society as "we" know it is becoming unhinged from its moorings and handed over to a fringe of ne'er-do-wells and special-interest groups.

Every victim needs an aggressor. And in the event that an aggressor does not exist, one must be invented. In these cases, it is a mythical "liberal establishment." Given the rightward shift in politics and economics on both sides of the Atlantic over the last thirty years, it is difficult to work out quite where this establishment resides.

One of the favorite punch-bags is the media. Given growing corporate centralization, the plurality of viewpoints available on the internet, the success of right-wing zealots such as Ann Coulter and Glenn Beck, and that of papers such as the *Sun* and the *Daily Mail* in the UK, and television channels such as Fox in the US, the Right's criticism of the media is difficult to take seriously. Even the right-wing media blames the media. In the US, they blame Hollywood; in the UK, they blame the BBC. Paradoxically, they particularly blame them for creating a grievance culture where people blame other people for what is happening to them.

The answer to the question of how the "liberal establishment" has attained such levels of social and political authority to be able to keep down white men, Christians and other powerful groups can be summed up in two words—"political correctness." Finding a working definition of political correctness is not easy. In the space of one month in 2006, the term "political correctness" was used in the British press on average ten times a day—twice as frequently as "Islamophobia," three times as often as "homophobia" and four times as often as "sexism." During that period, it referred to the ill treatment of rabbits, the teaching of Gaelic, Mozart's opera *La Clemenza di Tito*, a flower show in Paris and the naming of the Mazda 3 MPS.

But the most honest definition I have seen was by Dennis O'Keeffe in an Institute of Economic Affairs report called "Political Correctness and Public Finance" back in 2000. Political correctness is the "free world's latest fashionable ideology," he wrote. "[It is] a mix of extremist egalitarian doctrines such as feminism, anti-racism and multiculturalism. It is deeply threatening to social cohesion."

In a world where feminism and anti-racism are "extremist . . . doctrines," it is little wonder that some people might feel threatened when racism and sexism are challenged. You can imagine O'Keeffe's forebears lamenting the end of slavery after the American war of "political correctness" or lambasting those suffragettes for demanding the "politically correct" vote.

So political correctness simply becomes a coded shorthand for an attack on equality and civility. When Judge Graham Boal QC told the Criminal Bar Association dinner last year that an ideal candidate for promotion would have "the breasts of a lesbian, the backside of a homosexual and a large black penis," his words masqueraded as a joke about political correctness. When the Tory candidate for London mayor, Steven Norris, wanted to put an end to limits on a stop-and-search policy that was being used with such prejudice that the police had stopped both one of the country's few black lords and one of its few black bishops in a matter of weeks, he called for an end to "politically correct policing."

But while the objects of the Right's gripes are largely invented, their root cause does have some basis in reality. Thanks to the advances of various campaigns for equality over the years, the socially acceptable limits on what it is reasonable to say or do have tightened. In the past, racially offensive jokes, remarks about your female colleague's breasts or cracks about "spastics" were considered a reasonable element of daily banter both in and outside the workplace. Now they are not. We have abandoned them for the same reason we no longer burn witches at the stake or stick orphaned children in the poorhouse. We have moved on. Values change, societies develop and their language and behavior evolve with them. That's not political correctness but social and political progress. It was not imposed by liberal diktat but established by civic consensus. Those who are unwilling or unable to move on are welcome to their words and views. But like anyone else who engages in antisocial behavior, once they act on these impulses they must live with the consequences. Those who struggle with this are not so much living in the past as struggling to accept the present. For what they are really arguing for is the right both to be insensitive and for that insensitivity to go unchallenged. The first is their right—but, like all rights, it comes with both responsibilities and ramifications. The same freedom of speech that allows you to disparage large groups of people also allows those people to mobilize public opinion and legislation against you if you do so.

The most peculiar thing about political correctness is that, despite its rhetorical flabbiness, clichéd use and devalued currency, it has still maintained considerable potency as part of a general backlash. It has managed to silence many who believe in progressive change by branding them as unworthy, pedantic and controlling. Many liberals will start sentences with "I'm not politically correct but . . ." and then go on to make a compelling case for equality or cultural sensitivity, in the same way that many young women today say, "I'm not a feminist but . . ." before arguing why women should get equal pay for equal work. In short, it has managed to stigmatize both civility and equality.

In the end, the judicial committee voted 13–6 to confirm Sotomayor. Only one Republican, Lindsey Graham, voted for her. "This radical empathy standard stands in stark opposition to what most of us understand to be the proper role of the judiciary," said Senator Chuck Grassley. It was the first time in twenty-nine years that he had voted down a Supreme Court nominee.

It is difficult to relate to the very concept of empathy unless you recognize you have something to be empathetic with. It is also difficult to be empathetic unless you are capable of making a connection between your own experience and that of another. Either way, without sensitivity, your empathy won't be worth much. For those who think empathy is a bad thing, this is, of course, not a problem. For the rest of us, empathy has the potential to be the first, crucial step on the way to solidarity—not just feeling someone else's pain but working together to try and cure it.

In the full Senate, Sotomayor's nomination was passed by 68–31. Senator Inhofe, a Republican from Oklahoma, was one of the naysayers. He explained that he could not support the nomination of someone who was unable "to rule fairly without undue influence from one's own personal race, gender or political preferences." In 2002, Inhofe hailed the former segregationist presidential hopeful Strom Thurmond as a "great American" on his hundredth birthday. One can only assume that this was an expression of objective appreciation not unduly influenced by Inhofe's whiteness.

3. The Chronicles of Cablinasia

Identities do not emerge out of common sense but communities

A White person is any person who in appearance obviously is or who is generally accepted as a white person, other than a person who, although in appearance obviously a white person, is generally accepted as a Colored person.

– Population Registration Act, Department of Interior, South Africa, 1950

On 13 April 1997 Tiger Woods putted his way to golfing history in Augusta, Georgia. The fact that he was the first black winner of the US Masters was not even half of it. At twenty-one, he was the youngest; with a twelve-stroke lead, he was the most emphatic; and finishing eighteen under par, he was, quite simply, the best the world had ever seen.

But the fact that he was black definitely explained much of the excitement. Golf in the US was never just a game. Long regarded as the bastion of the white, Christian and middle class, it was a gatekeeper to respectability and networking open principally to local and national elites. Black players had only been allowed to compete in the Masters in Augusta since 1975. Until 1982, all the caddies in the tournament there had to be black. And until 1990, Augusta didn't allow black members and even then only conceded because, if they hadn't changed their policy, they would have lost the right to host the tournament.

Woods apparently understood the symbolic meaning of his victory beyond golf. He was quick to thank Charlie Sifford, Lee Elder and Ted Rhodes—three former black golfing giants who had never been granted full recognition for their achievements—for forcing at least some courses open. His sponsors were no less aware of his broader significance. Woods appeared in a commercial for Nike saying, "There are still courses in the United States that I am not allowed to play on because of the color of my skin."

Given the decisive nature of Woods' triumph, he was of course consumed both as an example of unrivaled sporting prowess (like Björn Borg, Michael Jordan or Pelé) and as a representative of racial breakthrough (like Althea Gibson, Jackie Robinson or Lewis Hamilton). His racial identity was apparently understood both by those who embraced his achievements and those who sought to disparage them.

"That little boy is driving well and he's putting well," said fellow golfer Fuzzy Zoeller, referring to Woods' performance. But looking ahead to the following year's Masters, when Woods would exercise the title holder's right to choose the menu for the Masters' Club Champions' Dinner, Zoeller went on to tell journalists, "So, you know what you guys do when he gets in here? You pat him on the back and say congratulations and enjoy it and tell him not to serve fried chicken next year. Got it?" As he turned away, he added, "Or collard greens or whatever the hell they serve."

Zoeller later explained, "People who know me know I'm a jokester. I just didn't deliver the line well." African-Americans certainly didn't see the funny side. Nor did the corporate world. Fearing a backlash from black customers, Kmart immediately ended Zoeller's sponsorship agreement.

But within a fortnight of black America gaining a new sporting hero, it seemed as though they had lost him again. From the revered perch of Oprah Winfrey's couch, Woods was asked whether it bothered him being termed "African-American." "It does," he said. "Growing up, I came up with this name: I'm a 'Cablinasian.'"

Woods is indeed a rich mix of racial and ethnic heritage. His father, Earl, was of African-American, Chinese and Native American descent. His mother, Kutilda, is of Thai, Chinese and Dutch descent. "Cablinasian" was a composite of Caucasian, black, Indian and Asian. When he was asked to fill out forms in school, he would tick African-American and Asian. "Those are the two I was raised under and the only two I know," he told Oprah. "I'm just who I am . . . whoever you see in front of you."

It's not difficult to see where Woods was coming from or to sympathize with what he was saying. Few people relish having their identity reduced to tickable boxes. "One notices the census-makers' passion for completeness and unambiguity," writes Benedict Anderson in *Imagined Communities*. "Hence their intolerance of multiple, politically 'transvestite,' blurred, or changing identifications. Hence the weird subcategory, under each racial group, of 'Others'—who, nonetheless, are absolutely not to be confused with other 'Others.' The fiction of the census is that everyone is in it, and that everyone has one—and only one—extremely clear place. No fractions."

This is not just true of race. Watch a British person's hand hover when they have to put a single designation for their nationality and see how basic the complexities can be. England, Scotland and Wales are not officially nations—even though they do have their own football and rugby teams. Scotland has its own parliament; Wales its own assembly; England has no political institutions of its own. Officially, along with the people of Northern Ireland, we are all citizens of the United Kingdom, yet there are relatively few who would describe themselves as such. A British Attitudes survey from 2007 revealed that only 44 percent of Britons felt British, as opposed to English, Scottish or Welsh, was "the best or only way to describe their national identity."

Any box-ticking exercise can be refined, and yet it will remain necessarily crude. By their nature, boxes seek to highlight not the particular but the general; their aim is not to understand how we feel but how we might be counted. And how we are counted is no neutral factor. It shifts with the balance of power and the tide of history. Where race is concerned, fractions have, in fact, played a part. In America, black people were once understood as three-fifths of a person. Until 1930, "mulatto" (one black parent and one white; the word references "mule"—half horse, half donkey) was a category on the US census. Until 1890, quadroons (one black grandparent) or octoroons (one black great-grandparent) were also included. But it should also go without saying that a census is not where a person's uniqueness will be displayed.

"By choosing to embrace all of who he is," argued Gary Kamiya in Salon.com, "an entity for which there is no name, except one that sounds like a tribe from the imaginary country of Narnia—Woods, the goofy 21-year-old with the golden-brown skin and the beautiful swing, has become a messenger for a larger truth: Our race does not make us who we are."

True. And yet, if that is the case, Woods' insistence represented not an advance but a retreat in our efforts to retire race as a restrictive category. For far from abolishing racial categories by coining "Cablinasian," he simply created a whole new category just for himself. We could all do that—but it would make a census a fairly worthless document. The reality is that no box on a form "makes us who we are." "A single white female aged between thirty-five and forty-four earning between $55,000 and $65,000 who was born in Boston and lives in San Francisco" is the kind of information one might glean from a census form. Neither her gender, age, salary, birthplace nor address makes this woman who she is, any more than does her race—even when put together. One would hope there is a whole lot more to her than the sum of what appears on the form: she may have grown up working class, understanding Russian but not speaking it, be gay, unhappy in her job, converting to Buddhism or bored with California. And yet, for a whole set of reasons related to town planning, taxation, class sizes, commercial investment and medical services—in short, allocation of resources—what we do learn from the boxes she has ticked is quite useful. "We are not ticking the box that we would use about ourselves," explained Chris Myant, a spokesman for the now-defunct Commission for Racial Equality, "but one that we see ourselves fitting into so that we can better understand society."

Like Woods, we are all "just who we are." And who we are is not simply a matter of our own creation. "Men make their own history," wrote Karl Marx in the *18th Brumaire of Louis Bonaparte*, "but they do not make it just as they please; they do not make it under circumstances chosen by themselves, but under given circumstances directly encountered and inherited from the past."

Some black Americans, not unreasonably, felt Woods was trying to write himself out of their story. Most recognized his right to call himself whatever he wished, but many also objected to the choice he had made. "When Tiger admits having a problem with being referred to as an African American, it is as if he thumbed his nose at an entire race of people," wrote Mary Mitchell of the *Chicago Sun-Times*. "His actions are as conflicting as they are confusing. On the one hand, Tiger Woods gladly accepted the mantle of hero. On the other, he wants to transcend race, at least the African-American part of it. Such a feat would be possible in a color-blind world. In such a place, I would not be a black columnist. There also would be no black politicians, ministers, leaders, athletes or businessmen. There would be no barriers and no barriers to break."

Elsewhere in the paper, the editorial writers disagreed, praising Woods, who would later become enmeshed in a series of sex scandals, for his ability to shed the confining skin of antiquated racial terminology and write himself into a bigger story. "Our view is that Woods represents the best of the American dream," claimed the editorial. "That we are a nation of immigrants—even forced to come as slaves—whose descendants have sloughed off old identities to become something new. He justly rejects attempts to pigeonhole him in the past. Tiger Woods is the embodiment of our melting pot and our cultural diversity ideals, and deserves to be called what he in fact is—an American." Given that there are more black people in the world than there are Americans, why "black" should be considered any more a pigeonhole than "American" is not clear.

At root, all identities are created by us to make sense of the world we live in. That doesn't mean that there are no differences between people. Black people generally look different to white people, who in turn look different to Asian people. Women have different bodies than men. Different religious groups draw from different spiritual stories and worship different kinds of gods. But the meaning assigned to these differences is a matter of social construction.

This is most obvious with national identity. Borders are created by people with the express intent of distinguishing one group from another. Many are literally straight lines drawn by a cartographer. Others plunge and rise with mountains and meander with streams. Either way, these borders are both arbitrary and definite. They are arbitrary because the cartographer could simply have drawn the line somewhere else. Indeed, one day in the future, the line may well be drawn elsewhere. Germany has expanded, contracted and expanded again during the last century, dropping and adding parts of Poland, France and Austria along the way, as well as dividing and then re-uniting. Throughout the developing world, borders were drawn by colonial powers with scant attention to ethnic or linguistic affiliation, leaving ample basis for conflicts for decades to come. In the small town of Lajitas in southern Texas, people go back and forth between Mexico and the United States every day across a small stretch of the Rio Grande to see family and to work. The afternoon I arrived there, a man was nipping back over the river and across one of the most fortified borders in the world to repay a debt to a friend. The next day, Ms Rodriguez rowed her two children (and a rooster) over to see their grandmother on the other side. In most frontier towns on this border, the population is more than 80 percent Latino. Whether you are in the US or Mexico makes little difference to your cell phone, which will pick up a signal wherever it can find it. Throughout southern Texas, Spanish is generally spoken and English is usually understood. Big belt buckles, big hats and cowboy boots are de rigueur on both sides.

But while the precise contours of these borders may have been conceived arbitrarily, once drawn they mark definite dividing lines. They may be defended by dogs, armed guards and huge fences, and you are usually required to have passports to cross them. People will literally risk their lives to get from one side to another, traipsing through deserts, clutching on to the bottom of trains or hiding in the cargo holds of planes. These borders can mark a drastic disparity in human rights and opportunities. The rod-straight line that separates Canada from the US was once the difference between freedom and slavery, conscription and a life without war. Geographically and culturally, the difference between Texas's borderlands and Mexico may be minimal but, economically and politically, it is huge. The average national income is four times higher, and the infant mortality rate three times lower on one side than on the other. "It's the most extreme economic precipice on the planet," says author and lecturer Mike Davis.

So while there is no essential difference between people on different sides of any national border, which side of the border they are on can make a huge difference to their lives. It is by attempting to pass off what is socially acquired and ephemeral on either side of the line as "national characteristics" that are eternal and innate that the nationalist and xenophobe peddle their wares. "Nationalism is not the awakening of nations into self-consciousness," writes Ernest Gellner in *Thought and Change*. "It invents nations where they did not exist."

Often it is on the basis of these inventions that resources are distributed and wars are fought. Ethnicity in Rwanda provides one of the more blatant examples. The political identities of the principal ethnic groups there—Hutus and Tutsis—were constructed by their colonial overlords. Because Tutsis tended to be taller, thinner and have finer features, a series of colonial interlopers decided they seemed so much like Europeans that they must be a "superior race." English "discoverer" John Hanning Speke delighted in their "fine oval faces, large eyes, and high noses, denoting the best blood of Abyssinia." Believing them to be descendants of Ham, Noah's disowned son, they were considered a sub-group of Caucasians and fit to rule over their shorter, more squat neighbors, the Hutus. And so a definite policy, from both the Church and the state, emerged during the twentieth century to favor the Tutsi as the "born rulers" of Rwanda.

"To be a Tutsi was thus to be in power, near power or simply to be identified with power," writes Mahmood Mamdani in *When Victims Become Killers*. "Just as to be a Hutu was more and more to be a subject." This was the basis of the power struggle that would eventually lead to the Rwandan genocide in which Hutus massacred Tutsis in their millions. The only trouble was there was really no sensible way of determining who was a Hutu and who was Tutsi. Not only did they speak the same language, live in the same areas and have the same religion, they had also intermarried and interbred over several generations. To maintain the clarity of difference within the murkiness of human relations, the rule was established that ethnic identity was passed through the father. If your father is a Tutsi and your mother a Hutu then you are a Tutsi, and vice versa.

"As the child takes on a unidimensional identity, that of the father, the identity of the mother—whether Hutu or Tutsi—is systematically erased," explains Mamdani. "So it happens that the child of generations of intermarriage and cohabitation between Hutu and Tutsi comes into this world unequivocally Hutu or Tutsi . . . If you go to Rwanda or Burundi, the purity of social definition is striking: everyone you meet identifies as either Hutu or Tutsi; there are no hybrids, no one is Hutsi." When the genocide was in full swing these were no minor distinctions. Hutu husbands were forced to slay Tutsi wives; Hutu wives of Tutsi husbands were slain by association. Entire communities were constructed to death.

Indeed, oftentimes, the emphasis on racial and ethnic differences is rivaled only by the negligible basis for those differences in biological fact. The outward differences of skin, eyes, lips, nose and other physical attributes are just that—outward. It is only thanks to the way race is constructed that these physical differences are transformed into racial characteristics. In 1998, the American Anthropological Association declared, "With the vast expansion of scientific knowledge in this century it has become clear that human populations are not unambiguous, clearly demarcated, biologically distinct groups. Evidence from the analysis of genetics (e.g. DNA) indicates that most physical variation, about 94%, lies within so-called racial groups. Conventional geographic 'racial' groupings differ from one another only in about 6% of their genes. This means there is greater genetic variation within 'racial' groups than between them." In short, we really are more alike than we are unalike.

If race is an arbitrary fiction, then "race-mixing" is a conceptual absurdity. "In neighboring populations there is much overlapping of genes and their phenotypic (physical) expressions," the AAA continues. "Throughout history whenever different groups have come into contact they have interbred. The continued sharing of genetic materials has maintained all of humankind as a single species." Put simply, to the extent to which "mixed race" makes any sense at all, we are all mixed race.

This is a fact well illustrated by this tale of two "white" girls: Bliss Broyard from Connecticut and Sandra Laing from Mpumalanga in

South Africa. Broyard was raised in the blue-blood, mono-racial world of Connecticut's twee suburbs and private schools. Her racial identity was ensconced in the comfort of insular whiteness; she had always known there were "others" but had never really considered them. "I'd never had a conversation about race," she confesses in her book *One Drop*. "In the world I was raised in, it was considered an impolite subject. The people I knew lowered their voices when referring to a black person. Although I grew up within an hour's drive of three of the poorest black communities in the United States—Bridgeport, New Haven and Hartford—those neighborhoods seemed as distant as a foreign country."

But in early adulthood, Broyard would discover that, on one level, she had a greater connection to those neighborhoods than she imagined. For on his deathbed, her father, Anatole, confessed that he was in fact a black man who had been passing as white throughout most of his adult life. This was quite common, particularly under segregation. "Every year approximately 12,000 white-skinned Negroes disappear," claimed Walter White, the former head of the NAACP, in a 1947 article "Why I Remain a Negro." "People whose absence cannot be explained by death or emigration . . . men and women who have decided that they will be happier and more successful if they flee from the proscription and humiliation which the American color line imposes on them."

Initially Broyard was thrilled at the news. It was "as though I'd been reading a fascinating history book and then discovered my own name in the index. I felt like I mattered in a way that I hadn't before." But then came the heavy lifting. The family her father had left behind, many of whom lived in the South, and her relationship to those poor black communities she had known of but never actually known, forced her to reassess everything she had once thought about herself. "If my father was black, what did that make me?" she asked, fearing inauthenticity in her new-found identity. Later she concluded she had "finally cracked the code: since my father was 'really' black, then I must 'really' be black too. Yet I still felt unsettled: I'd already experimented with describing myself as black on a few occasions and it hadn't gone over well."

When she went to New Orleans to trawl through local archives to find out more about her family history, she found that, however extraordinary the news was to her, it was not at all uncommon for white people to find they had black ancestors they weren't actually looking for. "I'd heard stories from a research assistant at the library about white people who started to cry on hearing the explanation about what the 'mu' [mulatto] stood for on the census record," she said.

The other "white" girl, Sandra Laing, was born to two white apartheid-supporting Afrikaner parents in the small town of Piet Retief near the Swazi border. Her grandparents were also white. Blood tests proved she was her father's daughter. Yet Sandra emerged dark-skinned with Afro hair—a black girl. And under the strict segregationist laws of apartheid, the fact that she had two white parents could only mean so much. Sandra was removed from her whites-only school and reclassified as "colored."

If there was ever a barefaced example of racial construction it was apartheid, where the state would assign you a racial category at birth that would determine every aspect of your life. If you objected to the decision, you could go to the Race Classification Appeals Board. The criteria the boards used to determine a person's race was based on anything from pseudo-science to social and cultural performance. Among the various checks was the pencil test (if a pencil stuck in your hair slid through when you bent forward, you were white; if not, you were colored), the fingernail test (the pinker the cuticles the blacker the person) and the scrotum test (assigning race on the basis of the shade of the testicular sac). Until 1966, the judgment hinged on a mixture of appearance and acceptance by the immediate community. In one instance, a Chinese man, David Song, was successfully reclassified as white after he produced an affidavit signed by 350 white neighbors and colleagues saying they accepted him as white.

Sandra's parents fought the reclassification hard. "Sandra has been brought up as a White," her father explained to the *Rand Daily Mail.* "She considers herself White. She is darker than we are, but in every way she has always been a White person." In this battle, Sandra's father had to weigh his love for his daughter against his devotion to white supremacy. "It is too tragic to countenance, this power possessed by the authorities which can suddenly change a little girl's happiness into misery." "If her appearance is due to some 'colored blood' in either of us, then it must be very far back among our forebears, and neither of us is aware of it," he told the Johannesburg *Sunday Times* in 1967. "If this is, in fact, so, does it make our family any different from so many others in South Africa?"

Eventually, Sandra would be reclassified as white. But in a country where everything was strictly segregated and nobody accepted her as white, this legalistic change was little more than a technicality. In time, she would reclassify herself back to colored.

Two white girls in two nations founded in no small part on racial classification and segregation discover that they are each, in different ways, black. Given their known genealogies, the one with the greatest claim to whiteness, Sandra Laing, would have the weakest case in the court of common sense. But then common sense has nothing to do with race. Few of us truly know our genealogies, beyond a certain point. And if, as Abraham Laing pointed out, his family is not that different from many in South Africa, where racial separation was so rigidly enforced, how familiar must it be elsewhere? If race-mixing was so prevalent in South Africa then what, ultimately, was apartheid really all about?

"Everybody is mixed but not everybody counts as mixed," says Paul Gilroy, professor of sociology at the London School of Economics. "The truth is that no one can say with any certainty where they come from." "Marble cake, crazy quilt and tutti-frutti," Roger Sanjek is quoted as saying in Judith Stone's book about Sandra Laing's experiences, *When She Was White*, "are all better metaphors of human physical variability than is the x number of races of humankind."

But in the US, South Africa and elsewhere, the meaning attached to these metaphors has always had its roots in politics and economics. "Fundamental to race is a hierarchy of power," writes Ariela Gross in *What Blood Won't Tell*. "Despite the language of racial difference and the neutrality of terms like 'racial categories' and 'boundaries,' central to racial thinking is not only the notion that the categories of white, black, brown, yellow and red mark meaningful distinctions among human beings but also that they reflect inferiority and superiority, a human Chain of Being, with white at the top and black on the bottom. Determining racial identity was about raising some people up that chain to put others down; enslaving some people to free others; taking land from some people to give it to others; robbing people of their dignity to give others a sense of supremacy."

This plays out in different ways between different groups in different places at different times. Where blacks and whites in the US are concerned, race was specifically constructed in order to preserve the power differential between master and slave and to protect the master's property and outward integrity, even as he consorted, usually by force, with his female slaves. To ensure that the progeny of these liaisons could never have a claim on the wealth of their fathers, racial classification was governed by the rules of hypodescent, or the "one-drop rule"—that anyone with even a single drop of black blood should be regarded as black. So while there were light-skinned black communities—particularly in places such as Louisiana—these would never have been considered "dark-skinned white communities." In a bid to keep tabs on mixed-race individuals' heritage, the slave-owning class created categories such as mulattos, quadroons and octoroons (those pesky fractions again). But these were not so much intermediate categories as subcategories: they were all gradations of blackness. There was never any suggestion that they could be related to white-ness, even though they clearly would not have been possible without white people.

Economically and politically, all of this made perfect sense. In-tellectually, it was and remains a nonsense. As Barbara J. Fields pointed out in her landmark essay, "Ideology and Race in American History," it meant that "a black woman cannot give birth to a white child" while "a white woman [is] capable of giving birth to a black child."

So goes the apocryphal story of an American official who visited a Haitian statesman in the thirties:

"What percentage of Haiti's population is white?" the American asked.
    "Ninety five percent," said the Haitian.

"I don't understand—how on earth did you come up with that figure?" asked the baffled American.

"Well—how do you measure blackness in the United States?'

"Anyone with a black ancestor."

"Well, that's exactly how we measure whiteness," the Haitian replied. "Anyone with a white ancestor."

Both arbitrary in its conception and definite in its application, "one drop" is a pernicious and easily ridiculed rule. But no more or less pernicious and ridiculous than the rule that says everyone born this side of a line is Mexican and the other, American. Nonetheless, "one drop" was the rule, and in terms of how race is generally understood it remains so to this day. You can't change those rules by fiat any more than you can proclaim that women will no longer be judged by their looks. Choosing to ignore something or even declaring it invalid does not abolish it. Rules, mores and traditions don't simply expire because they are wrong. They disappear because the material reality that gave rise to them ceases to exist. To acknowledge a construct is not the same thing as to accept its intellectual or moral validity. Nor does it mean that the rules cannot change. The construction of race in the US has evolved over time. There is nothing to suggest it won't keep doing so.

In this respect, Woods' decision to come out as a Cablinasian could not have been more timely. The day before he was on *Oprah*, Congress held a hearing to explore how the federal government measures race and ethnicity. "Tiger Woods is not alone in wanting the racial background of both his parents and all his relatives reflected in how people describe him," said Douglas Besharov of the right-wing American Enterprise Institute.

On this point, Besharov was quite right. In the ten years after the Supreme Court's 1967 decision of Loving *vs* Virginia declared bans on mixed-race marriage to be unconstitutional, various strands of a mixed-race movement emerged in the US. Some were started by mixed-race couples, others by those who adopted across the color line, yet others by mixed-race people themselves. Through various networks, they provided advice and support and increasingly sought to make their voices heard in national and political forums. From the late eighties to the mid-nineties, one of their central priorities was to ensure that government bodies gave the option of putting mixed race alongside the existing black, white, Native American, Alaskan Native, Asian, Pacific Islander and Other on official forms. This battle reached its greatest intensity in the mid-nineties as activists fought for a specific "multiracial" category on the census.

"Tiger Woods could not have come at a better time. The public can now see a face of what it means to be multiracial," said Susan Graham, the executive director of Project Race, which supported the new category, at the time. "Whether he wants to or not, he is sort of becoming the poster person for multiracial identity," said Ramona Douglass, the president of the Association of MultiEthnic Americans (AMEA). Following the hearing in 1997, one Republican, Tom Petri, introduced legislation backing the multiracial check-off for the 2000 census. He called it the "Tiger Woods bill."

Some made great claims for what the inclusion of such a category might achieve. Amitai Etzioni of American University, in Washington, DC, argued that it had "the potential to soften the racial lines that now divide America by rendering them more like economic differences and less like harsh, almost immutable, caste lines." Rather than change the material realities that give the constructs of race and racism their meaning, the tortured logic went that, if you constructed race differently on a form, then maybe those realities and our understanding of them would change.

Others, on the Right, saw the introduction of the category as a Trojan horse for the elimination of affirmative action. "The main effect of the multiracial check-off is that it will doom affirmative action, already on the run," argued James Glassman in the *Washington Post*. For that very reason, many civil rights leaders argued against the multiracial box, viewing it as a direct assault on their ability to redress racial inequality that would dilute resources earmarked for minorities. "It would be much more difficult with this additional category to measure the effects of discrimination in our community and to be able to adequately redress them," explained the NAACP leader, Kweisi Mfume. "The Supreme Court has required now for a decade that in order to find on behalf of the plaintiff alleging discrimination that there be a history of discrimination, and there has not been a history of discrimination against 'mixed race' people."

This by no means suggests that being mixed race in the US might not represent a particular personal experience. For some, it is the most meaningful way they have found of describing their familial history, cultural influences and racial heritage. They may even feel that for others to describe them in some other way would deny a crucial part of who or what they are. For example, several mixed-race people interviewed for this book say they have struggled fully to "fit in," socially or culturally, to the different communities from which their parents came.

"The thing you end up having in common is treatment. Being accepted or rejected by other family members," says Jennifer Nobles, the president of Multiracial Americans of Southern California. "Finding yourself being asked to choose between either/or group. Am I more of this or more of that? There are a lot of people out there who feel they don't have a place. They want to have a community where they can say: 'Oh I feel that too.'" This, explains Nobles, would be what a biracial person with Korean and Latino parents might have in common with Nobles herself, who is a mix of Sri Lankan and African-American. The feelings of not quite belonging and demands for authenticity were pervasive, she said, regardless of the ethnic or racial mix.

But among those who are supposed to own it, the category is anything but settled. Drawing on a study of the racial identifications of different types of mixed young people in Britain, Professor Miri Song concluded: "While there is evidence of a growing consciousness and interest in being mixed, we cannot (yet) speak of a coherent mixed group or experience in Britain." Champions of black culture and black politics, including Malcolm X, Bob Marley and Fard Muhammad (the founder of the black nationalist Nation of Islam) all had white parents or grandparents whom they knew of. "My whole life it would have been easier to identify as biracial," explains Danzy Senna, author of *Caucasia*, whose father is Afro-Mexican and mother is Irish-American. "But I didn't feel half and half. I grew up in Boston in this very stratified world with very virulent racism. Blackness is the context in which I was born and the context in which I was raised. We're all a function of history, we're not born into a vacuum."

Meanwhile, when the US census put out trial questionnaires with the multiracial box on it, they found that different people understood "multiracial" to mean very different things. "One of the largest percentages of people who filled out the multiracial category were people who would not generally be considered multiracial at all," said Ruth B. McKay, an anthropologist at the Bureau of Labor Statistics. "They were people whose parents were of Irish and Italian origin or white American and French—people who are generally considered white. They were mixing race and ethnicity, which just shows how much of an education campaign we would have to launch if we were ever going to get this to work effectively."

No identity is homogeneous. But for a social identity (as opposed to a personal one) to be viable it cannot be so porous that large numbers of those whom it should include fail to recognize it as meaningful while large numbers whom it should not include believe they are part of it.

Take the Roma. As with the people of any diaspora, they have been heavily influenced by the places they have settled. In Macedonia, the vast majority speak Romani, while in Hungary, 80 percent speak only Hungarian. Religion is an important aspect of Romani culture, but precisely which faith is shaped more by geography than ethnicity—most Roma in Croatia are Catholic; in Bosnia they are Muslim; and in Serbia they are Orthodox. Many, particularly in Eastern Europe, have the skin tone of an Indian or a Sri Lankan; others may appear white. Some in the Roma community dispute that India is their common homeland; others embrace it. Yet for all that, the Roma bear the crucial test for a meaningful identity—they know who one another are, and everybody else knows who they are too. Like Bliss Broyard, Sandra Laing or the residents of Lajitas, the precise definition of who belongs and who does not frays with the complexity of human difference. But they are as able to discriminate between themselves and a *gadje* (non-Roma) as the state and civil society are able to discriminate against them.

Nothing really coheres multiracial people in the US in the same way. The stories of not quite belonging in both parents' milieus might be a common experience but not one that is exclusive to those who are multiracial. Indeed, those sentiments could be just as evident among children whose parents are the same race but from different countries or religions as among children whose parents are different races but were raised in the same town. Unlike the Roma, there is no consensus among people with parents of different races about which community they belong to, nor any consensus among the rest of society about how one might identify them. In short, if there is a multiracial community in the US then no one seems to know where it is or who is in it, including a significant portion of those in whose name it was created.

Not all of our personal identities, some of which are extremely important to us, are necessarily also social and political identities. That does not make them necessarily less important to us as individuals but it does make a difference to their currency. Take names. In 2009, 37-year-old Eileen De Bont legally changed her name to "Pudsey Bear" after the BBC's Children in Need mascot. She changed her driver's license, bank cards, credit cards and tax forms, but when she went to change her passport, the UK Identity and Passport Service wrote a letter addressed to "Mrs Bear" refusing the request: "It is deemed to be a frivolous change of name, which would bring IPS into disrepute. It could also pose problems for you at border control in some countries," they wrote.

"IPS is not questioning the validity of the deed poll, however it is not prepared to issue a passport in a frivolous name which could compromise our mission statement 'safeguarding your identity.'" Mrs Bear insisted this was her new identity. She was devastated, but her personal setback did not really affect anyone other than herself. "I love my new name," she told the *Daily Telegraph*. "It has become part of my life. It is who I am. My girls both call me 'Mummy Bear.'"

As I pointed out earlier with Irish names in Northern Ireland, however, in a different context, your name can be a potent signifier of your identity. In a different place and a different time, the same could be true for Muslims, Jews and many others. Think of the consequences of announcing a specifically Catholic, Protestant, Jewish or Muslim name in a politically sensitive region.

So the extent to which "mixed race" is a personal identity as opposed to a social one is not a point of principle. In a different place, with a different history, where race was constructed in a different way, a social identity could and has emerged from a group that is "racially mixed."

Just a twenty-minute drive from the center of South Africa's Cape Town, beyond the shadow of Table Mountain, lies Silverstream Road. If ever you were looking for an example of how race could be constructed in such a way as to give "mixed-race people" their own distinct particular space, then this is it. On one side is the township of Gugulethu—98 percent black, 94 percent Xhosa-speaking. On the other is Manenberg—94 percent colored, 72 percent Afrikaans-speaking. Two huge communities divided by one relatively narrow street and a lot of history.

Silverstream Road acts not merely as a geographical border, it divides on the basis of race, language, religion, economics and history. Gugulethu and Manenberg occupy adjacent territory and yet vastly different cultural spaces. The South African census bears this out. Unlike the "two or more races" category in the US, when broken down statistically, colored life is rooted in a distinct experience. When compared with blacks, coloreds live in a state of relative privilege. According to the 2001 census, coloreds in the Western Cape (where Cape Town is situated) are significantly more likely to have some education than blacks, significantly more likely to be employed and earn incomes considerably higher than blacks, with 40 percent earning more than R1,500 (£133) a month, compared with 23 percent of blacks. They are more than twice as likely to have piped water in their house and more than three times as likely to have a phone at home.

As was the case with the New Haven firefighter Frank Ricci,

however, the key word when looking at living standards here is "relative." For such figures tell us how bad things are for blacks rather than how great things are for coloreds. Compared with that of whites, the situation of coloreds is dire. The same census shows that coloreds are more than four times less likely to have graduated from school than whites and five times more likely to be unemployed. Their incomes are substantially lower than those of whites, who are more than twice as likely to earn more than R1,500 a month or to have a phone in the house than coloreds and thirty times less likely to have to draw water from a pipe.

"In this country everything is about the scramble for resources," explains Ryland Fisher, the colored former editor of *Cape Times*. "Most of the economy in South Africa is in white hands. We're fighting for the last 10 percent. The colored community has been neglected by the government. Black people think coloreds are getting the jobs. Colored people think black people are getting the jobs." Such is the legacy of apartheid.

"Colored" has always been a problematic term. Until relatively recently, it was generally uttered with theatrical awkwardness. People would say it while airbrushing in quotation marks with their fingers. Others would say, "so-called colored." On the one hand, people didn't want to use it; on the other, they had no other words for a group of people who had formed a community, even if it was not on their own terms. So "colored" had currency, albeit a devalued one.

Apartheid didn't create coloreds. For that we must look to slave routes and slave roots. Standing at the tip of a continent, at the helm of two oceans, Cape Town became a crucial waystation for traders in a range of cargo, including human beings, from midway through the seventeenth century. With relatively few white female settlers, it was not long before the racial and gender hierarchies of the day replicated themselves horizontally come nightfall.

Alongside those who were imported were the native KhoiKhoi and San peoples, who were conquered, dispossessed and subjugated. Before long, thanks to miscegenation, both forced and voluntary, a caste of people with varied racial and ethnic heritage emerged whose existence gave lie to the prevailing norms of racial segregation. Since many worked on settlers' farms, eventually, they started to speak the settlers' language (Afrikaans) and worship in their church (the Dutch Reformed Church). No one ever mistook them for white (apart from the few who were very light-skinned). But few mistook them for black either (apart from those who were very dark-skinned).

The result was a racially intermediate status, particularly prevalent in the Western Cape, home to 60 percent of the nation's coloreds, which became concretized under colonialism and then formalized under apartheid. "For me, growing up colored meant knowing that I was *not only* not white, but *less than white*; *not only* not black, but *better than black*," writes Zimitri Erasmus in the introduction to *Colored by History, Shaped by Place*. "Colored identity has never been seen as an identity 'in its own right.' It has been negatively defined in terms of 'lack' or taint or in terms of a remainder of excess which does not fit a classificatory scheme."

Accusations of inauthenticity came from whites and blacks. In 1983, Marike de Klerk, wife of the apartheid leader F. W. de Klerk, described coloreds as "a negative group. The definition of a colored in the population register is someone who is not black, and is not white and is also not Indian, in other words a no-person. They are the leftovers. They are the people who were left after the nations were sorted out. They are the rest."

"Coloreds don't know where they come from," Hombi Ntshoko, a black woman from Langa, told a researcher for the book *Voices from the Communities*. "We know where we come from. Whites know where they come from. But these coloreds don't know whether they are black or white."

While apartheid didn't create coloreds, it played a decisive role in creating the bureaucratic boundaries that would construct the meaning of what it was to be colored. "There were 8 different types of coloreds," points out Henry Jeffreys, the colored editor of the formerly apartheid-supporting Afrikaaner-language paper *Die Burger*. "When they ran out of things to call them they called them 'Other Colored.' My brother and sister were called 'Other Colored' but I was called 'Cape Colored.'"

It was this combination of who coloreds were and weren't and what they could and couldn't do that lent social, economic and political significance to their condition. They didn't just feel different; in almost every aspect of their lives they shared a common experience of difference. "They didn't have the vote," explained Reggie September, who founded the South African Colored People's Organization in 1953 (which was affiliated with the African National Congress), as he detailed the many ways in which coloreds constituted a particular, known group. "They were segregated and most of them lived in terrible conditions. They couldn't come to a place like this," he said, waving an arm across the upscale hotel restaurant in Cape Town where we were eating. "They went to colored schools and colored churches. They were separate from everybody else. We were mixed long enough to be a separate community. We had our own cricket teams, football teams. It's the way it's always been. It's a very problematic community."

With the coloreds' particular fusion of religions, language, race and status came some degree of cultural autonomy; small but telling pointers to a life lived slightly differently. There is the Gatsby, a huge sandwich made of French loaf filled with chips, salad and then meat or fish, which is popular in Cape Town; the passion gap, the extracted front teeth that peer out from the smiles of young colored men (I never found a satisfactory explanation for why this should be); the swirlkos, doo-rags wrapped around your hair to stop it going puffy at night; and the names that correspond either to months of the year or are taken from classical (Western) civilizations, such as Adonis, Apollis and Cupido.

This is the kind of material that Melanie Jones, a colored comedienne, uses when she's on the circuit. "When a chick from the Cape Flats goes on a date the guy will come to pick her up in a 1972 convertible," she explains, reciting one of her routines. "Not one where the top goes down. But one they have converted themselves. Colored guys are always working on their cars." How would they be different to black or white guys? "Black people would either be in taxis or BMWs. White people have their own cars and if it breaks down they buy new ones," she says.

None of these common attributes make coloreds homogeneous.

The colored community comprises Muslims, Christians, Indians, Malays and pretty much the full range of skin tones from latte to five past midnight. One in ten is Muslim; one in five belongs to the Dutch Reform Church; one in six speaks English. "I'm still struggling to find out exactly what it means," confesses Ryland Fisher. "There are some coloreds who are whiter than most white people and others who are darker than most black people. It can't be about hair texture. And if you go to Durban you'll find coloreds who don't speak Afrikaans at all."

The precise nature of colored identity is deeply contested. Some insist it is purely racial; others that it is primarily political; others that it has a strong cultural element. But the one thing you won't find is anyone suggesting that it is not an identity at all. For all their differences, everybody knows who coloreds are (apart from the "play-whites" who can pass). While there are large ethnic, religious and class variations among them, nonetheless they share enough of a common experience that it is possible to talk about them as a group. Moreover, they know who they are. The issue is not just that they feel different. Their particular racial identity is rooted in a material reality. The nature of that identity may be contested, but the arguments are not existential. Two people who are designated colored may have different views about what that means or whether the term should be used, but no one that I met in Cape Town ever denied the existence of the category itself.

Paradoxically, the end of apartheid did not deliver a death blow to colored identity but instead breathed new life into it. Emerging from the dead weight of official segregation, coloreds started to claim the word and the experience for themselves; to be not just an intermediate category between black and white but an identity beyond them and on its own terms. "In the past they used to do airquotes but they just don't do that anymore," says Fisher. "After '94 there was no longer a need for these ambiguous parts of our identity. There's no more so-called. Colored became something they could feel comfortable with."

Quite what that "something" would be, however, still needs to be worked out. "If I'm not 'so-called' then what am I?" asks Revd

Michael Weeder, a long-time activist in the colored community:

After 1994, everybody was into ethnic identity. Everyone became more Portuguese, Xhosa, Zulu. It was cool. But if I'm going to go with anything I'm going with colored because it takes me somewhere in Africa. It's not the definitive thing. It's not the only thing. But it's the community that I knew exclusively in my formative years. Colored only made sense here. Elsewhere it made no sense. So we reclaimed it. It won't disappear. We've taken it. We're working with it. The term's always been here and probably always will be here. But it will always be qualified differently. It will always be understood differently. We've all been tainted by color. Colored will still be used but not the way it has been used in the past . . . None of us escapes the influences of living in a cosmopolitan world. In South Africa everybody's a creole. They're just not aware of it.

Back in that most cosmopolitan of nations, the United States, Congress passed a version of the Tiger Woods bill. With multiracial people in mind, the census bureau decided to amend its categories for 2000 to include the option of ticking two or more races and specifying which ones. In the end, only 2.4 percent of Americans claimed it—more than the Native American and Pacific Islander populations put together but still less than half of those who chose "other." Meanwhile, the proportion of African-Americans effectively remained unchanged (it actually rose by an insignificant 0.24 percent). But unlike the other racial groups on the census, about whom some generalizations concerning income, health and poverty could be drawn, the data from the two races or more category offered no coherent narrative. In many of the nation's most racially and ethnically diverse states, relatively few saw fit to dignify their diverse racial heritage with a tick in a box. The ten states in which people were most likely to tick two races or more did not include any of the ten states with the highest proportion of African-Americans, or Florida, Texas, New York, Arizona or Illinois, which are among the most racially diverse states in the nation. The 2010 US census showed a sharp increase in the number of those who identified as two races or more to one of the fastest growing demographic groups. But there was no suggestion of any pattern relating to broadly shared material circumstances for that group.

Nonetheless, in this entire saga, two important principles had been established. First, everyone has the right to call themselves whatever they want. If Woods wants to call himself Cablinasian, or Teresa Heinz Kerry (the white millionaire wife of former Democratic hopeful John Kerry who was born in Mozambique) wants to call herself African-American, then we should respect that. The same goes for transsexuals who want to call themselves women and Scots who want to call themselves Brits.

We should honor self-definition not to humor the subject but because it is infinitely preferable to allowing anyone to be defined by others. "The human approach to experience is categorical," argued anthropologist Harry Wolcott. "What we don't label others will, leaving us at their mercy. We are better off to supply labels of our own and to be up front about the identifications we seek." Young people born and raised in France whose parents or even grandparents are from North Africa are often referred to by other French people as immigrants, even if they've never left the country. Similarly, white people born and raised in Africa may be branded settlers even if their families have lived there for generations. These flawed descriptions matter. The more exclusion is embedded in language, the harder it is to extract it from politics.

Left to their own devices, people's self-definition may change a great deal depending on place and time. Over the years, "negro" has become "colored" has become "black" has become "African-American," just as "homosexual" has become "gay" has become "queer" has become "LGBT" (Lesbian, Gay, Bisexual, Transgender), with the occasional addition of another couple of Qs for "Queer and Questioning." In Eastern Europe, the term "gypsy" is regarded as an insult by the Roma; in Britain, Roma interests are represented by the Gypsy Council. Anybody has the right to challenge these identities (indeed that is how they evolve and develop), but nobody has the right to tell someone else that they are something they have no interest in being.

The second important principle is that with this right comes at least one responsibility—that if you want your identity to have any broader relevance beyond yourself, it must at least make sense. I found this out the hard way when I was seventeen and living in Sudan. Up until that time, I never described myself as British, even though I was born there. During my childhood, so many white British people had constantly reminded me of my "foreignness"— "Go back to where you came from"; "Where are you from originally?"—that Britishness didn't seem like a viable thing to claim. So instead, I told people I was Barbadian, where I had been for just six weeks on holiday as a four-year-old.

However, when I went to Sudan, the fact that I was a black man who did not speak Arabic would routinely prompt a question about where I was from. Initially, I told them Barbados. They had never heard of it. A few would ask what it was like. I would make something up from memory. Then I started saying that my mother was from Jamaica, because, thanks to Bob Marley, they had heard of Jamaica. Before long, I was claiming I was from a place I had never been to and where I had no family. As a response to such a simple question, this was clearly unsustainable. In the end, I had simply to admit that I was indeed British and reorganize my sense of self accordingly.

Similarly, those who insist that because Barack Obama has a white mother and grandmother who raised him he could just as easily be described as another white president as the first black president are in a losing battle with credibility. "Obama's chosen to identify as an African-American male," explains Jennifer Nobles, the campaigner for multiracialism. "It's the same thing with Halle Berry. That's their choice and it makes sense. But he could identify as white if he wanted. The trouble is no one would receive it that way."

"But if no one would receive it that way, then it would have no meaning," I suggested.

"In theory he could call himself white, but in reality it doesn't work because people see he's that way and understand him that way. On paper he could be the next white president."

"And where could that theory be applied?" I asked. "Who would look at that piece of paper and understand it?"

Nobles shrugged. She conceded that the distinction between how he might describe himself and how that description would be comprehended was a problem. But, according to her, it was only a problem because of how everyone else misunderstood race rather than how she understood it. This discrepancy cannot stand.

"A tree, whatever the circumstances, does not become a legume, a vine, or a cow," explains Kwame Anthony Appiah in *The Ethics of Identity*. "The reasonable middle view is that constructing an identity is a good thing (if self-authorship is a good thing) but that the identity must make some kind of sense. And for it to make sense, it must be an identity constructed in response to facts outside oneself, things that are beyond one's own choices."

A society in which "Cablinasian" makes sense has yet to be created. Like a Rwanda full of Hutsis, it exists only in the imagination. That does not necessarily mean that such a society could not or should not emerge. But "the facts beyond one's own choice" do not yet allow it. Identities may be constructed and can be built differently. But we can only work with the materials available.

4. Blessed Are the Gatekeepers

There is no such thing as authenticity, but there are
plenty of people trying to enforce it

I have been German, I have been stateless, and I have been British. I am
now American. But I was always a Jew, and always will remain a Jew.

— Hermann Gottfried, fled Germany in 1939 on children's transport for
Great Britain, quoted in *What We Knew*, by
Eric A. Johnson and Karl-Heinz Reuband

In the late sixties, Emil Fackenheim, German-born concentration-
camp survivor, noted Jewish philosopher and Reform rabbi, decided
that the Jewish faith needed a 614th mitzvah. To many, the first 613
were plenty. The commandments, which lay down the laws and
ethics contained in the Torah and provide the framework for Judaism,
include everything from not committing adultery to not eating fruit
from a tree during its first three years. But Fackenheim thought that
the Holocaust necessitated a new one: "Thou shalt not hand Hitler
posthumous victories. To despair of the God of Israel is to continue
Hitler's work for him."

Fackenheim, who was arrested on Kristallnacht and escaped to
Canada via Scotland in 1939, would later elaborate in the Charles F.
Deems Lectures at New York University:

If the 614th commandment is binding upon the authentic Jew, then we are,
first, commanded to survive as Jews, lest the Jewish people perish. We are
commanded, secondly, to remember in our very guts and bones the martyrs
of the Holocaust, lest their memory perish. We are forbidden, thirdly, to
deny or despair of God, however much we may have to contend with him
or with belief in him, lest Judaism perish. We are forbidden, finally, to

despair of the world as the place which is to become the kingdom of God, lest we help make it a meaningless place in which God is dead or irrelevant and everything is permitted. To abandon any of these imperatives, in response to Hitler's victory at Auschwitz, would be to hand him yet other, posthumous victories.

Such a theory was not without contention, not least because one of the mitzvoth already prohibits adding to the commandments. Some argued that it granted too much power to Hitler and the Holocaust in shaping Jewish identity. "We abuse the Holocaust when it becomes a cudgel against others who have their claims of suffering," argued Rabbi Harold Schulweis in a speech to the Jewish Council for Public Affairs. "The Shoah must not be misused in the contest of one-downsmanship with other victims of brutality . . . The Shoah has become our instant raison d'être, the short-cut answer to the penetrating questions of our children: "Why should I not marry out of the faith? Why should I join a synagogue? Why should I support Israel? Why should I be Jewish?" We have relied on a singular imperative: "Thou shalt not give Hitler a posthumous victory." That answer will not work. To live in spite, to say 'no' to Hitler is a far cry from living 'yes' to Judaism."

Some also used Fackenheim's exhortations to pressure Jews not to marry out of the faith (particularly Jewish men, because Judaism is passed through the mother) and thereby deplete the number of potential Jews. There is a real irony in this. For this famed Jewish scholar, Fackenheim, married a Gentile who had not converted when his son, Joseph, was born in Canada. Joseph (generally known as Yossi) was converted to Judaism when he was two years old by a rabbinical court in Toronto. After a short blip, the Jewish lineage of the Fackenheim name had been restored and protected. The Fackenheims moved to Israel when Joseph was four, and he became a citizen. Joseph married a fellow Israeli when he was twenty-one and then, after seven years, they decided to divorce.

Israel makes no provision for civil ceremonies for life-cycle events of this kind. When the state was founded, the political wing of Zionism reached an agreement with the religious wing to give the latter discrete areas of autonomy over Kashrut (dietary laws), Shabbat (the day of rest),

burial, marriage, divorce, and a few other matters. The Israeli Chief
Rabbinate is strictly Orthodox and, as Joseph was about to discover,
extremely powerful. When he went for his divorce he was questioned
extensively about how well he kept kosher and whether he observes
Shabbat, about what he eats and how often he worships. The judge,
Yissachar Dov Hagar, then went on to grill him about Shakespeare.
Fackenheim was at drama school in London and had expressed a fondness
for the bard: the one who created Shylock, the venal moneylender in
The Merchant of Venice. What decent Jew could possibly like Shakespeare,
wondered Hagar, insinuating that Joseph might even be an anti-Semite.
"This went on for four or five hours," Joseph told the *Toronto Star*. "I
put up with it because my wife needed a divorce."

He needn't have bothered. Unimpressed by his answers, Hagar
ruled that, under Jewish law, he couldn't grant Joseph a divorce
because, under Jewish law, he should never have been married in the
first place. In fact, Hagar decreed, Joseph was not Jewish and never
had been. And so it was that the son of the scholar, whose life's work
was dedicated to embedding Jewish resistance to Hitler's genocide
into the religion itself, found himself cast out of the faith altogether.

What he thought would be a routine matter had "unnecessarily
turned into a humiliating expulsion" from the Jewish people, Joseph
later said. "The judge also made derogatory remarks about my profession," he told the Israeli newspaper *Haaretz*. "I came completely
unprepared and didn't think for one minute I'd walk out with a
document expelling me from my people." Hagar eventually granted
the divorce, but added an attachment voiding the marriage that
referred to "Yossi the convert."

"It's kind of the perfect irony that my father's life's work was about
keeping the unity of the Jewish people," said Joseph. "My parents
converted me into Orthodox Judaism specifically so that I would not
have these problems later on. I have friends, converts in Israel, who
live in fear. It's the end of them," he told the *Toronto Star*. "I don't
need [the Rabbinate] to tell me I'm Jewish. I'm Jewish."

Unfortunately for Mr Fackenheim, only one of those last two
statements is true. On the one hand, Joseph's claims to Jewishness are
undeniably strong. He was converted to Judaism as a toddler, raised

as a Jew, understands himself to be a Jew, and both Jews and Gentiles who know him understand him to be a Jew. For the purposes of his everyday life, he is Jewish.

But, in Israel, there is more to being Jewish than that. Israel is a Jewish state. That is not just an incidental description but its deliberate intention. The express aim of its political class and popular culture is to keep it that way. So the question of who is deemed to be Jewish and by whom is of no small importance. Indeed, it is an affair of state. And how Jewishness is defined in turn defines the state. To live a full life in Israel, Joseph needs an authority to sign off on his Jewishness. In short, he does need the Rabbinate to tell him he's Jewish.

Joseph is not alone. More than forty thousand conversions were annulled by the Rabbinical High Court in 2008 after it ruled that the rabbi charged with overseeing them had been too lenient. "Like so many other things going on in Israel and Jerusalem in particular, it is a territorial struggle over who is a Jew in this country, who decides who is a rabbi," Anat Hoffman, executive director of the Israel Religious Action Center in Jerusalem, told the *Toronto Star*. "How could that be that the son of a great thinker, a rabbi, a celebrated professor, will find himself at his age after living most of his life in Israel having his Judaism revoked retroactively?"

But there is more to the outcome of this struggle than bureaucratic jockeying. "They're not just telling someone you can't have a driving license because you failed an eye test," explains Rabbi Seth Farber, an American-born Orthodox Jew whose organization, ITIM, helps people who feel they have been mistreated by the Rabbinate. "They're rejecting someone's whole identity. They're saying you're not Jewish."

Every identity has its gatekeepers, the arbiters of who does or does not belong, on what basis and to what end. As in the case of the apartheid-era race-classification boards which thrice reclassified Sandra Laing—from white to colored, colored to white (at her father's insistence) and then back to colored again (at her own)—once an identity has been constructed, its perimeters must be guarded to make sure they are not breached. Gatekeepers establish the basis for both inclusion and exclusion.

Sometimes, as is the case with the Rabbinate, they are official, the holders of stamps and seals and dispensers of certificates that carry the imprimatur of the state. In 2009, the United Kingdom appointed its first identity commissioner, whose task was to ensure that the state was dispensing official identities in a reliable, responsible and orderly fashion.

These are the people who not only designate which boxes are available to tick but decide what it takes to qualify to fit in them. When the French government denied citizenship in 2008 to the Moroccan mother of three French-born children because she wore a burqa and practiced a radical form of Islam, according to the French daily *Le Monde*, it was the first time the intensity of a person's religiosity had been regarded as a conclusive factor in their ability to assimilate into France. The woman's application for French nationality had been denied in 2005 on the grounds of "insufficient assimilation" after social service reports claimed she lived in "total submission" to her husband. She appealed, invoking the constitutional right to religious freedom and insisting that she had never harbored a desire to challenge France's fundamental values. But after three years, the Council of State, France's highest administrative body, upheld the ruling. "She has adopted a radical practice of her religion, incompatible with essential values of the French community, particularly the principle of equality of the sexes," it said. The legal expert who reported to the Council of State said the woman's interviews with social services revealed that "she lives almost as a recluse, isolated from French society."

The report said, "She has no idea about the secular state or the right to vote. She lives in total submission to her male relatives. She seems to find this normal and the idea of challenging it has never crossed her mind." Daniele Lochak, a law professor not involved in the case, argued that to consider excessive submission to men as a reason not to grant citizenship was bizarre. "If you follow that to its logical conclusion it means that women whose partners beat them are also not worthy of being French," she told *Le Monde*.

These official gatekeepers hold great power. For with certain pieces of paper come certain rights. Proving that you are eligible for those papers can be a great challenge, and not being eligible can cast you into a life of destitution and desperation. The Western world is full of people who are excluded precisely because they have no valid identity. In France, such people formed a movement of *sans papiers*— literally, people without papers; in the US, liberals call them "undocumented workers" while conservatives brand them "illegals": no noun necessary, the description of their citizenship status, or lack of it, conveys all you need to know.

Proving that you are who you say you are—or in Joseph's case who you think you are—is no easy task. Even the US president has struggled to convince a significant minority of Americans that he was born in the country—despite an independently verified birth certificate and birth announcements in his local newspaper. Imagine how difficult it would be for someone seeking asylum from a country with a less efficient bureaucracy to prove their identity to the US immigration service.

A lot of Seth Farber's work at ITIM involves excavating family records across generations and continents, sending people to take pictures of grandparents' gravestones, asking local rabbis to bear witness and telling people to take their chances at the county courthouse. All efforts are made to sew together the necessary documentary evidence which Jews will need to tell the story of their lives and which can, in turn, prove their identity to the Rabbinate.

Gatekeepers, however, need not be official. They can just as easily appoint themselves, with varying degrees of credibility, to be the custodians of an identity's authenticity, imposing the cultural standards and behavioral norms which they hope will plug the porous borders, cast out the impostors, intruders and interlopers and thereby impose a notional conformity for those on the inside. So real men don't cry, a true Englishman is reserved, and a Jew worthy of the name does not like Shakespeare.

This self-designated, unofficial role is brilliantly illustrated in *The American Directory of Certified Uncle Toms*, published by the Council on Black Internal Affairs, which was set up following the Million Man March in 1995. The book comes with the subtitle "Being a review of the history, antics and attitudes of handkerchief heads, Aunt Jemimas,

head negroes in charge and house negroes against the freedom of the
black race." The council set the lofty target of monitoring "the
progress of the black race toward its inevitable freedom." The book,
wittily written as it is, remains a landmark document in the history
of internal race regulation. It ranks over fifty prominent black figures,
past and present, according to a five-star Uncle Tom rating, with five
being the worst. Michael Jackson, who had plastic surgery which
effaced many of his black features, got one star; Bayard Rustin, the
gay activist who organized the march on Washington at which King
made his "I have a dream" speech, got five; W. E. B. Du Bois, a pioneer
of Pan-Africanism who died in Ghana working on an Encyclopedia
Africana, was also, according to the authors, a five-star Uncle Tom.

Colin Powell (five stars) becomes "an official, government-issue
Uncle Tom"; Maya Angelou (two stars) is "the much glorified but
innocuous negro emissary of ebony culture"; and Oprah Winfrey
(four stars) is "the best unambiguously black ambassador of plantation
placidity since Hattie McDaniel gushed over Scarlett in *Gone With
the Wind.*" The book promises not only constant vigilance—"More
will be nominated. More will be exposed. More will be certified"—
but also redemption: "Only by refashioning his mind and recasting
his role in black affairs can the Uncle Tom declare himself to be a
friend of his own black race." Such is the role of the cultural gatekeeper: to refashion the mind or, failing that, to expose the heresy
of those who refuse to comply.

There is, however, a connection between official and cultural
gatekeeping. For the official gatekeepers to maintain credibility and
political support, the process by which they determine who is in and
who is out must be underpinned by some notion of who is worthy
of inclusion or exclusion in the population at large.

This was illustrated in the findings of a 2007 UK Home Office
report, *Exploring the Decision-making of Immigration Officers*, examining
the process by which the ultimate national gatekeepers determine
which foreigners should be questioned at UK ports of entry. The
officers claimed they based their decisions on "instinct" or "intuition"
about people who "look the part." "We're making decisions based
on . . . a balance of probability," said one immigration officer. These

instincts did not come from nowhere. This was a period when EU expansion and Third World deprivation had made immigration a hot-button political issue. Popular fears that poor foreigners were coming to the UK and either undercutting British workers' wages or drawing money from an already depleted welfare system had sparked a dramatic increase in support for the far right and a more xenophobic tone across the political spectrum. In such a climate, deciding whether someone "looks the part" is a matter of guessing whether that someone can "pay their way." At a time when nearly half the planet live on less than $2 a day, the principal role of these gatekeepers is to keep the poor out and wave the wealthy through. In the study, they freely admitted as much, saying they have learned to "no longer . . . ask a well-traveled American businessman how much money he has brought with him or for details of his bank balance." "For some [immigration officers]," the report concluded, "credibility is essentially a matter of economics."

It is an explicit admission that the West (for, in this respect, Britain is no different to most other developed nations) is in lockdown, in order to protect itself from the massive global underclass it has helped create through colonialism and neo-liberal globalization. During the Cold War, one of the central criticisms of the Eastern Bloc was that it denied the basic right to freedom of movement. But as soon as the Berlin Wall came down, we just built another obstacle to replace it. Politics once kept people in; now economics keeps them out. Poor people—and that is most of the world—are simply not supposed to travel to the West any more.

This, the report illustrated, has repercussions in terms of race and gender. To appear wealthy, women had to perform their femininity in a certain way. "American ladies who've got loads of jewellery on . . . their hair is perfect . . . their make up is perfect and their clothes are really nice," were waved through. Young women in "white stilettos and short skirts," however, could be prostitutes and were more likely to be questioned. No such performance of race, however, was necessary. The officers saw all they needed in the travelers' faces. Non-white South Africans were ten times more likely, and non-white Canadians nine times more likely to be subjected to further questioning than their white countrymen. (The disparity for black and white Americans was much smaller, presumably because the officers assumed all Americans are reasonably wealthy.) The authors of the report insisted that this has nothing to do with racism, claiming that the imbalance was because black people were more likely to be poor and therefore more likely to be seeking work or drawing on public funds. But if that really was the aim, then the officers were failing even on their own terms. When the figures were adjusted to take the occupation of the traveler into account, the discrepancy widened dramatically in the wrong direction. Professional non-white South Africans became eighteen times, and non-white Canadians thirteen and a half times more likely to be stopped than non-professionals. Moreover, when translated into sterling, the mean income of a non-white Canadian is almost double that of a white South African. Yet a black Canadian was four times more likely to be stopped than a white South African. Thanks to their prejudices, the immigration officers were actually letting in poorer people because they were white.

The immigration officers were not following the strict letter of any law or government edict. But when it came down to it, their "intuition" as gatekeepers was in keeping with both the government's intentions and rising popular sentiment. This was exemplified during a particularly contentious edition of the BBC's flagship politics discussion program *Question Time*, where the extreme-right British National Party gained an invitation for the first time. Representatives from each of the main parties expressed their disgust at the BNP's racism—then each in turn sought to establish their anti-immigration credentials so as not to be outflanked.

Had the officers been keeping out rich white Americans and letting in poor black South Africans with converse consistency, there would have been an uproar. Their task is not to be fair but to keep gate—to defend the integrity of our borders from unwanted intruders. Whether official or self-styled, metaphorical or literal, that is the role of the gatekeeper: to make the conclusive decision between banishment and belonging; to discriminate between and, when necessary, to discriminate against.

★

And so it was that when Fackenheim went before Hagar, he stood not just before a rabbinical judge but on a long-standing cultural, political and societal faultline between secular and religious that runs through the entire state of Israel. The issue of how Jewish both Israel and its citizens should be is constantly being negotiated both within its borders and between the state and the Jewish diaspora.

It wasn't always this way. At one stage in the diaspora, those who claimed to be Jewish were accepted on trust. "If he lived among us, was a partner in our society and said he was one of us, we assumed he was right," Zvi Zovar, a professor of law and Jewish studies at Bar-Ilan University told *The New York Times*. The position of Avraham Yeshayahu Karelitz, leading ultra-Orthodox rabbi in the area both before and after the state of Israel was created, was that anyone who came claiming to be Jewish should be allowed to marry within the Jewish faith, "even if nothing is known of his family." Since, in most parts of the world, being a Jew carried heavy penalties, including segregation, exclusion and even death, there was little incentive to falsely claim Jewish heritage. Back then, no gatekeeper was necessary—the gate was always open.

But the creation of the state of Israel demanded a tighter ship. In 1950, shortly after it was founded, the Knesset (national parliament) established the Law of Return, which made Israel not only the actual new home to many Jews but the potential home to any Jew. Back then anyone whose mother was Jewish or who had converted to Judaism was generally considered to be a Jew. Over time, the definitions of how Jewish you had to be to be a citizen of Israel evolved, and diverged away from how Jewish you needed to be to satisfy the rabbinical courts. In 1970, following a series of contentious Supreme Court cases, the Knesset broadened the scope to include the spouses and children and grandchildren of Jews and the spouses of children and grandchildren of Jews; one Jewish grandparent, male or female, was enough to earn immediate citizenship. The new law covered everyone who would have been persecuted as a Jew under the Nuremberg Laws, the Nazi rulings that paved the way for the Holocaust. Meanwhile, those who converted away from Judaism to another religion, regardless of what religion their parents were, became ineligible for Israeli citizenship on the basis of the Law of Return, even as they remained Jewish in the eyes of the Rabbinate.

"The Law of Return means there's a place in the world where Jews can immigrate," explains Farber. "That is a great thing. But the realities and complexities of the Enlightenment age present a real challenge because Jewish identity is so complex." This tension between the civil and religious sections of the state simmers constantly and occasionally boils over. The truth is that relatively few Jews would have passed the tests for observance that Hagar set down. In 2007, a poll by the Israel Democracy Institute found that only 27 percent of Israeli Jews kept Shabbat in accordance with Halachic laws, while 20 percent kept it to some degree and 53 percent said they did not keep it at all.

The archetypal Jewish Israeli against whom Fackenheim was being tested was a rarity. According to 2008 Guttman polls, 51 percent of Israeli Jews regard themselves as secular, 10 percent as Orthodox, 9 percent as ultra-Orthodox and 30 percent as traditional. In other words, the people who have been appointed to the task of determining the level of Jewishness one needs to live and exhibit in order to be judged truly Jewish themselves represent a minority in Israeli Jewry. Their job became much harder in 2008, after a Danish woman known only as Yael (she did not want to give her full name or Hebrew name for fear of retribution) filed for divorce at the rabbinical court in the port city of Ashdod. Yael was not born Jewish but had married a Jew and converted fifteen years earlier. The judge asked her a few questions about her conversion and then, evidently unimpressed, probed her on her observance. Left with the impression that she did not observe Shabbat or otherwise meet the standards he believed worthy of a Jewish convert, he ruled her conversion invalid. As with Joseph, this meant her marriage was not valid. It also meant that her children were now no longer Jewish either.

Yael had been converted by Chaim Druckman, head of the National Conversion Authority, whose primary task was to try to establish universal standards for conversion, in light of the arrival of roughly 300,000 immigrants from the former Soviet Union. Druckman took a less hardline position than others in the Rabbinate where Soviet Jews were concerned, on the basis that the political climate in which they grew up did not allow many of them to practice their religion freely. "There is a commandment to love every Jew and there is a special commandment to love the convert," he said.

Not everyone felt the same way. One judge on the High Rabbinical Court, Rabbi Avraham Sherman, told a conference dedicated to "Strengthening the Walls of Conversion" that the new immigrants were "in the vast majority gentiles who want to convert out of self-interest," and said that the Orthodox rabbis who wanted to convert them were suffering from a "false and distorted perspective, a lack of understanding of halakha," or Jewish law: "There is no logic to telling tens of thousands of goyim [non-Jews] who grew up on heresy, hate of religion, liberalism, communism, socialism, that suddenly they can undergo a revolution deep in their souls. There is no such reality."

Sherman was part of the three-judge panel that upheld Ashdod's decision to invalidate Yael's conversion. But in their fifty-page verdict, they went even further, disqualifying all conversions performed by Druckman and one other rabbi since 1999, effectively annulling forty thousand. "Nobody really checked how many of these 300,000 people really wanted to be Jews," said Rabbi Eliyahu Ben-Dahan, director of the rabbinical courts, referring to the Soviet immigrants. In other words, forty thousand people were first told they were Jewish and then told they were not. The gatekeeper giveth. And the gatekeeper taketh away.

Not surprisingly, this caused considerable concern throughout the diaspora. "I'm very worried," Yael told the Associated Press. She was born in Maryland into a non-religious household, to a Jewish father and non-Jewish mother, and had undergone an exacting conversion process, taken a Hebrew name, kept kosher, changed her wardrobe to conform to Orthodox custom and moved to Israel. In her daily life, she was more observant than most Israeli Jews. But now her Jewishness was being denied. "I probably will not be able to get married in Israel. God forbid, if I die, will I be allowed a Jewish burial?"

It is a common trait of the gatekeeper that the threshold they demand for entry is far higher than the norm for those on the inside. A 2009

Home Office consultation paper, "Earning the Right to Stay," proposed a points system to determine who was qualified to remain in the country. An application could be fast-tracked if the applicant became involved in political life, did voluntary or community work and spoke English; a number of points was awarded depending on earning potential and qualifications. But the paper also suggested deducting points from those who demonstrated an "active disregard for UK values." Quite what those values are or what an "active disregard" would mean was never made clear. It does not mean criminal activity, so presumably it describes an action that is legal yet disrespectful. As someone who feels uncomfortable standing for the British national anthem or saluting the flag—I don't believe in the monarchy, and the flag to me is the emblem of colonialism that dominated my mother's native land of Barbados—I guess that could mean me.

But I am already inside. There is nothing much the gatekeeper can do about me; they can only raise the bar for entry of others in a bid to set a new norm. Indeed, at times, that does seem to be precisely the task they have set themselves. At the launch of a blueprint for UK citizenship tests for new immigrants in 2003, then home secretary David Blunkett as much as admitted that the tests had little to do with immigration: "I want to see a greater pride from British people about their own culture and identity—English, Welsh, Scottish and Irish—so that people can actually celebrate their own sense of identity much more clearly and have the confidence to celebrate and welcome other people." In other words, newcomers were to be tested so that British people could feel better about themselves.

At times the role of the gatekeeper is not so much to enforce the rules of entry but to replicate the presence of the gate. In the United States the border between US and Mexico is not just a physical space that separates the countries but a political space that reproduces itself throughout the country. Immigration officers mount raids, local councils pass ordinances and states enforce their own strictures. In 2010 Arizona passed one of the most severe anti-immigrant laws in the country, making it a state misdemeanor for an alien to be in the state without carrying the required documents. It also obligated the police to attempt to determine someone's immigration status if there is reasonable suspicion the person is an illegal alien—as though citizenship is a condition that can be reasonably divined by sight.

While the physical border marks a geographically fixed, if historically fluid, area, the political border is more arbitrary. It divides families, terrorizes communities and cannot be effectively enforced without ethnic profiling. "I can tell an illegal just by looking at them," a Minuteman from the anti-immigration vigilante group once told me in New Mexico. "It's like wild dog versus tame dog. They just don't have the same kind of look."

A few years earlier when I met Republican congressional hopeful and Minuteman Randy Graf in Tucson, Arizona, I asked him how he expected to deport 11 million undocumented migrants; he shrugged. "We don't need to deport them," he explained. "All we have to do is enforce our employment laws and pretty soon they won't be able to get a job and will self-deport." Erect gates everywhere for certain people until they give up.

The push for authenticity runs deep in identity politics and corrodes from the inside. At its most powerful and insidious, it creates a form of self-policing whereby everyone assumes that everyone else is meeting an abstract ideal standard apart from them. At its root, it insists that who we are necessarily determines what we do and how we think. Assuming that there is a single, particular way to be Jewish, or at the very least a behavioral standard below which no one may be considered Jewish, it seeks both to set that standard and to decide on the penalties for not meeting it. Judge. Jury. Executioner.

Having established that there are certain ways people of a certain identity need to be, it follows that those who do not conform are impostors. It's the logic that guides the peer pressure that at different times has made it "unmaternal" for Western mothers to work; "uncool" for black kids to do well at school; or "un-American" for US citizens to believe in socialism. The bar is always arbitrary, mythical and illusive. The "real" mother, black kid or American is simply a figment of the gatekeeper's imagination—but that does not stop people trying to invent them, or those on the inside fearing that such an archetype might actually exist.

These narrow definitions and restrictive framings never made sense.

Authenticity of this nature requires isolation: a defense from the influences of the outside world. But people are social animals, and when they mix they take their culture and values with them. "The 'emblems' of a cultural identity often result from borrowing," writes Jean-François Bayart in *The Illusion of Cultural Identity*. "Portuguese *azulejo* tiles, for instance: the technique is of Arab origin and the blue comes from China, which had itself borrowed it from Persia. The tomato, which is as typical of Mediterranean cuisine as olives, bread and wine, was imported from the Americas by the Spanish and its name is Aztec in origin."

Now, thanks to new technologies and the advanced state of neo-liberal globalization—in which, notwithstanding the large numbers who are excluded, a broad spectrum of people travel, communicate and reproduce more often and more easily than ever before—the borders, categories and affiliations which gatekeepers seek to protect are less solid than ever.

And what is true for culture is no less true for politics. Just as being a Latina is no guarantee of having wisdom or good legal judgment, identities hold no inherent political position, cultural value or philosophical approach. Muslims may support the war in Iraq; women may be against abortion rights; and black Europeans may be in favor of far-right anti-immigration parties. There is nothing intrinsic in religious adherence, chromosomal composition or melanin content to suggest that support for such political positions represents some form of psychological deficiency. The fact that it is statistically unlikely owes more to the perceived material interests of those groups than to any genetic predisposition to the politics.

This point is well illustrated in the relationship between Jews and Zionism. The notion of a state of Israel was a contentious and hard-fought issue among Jews; for a long time there was no consensus. The Board of Deputies of British Jews, for example, did not have a Zionist majority until 1939. "It is easy to forget that Zionism and the possibility of a sovereign Jewish state were once deeply divisive issues in Jewish life in this country," argued a 1997 Institute for Jewish Policy Research document on the attachment of British Jews to Israel.

The date at which the Board of Deputies shifted was significant.

It was the year Britain entered the Second World War. The genocidal horrors that would be visited on Jewish people by Nazi Germany and their eager collaborators, and the failure of the rest of the world to come to the Jews' assistance, convinced sufficient numbers among them that they needed a state of their own or risked extinction, and won them over to the cause of the creation of the state of Israel. Put bluntly, European anti-Semitism played a decisive role in making Zionism popular and possible.

This should hardly come as a surprise. Attacked as Jews, people defended themselves as Jews. There is nothing exclusive to Judaism about this. When a group of people feel besieged, they are likely to rally around whatever it is that has made them a targeted group. After the terrorist attacks of 9/11, patriotism in America took on a new force. Within a week the country started running out of American flags (many of which were made in China). One poll showed that people were more likely to have displayed the flag than comforted their family.

When a TV station in Long Island told its presenters not to wear flag pins, in order to protect the station's credibility as an impartial news provider, it faced threats of a boycott. "We don't want anyone to get the false impression that our patriotic emotions cloud our reporting of the facts," said Patrick Dolan, senior vice-president of Cable Systems Corporation, which owns the station, on air on 19 September. Over the next few days, the corporation suffered a severe backlash, as several firms threatened to pull their advertisements because they felt the station was insufficiently patriotic. These businesses had, for the most part, been alerted to the situation by their customers. T. Walker Lloyd, the executive secretary of the Long Island Advertising Club, had little patience for Mr Dolan's reasoning. "I'm really angry that here's somebody saying we have to be even-handed," he told *The New York Times*. "If he said these things after Pearl Harbor, he'd have been lynched."

Some years later, respected television anchorman Dan Rather described the patriotic fervor that swept the country in dramatic terms: "It is an obscene comparison . . . but you know there was a time in South Africa that people would put flaming tires around people's necks if they dissented," said Rather. "And in some ways the fear is that you will be necklaced here, you will have a flaming tire of lack of patriotism put around your neck."

Any group that feels under threat will retreat to its camp and may well then come out swinging. The scope for dissent is diminished and the role of the gatekeeper enhanced. So, as Zionism became the firm consensus among world Jewry following the Holocaust, the space for criticizing it within the Jewish community became ever more narrow, until it almost disappeared altogether.

Jews who would once have been in the majority in their opposition to the creation of the state of Israel became labeled unstable "self-haters." To be Jewish and oppose Zionism was regarded as a psychological condition rather than a political position. The notion that the creation of Israel had ever been contested among Jews, let alone that it retains some dissenters, has effectively been banished from the public square. The result is effectively to lock support for Israel into Jewish identity by suggesting that Zionism has always been the only home for sane Jews. So, even though Zionism never held a monopoly on Jewish thought (according to a poll by the Institute for Jewish Policy Research, in 1995, 19 percent of British Jews had either negative feelings towards Israel or no special attachment), in the space of a few generations, it has secured a virtual monopoly on public discussion within the Jewish community. "Jewish critics of Zionism and Israel have been treated by the Jewish establishment as, at best, innocent oddballs [and] at worst some critics have stood accused of being irresponsible, crazy and 'self-hating,' if not downright disloyal," writes Adam Shatz in the introduction to *Prophets Outcast*.

With time, this restrictive discourse extended to take in almost any criticism of Israel's actions. When Richard Goldstone, a South African Jew and Zionist, conducted a report into the war in Gaza that turned out to be critical of Israel's actions, as well as those of the Palestinians, Israeli finance minister Yuval Steinitz told the *Jewish Week*: "Not all Jews are perfect. Some people can be unfair, unjust, unbalanced and even of bad character. So it is with Jews. Just as a non-Jew can be anti-Semitic, a Jew can also be anti-Semitic and discriminate against our people and despise and hate our people."

Paradoxically, the demands of the Zionist project have contributed considerably to the current debate in Israel over who qualifies to be a Jew and who is qualified to make the decision. For Israel to remain a Jewish state, as opposed to a state in which large numbers of Jews happen to live, Jews have to remain in a majority. In the eyes of some, that goal has been threatened by the growth in the country's Arab or Palestinian population (an Israel Democracy Institute study showed that 45 percent identify first as Arab while only 24 percent define themselves primarily as Palestinian). In 2008, Arab Israeli citizens constituted around 20 percent of the population and identified themselves primarily as Palestinian by nationality and Israeli by citizenship. For several decades, they had a significantly higher birth rate than the Jewish population, sparking fears among some Israelis that they could one day outnumber Jews and thereby pose an existential threat to Israel.

"The Israeli Arabs are a time bomb," Israeli historian Benny Morris told *Haaretz*: "Their slide into complete Palestinization has made them an emissary of the enemy that is among us. They are a potential fifth column. In both demographic and security terms they are liable to undermine the state. So that if Israel again finds itself in a situation of existential threat, as in 1948, it may be forced to act as it did then. If we are attacked by Egypt (after an Islamist revolution in Cairo) and by Syria, and chemical and biological missiles slam into our cities, and at the same time Israeli Palestinians attack us from behind, I can see an expulsion situation. It could happen. If the threat to Israel is existential, expulsion will be justified."

Israeli premier Benjamin Netanyahu has also referred to Arab Israelis as a "demographic threat', claiming that if they rose much beyond 20 percent of the population they would one day threaten Israel's raison d'être. These concerns continued even as the birth rate of Israel's Arab population slowed and the Jewish birth rate increased.

It is widely argued that the motivation behind the Knesset loosening the definition of who qualifies as Jewish and can therefore enjoy the Law of Return in 1970 was at least in part to ensure a permanent Jewish majority in Israel. It has also been understood as an attempt by the more secular leadership to limit the influence of religious groups. These two goals are by no means mutually exclusive. "The Law of Return provides an easy way to immigrate," explains Farber. "Given the demographic balance and the importance of maintaining a Jewish majority, the state has a strong incentive to lower the bar."

The net result has been little change to the levels of religiosity. According to the Israel Democracy Institute, the rate of observance remained fairly constant between 1999 and 2008, with a 1 percent increase in those who consider themselves partially, non- or only slightly observant (69 percent) and in those who consider themselves fully observant (13 percent) and a 2 percent drop in those who consider themselves very observant, to 18 percent.

The reason for this can be found in two countervailing trends, which effectively cancel each other out numerically and antagonize each other socially and culturally. On the one hand, there has been the mass migration of Jews from the former Soviet Union, where "being a Jew" was considered not just a religion but a nationality, like being a Russian, a Tartar or a Ukrainian. The impetus for many of these immigrants to come to Israel was primarily economic rather than religious, and their attachment to Judaism, compared with other Israelis', was relatively weak. In 2007, a survey conducted by the Forum for Immigrant Parents revealed that 82 percent of high school students who immigrated to Israel from the former Soviet Union saw nothing worth learning from in Israeli culture; 40 percent saw no need to study Jewish tradition or the Bible; and 45 percent thought they had no future in Israel—while more than a quarter did not define themselves as Jewish. That last figure chimes with Israeli officials' estimates that more than one in four Soviet immigrants were not practicing Jews and many were not Jews at all. According to the Guttman poll, 75 percent of those from the former Soviet Union regarded themselves as secular, as opposed to 44 percent of native Israelis.

"Until 1989, the overwhelming majority of people who sought to come to Israel through the aliyah [organized immigration to first Palestine and then, after 1948, Israel] were born Jewish, with their mother being Jewish," explains Farber. "In 1989, there was huge immigration from the Soviet Union, with many who were Jewish on their paternal side. All of a sudden, literally people said, 'Oh my God.'" By 1998, more than half the immigrants to Israel did not have a Jewish mother. "Until then, pretty much everyone who came saw themselves as Jews," added Farber. "They served in the IDF [Israeli Defense Forces], and celebrated Jewish holidays. So then we had to be much more suspect about who was coming in."

On the other hand, there continues to be a high birth rate among more religious and traditional Jews, particularly the ultra-Orthodox. So while the levels of religiosity have remained proportionally static, the intensity of religious feelings on one side and degree of ambivalence on the other has made for a far more polarized society, creating new fissures both within the Orthodox movement and between Jews in Israel and those elsewhere. Among those who consider themselves religious, the ultra-Orthodox now hold more sway. Thirty years ago, ultra-Orthodox parties held just 5 of 120 seats in the Knesset. Today they have three times that number. Since appointments to the rabbinical courts are essentially political, this has a significant impact on the importance the courts attach to things such as observance.

Joseph's experience, and the forty thousand annulments, also indicates a significant cleavage between what it means to be Jewish in Israel compared with in the diaspora. Outside Israel, the Orthodox are smaller in number and have no state power. Moreover, in most Western countries, Jews are raised in far more secular surroundings, where marriage outside the faith and the need to negotiate a minority status have arguably produced a more fluid sense of what it means to be Jewish. "In the United States and also in Western Europe there are many kinds of Jews," Professor Menachem Friedman, a sociologist of religion at Bar-Ilan University, told *The New York Times*. "People can change religions and identities quickly."

This has made the Rabbinate increasingly skeptical of the credentials of even Orthodox rabbis abroad and the validity of their conversions. Farber believes that the very pillars of American Jewry, who run the country's principal philanthropic and cultural organizations, would be turned down by the Rabbinate. "Eighty percent of the federation leaders probably wouldn't be able to reach the bar," says Farber. "With the Rabbinate, the question is what is an acceptable conversion and what is not. In other words, who is the gatekeeper and who isn't."

Given the amount of political and financial support Jewish Americans give to Israel, this is rapidly developing into an important schism between the diaspora and Israel. "Few crises have so divided Israel from the North American Jewish community," a representative of the United Jewish Communities, an umbrella group that raises hundreds of millions of dollars for Israel every year, wrote to the former prime minister Ehud Olmert shortly after the annulments.

It has also exposed an isolationist streak within the Rabbinate that is hard to distinguish from xenophobia. "When they want to marry, they will do everything possible to deceive," said Rabbi Yosef Sheinin, the chief rabbi of Ashdod, where Yael's conversion had been rejected, referring to immigrants from the former Soviet Union. "They are to be assumed to be cheaters."

During the period when Joseph's divorce was denied, these contradictions played themselves out in various ways around the country. There were street battles between ultra-Orthodox Jews and mounted police in Jerusalem. Strictly observant Jews don't work, turn on electrical appliances, spend money or drive from sundown on Friday to sundown on Saturday. When Jerusalem city council decided to pay someone to open a car park on the Sabbath to cater for tourists, it sparked disturbances. The protesters branded the police Nazis, murderers and Zionist Gestapo; the police responded by throwing them in bushes and dousing them with pepper spray. Secularists have held counterprotests, including confronting the religious imposition of a seating policy on local buses. In one ultra-Orthodox area, Ramot D, some public buses are designated as "*mehadrin*," or strictly kosher, which means men sit in the front and women go to the back. In a reprise of the Freedom Rides of the US civil rights era, the secular activists rode the number 40 bus—which is *mehadrin*—with the women in the front and the men at the back. The separation policy is being challenged in Israel's Supreme Court.

Elsewhere, in 2007, a gang of eight youths aged between sixteen and twenty-one from Petah Tikva, near Tel Aviv, were arrested after executing a spate of homophobic, anti-Semitic and racist attacks, including beating up gays and ultra-Orthodox and Ethiopian

Jews, as well as spraying a swastika on a synagogue. All eight were Jewish under Israeli law. Indeed, one of them came from a deeply Zionist family, was a straight-A student in Jewish religious studies and had a grandmother who had survived the Holocaust. His Ukrainian grandmother related how she was only six when the Nazis herded her and other Jewish families into open pits: "The Nazis stood all the Jews they had rounded up and began to shoot them. I was saved by a miracle because someone fell on me and hid me. I know who the Nazis are, I went through it, and my grandson knows that very well." She insisted that he had been intimidated into joining the neo-Nazis but was "terrified" of them and "didn't know how to get out."

The leader of the gang, nineteen-year-old Eli Boynatov, was nicknamed "Eli the Nazi." The gang had videoed their violent acts. In one recording, Eli spews self-loathing: "My grandfather was a half-Jewboy. I will not have children so that this trash will not be born with even a tiny percent of Jewboy blood." All eight boys were from the former Soviet Union.

It is the gatekeeper's task to make sense of this chaos; to deny the complexity, ignore the variety, suppress the unruliness and enforce the archetype—to impose the standard by which all ways of being may be measured. The fact that an archetype, by its very nature, exists only as a composite character in the imagination of its creator is less important to the gatekeeper than the notion that it should exist. For them, the reason it does not exist has nothing to do with human diversity and everything to do with human weakness. Out there somewhere is the Israeli Jew that Joseph Fackenheim might have been if only his father had married within the faith, if only he had been converted by a more trusted rabbi or in a different country, if only he were more conscientious in his observation of Sabbath and not quite so keen on Shakespeare. "The problem I have is not proving that people are Jewish," explains Rabbi Farber. "The problem is certifying that they are Jewish to a certain threshold."

The trouble is, the threshold keeps on changing. The gatekeepers adjust their rules of entry according to the political, economic and social demands of their time, even as they insist they are authenticating a timeless truth—in this case, "Jewishness." Who gets in and who does not is rooted less in facts than in context.

"One guy went to get married," recalls Farber. "His biological brother had got married in the same place just two years earlier. But the rabbi said there was no guarantee that he would qualify, because the rules had changed. 'What are you going to do about his brother then?' I asked. 'Because they have the exact same story.' The judge shrugged and said: 'We're not going to touch that.'"

5. The Truth in Her Eyes

The only certain thing about any identity is that it will keep on changing

It happened, I think, sometime in the mid-90s. I went to bed in one country and woke up in a different one.

– Roddy Doyle, *The Deportees and Other Stories*

In Ireland, back in the mid-nineteenth century, shortly before the potato famine, the son of a wealthy Irish Protestant merchant, William Mulchinock, became besotted with a Catholic cobbler's daughter, Mary O'Connor. William was something of a wastrel—a poet, dreamer and drinker. Mary worked for his family, first as a kitchenmaid and later as a nanny to his nieces and nephews.

Sometimes they would meet by the well in Tralee, a small town on the northern edge of the Dingle peninsula that was nonetheless the largest town in County Kerry. Occasionally, he would take her dancing in Clahane at the top of the glen. William proposed to Mary, but she refused—not because she didn't love him but because she felt the barriers of class and religion were too strong for a marriage to work and he would resent her for the consequences. William persisted, entranced by her lustrous eyes.

One moonlit evening, he took Mary out, once again declared his undying love and, by some accounts, persuaded her to marry him. It was a night that would later be immortalized in a verse penned by Mulchinock:

> The pale moon was rising above the green mountain,
> The sun was declining beneath the blue sea,
> When I strayed with my love to the pure crystal fountain,
> That stands in the beautiful vale of Tralee.

She was lovely and fair as the rose of the summer,
Yet 'twas not her beauty alone that won me,
Oh no, 'twas the truth in her eyes ever dawning,
That made me love Mary, the Rose of Tralee.

The cool shades of evening their mantle were spreading,
And Mary all smiling was listening to me.
The moon through the valley her pale rays were shredding,
When I won the heart of the Rose of Tralee.

Sadly, it was not to be. The next evening, at a packed political meeting in town held by those advocating repeal of the Act of Union between Britain and Ireland, a deadly scuffle broke out and William was accused of landing the fatal blow. He fled the country, ending up in India, where he worked as a war correspondent on the North-West Frontier and befriended a powerful man from Limerick who managed to pull some strings back home. William was pardoned for the murder and returned to County Kerry triumphantly in the early spring of 1849, with a view to rehabilitating himself and claiming his bride-to-be. He stopped off on the way for a cognac at the Kings Arms in Tralee and there saw a funeral cortege pass by. The body was Mary's . . . It is a story in the best Irish narrative tradition, containing in equal parts politics, passion, repression, religion, regret and misery. And little more than a century later, it spawned an Irish institution—the Rose of Tralee competition.

Once a year, since 1959, the Irish diaspora and national media descend on this town to watch judges put young women through their paces in search of Mary's modern likeness. Call it a beauty pageant, and the organizers will correct you firmly, instructing you that it all comes back to Mulchinock's ballad. "That is still basically what the judges are looking for," says Niall O'Loingsigh, the former chairman and marketing manager of the festival. "The truth in her eyes. A well-rounded personality that can represent the Irish diaspora at home and abroad." In short, it is the search for the embodiment of quintessential Irish womanhood—chaste, charming, accomplished and comely. The kind of woman you can take home to meet the family or take around the world to showcase a diaspora.

The first Rose of Tralee festival, half a century ago, had just four contestants—from Tralee, Dublin, London and Birmingham—with only those who originally hailed from Tralee allowed to compete. In the early sixties, the organizers opened it up to women from County Kerry and, by the end of the decade, anyone of Irish birth or ancestry was eligible. Since then, the festival has penetrated ever deeper into the diaspora. Today, England and Ireland are literally not even the half of it. In 2008, there were thirty-one Roses: nine from Ireland, nine from the United States, five from Australia, four from England, and the remaining four from Canada, Dubai, New Zealand and Luxembourg. That year, over two nights, 684,000 people tuned in to watch on television—just over half the number who tuned in fifteen years ago but still a sizable figure in a country of just 4.5 million people.

To enter the Rose of Tralee competition, you must be an unmarried woman under the age of twenty-seven and have some claim to Irish ancestry. From Tipperary to Texas, hopefuls attend heats. The winners come to Tralee, where each one is assigned a male escort, chosen because they are "debonair, diplomatic, can carry a conversation and have a roguish side." The Roses may be called on to perform party pieces, parade in evening wear and make the kind of chit-chat that works well on a public stage before a live audience. In 2008, when I attended, Rita Talty from New Jersey sang "Jumbo Breakfast Roll," Aislinn Ryan from New Zealand did a jig from *Riverdance*, Carol Ann Keenan from Louth played "Bare Necessities" on her cornet and Fiona McConnell from Liverpool strummed and sang "The Lakes of Ponchartrain." There are no swimsuits or ostentatious flashes of flesh.

"The Rose is Ireland's answer to the perennial problem of how to present sexuality as a tame beast with which to milk the global wallets of the old diaspora by reassuring us that wherever we roam, there'll always be a welcome mat and a fine, economically dependent female to warm the pot without giving you backchat," explains columnist Medb Ruane. "The good girl with personality can be chatty, but not too talkative, clever but not too smart. You have to come across as very gentle and unthreatening. That's the key. Deep cleavages and big slits in your skirt are not good. They don't want *Baywatch* babes. You've got to have breasts but not show them." Such was the parody in the television show *Father Ted*, set on a remote Irish island, where the "Lovely Girls Competition" is decided by a "lovely laugh tie-break."

While the resemblance to Miss World is reasonably denied, it remains apt. "The argument that it is a cultural—not a beauty—pageant is common in cultural pageants such as those that purport to reward cultural 'authenticity,' cultural practices and preserve cultural traditions," writes Rebecca Chiyoko King-O'Riain, a senior lecturer at Maynooth University, in her essay "Making the Perfect Queen." "However, they do so by choosing a woman as a symbol of all of this 'culture.'"

The thing is, over the past twenty years, that "culture" has undergone a huge transformation. Socially, sexually, economically, professionally and politically, women's lives have arguably changed more in Ireland in the course of a generation than anywhere else in the Western world. So while the search has continued unabated for half a century, what the organizers are looking for has changed considerably. It had to. The Rose they once sought barely exists.

On a macro-level, the nation's economic boom altered Ireland's relationship to the rest of the world. On a micro-level, this in turn revolutionized women's relationships with their own bodies, other women and, of course, men. "[Women] became more visible in the public world. Ireland had two women presidents in a row [the first, Mary Robinson, in 1990] and a woman Tánaiste [deputy prime minister]," writes *Irish Times* columnist Fintan O'Toole. "The first female editor of a national newspaper, Geraldine Kennedy of the *Irish Times*, was appointed . . . Young women were more assertive, less demure and allegedly more hedonistic."

This shift was dramatic. As recently as 1970, Irish fertility rates were the highest in the Western world. One third of all births in Dublin's maternity hospitals in 1960 were the fifth birth or more. In Europe, only women in Albania—a poor, rural Communist dictatorship—had more children. When Ireland joined the European Union in 1973, the graphs had to be recalibrated to accommodate this new fertile nation. The unrivaled power of the Catholic Church made obtaining birth control a convoluted process and imposed severe restrictions on women's autonomy. It was illegal to buy contraceptives until 1979—although family planning clinics were allowed to distribute them for free and ask for a donation, and doctors could dispense the Pill, but only to regulate periods. Divorce was unconstitutional until 1996. "It was the mother who became the organizational link between the newly institutionalized power of the Roman Catholic Church and the individual farming family," wrote Tom Inglis in *Moral Monopoly*. "It was she who instilled and maintained in her husband and children all that was disciplined, moral and civil." And with the Catholic Church and the state so inextricably intertwined, the woman's place in the home became a goal enshrined in the constitution. Article 41.2, subsections 1 and 2 read: "The State recognizes that by her life within the home, woman gives to the State a support without which the common good cannot be achieved"; and "The State shall therefore endeavour to ensure that mothers shall not be obliged by economic necessity to engage in labor to the neglect of their duties in the home."

As recently as 1983, a secondary-school teacher, Eileen Flynn, was fired by the religious order that employed her because she was living with and became pregnant by a married man whose wife had left him. In 1991, the Virgin Megastore in Dublin was fined I£500 for selling condoms to unmarried people in Dublin. Madonna's book *Sex* was banned until 2004.

"It's amazing sometimes to think how recently unmarried pregnant women would have their children taken away from them at birth," recalls Mary Dowling, secretary of the management committee at the Tralee Women's Resource Centre. "According to the Catholic Church, women were there to produce children, so we just didn't exist in our own right." But then came the changes. Shifts in the opportunities open to Irish women were as radical in pace as they were in scale.

Rapidly, the link between marriage and childbirth became decoupled. Almost a third of all births in 2007 were outside marriage, compared with just under 3 percent in 1971. And just over half of all births outside marriage in 2007 were to cohabiting parents. "The teenage unmarried mother phenomenon is declining in relative salience while non-marital births have increased," wrote Michael

O'Connell in *Changed Utterly*. "The firm association between parenthood and marriage is also loosening." In short, motherhood became more of a choice than a destiny.

On average, Irish women now have children considerably later, and far fewer of them. Today the fertility rate is still the second highest in the EU, but it is edging closer to the norm. All this means that women are more likely and able to work. Female participation in the workforce has grown considerably. In 1981, it was just under 30 percent; in 1994, the rate was just 39 percent; by 2006, it was 53 percent. That's still below the European average, but it's a considerable increase nonetheless and double what it was in the eighties.

These developments did of course happen elsewhere too. Throughout the West, women's lives were transformed by feminism and reproductive rights, and the job opportunities and move towards equality that came with them. What was different about Ireland is that these developments took place much later than elsewhere (almost by a generation) and then took place so quickly (within a generation). "The irony of Irish studies is that women are now considered to have suddenly changed from being late developers to rapid developers," writes Linda Connolly in *The Irish Women's Movement*. "Irish women internationally today have an image of prosperity, mobility and modernity."

In short, girls grew up thinking certain things were possible only to leave school and find a whole new world waiting for them which their mothers would barely have recognized. "Ireland is a totally different place compared to when I took part [in the competition]," explained the first Rose of Tralee, Alice O'Sullivan from Dublin. "Now we see confident women from exotic places and, I must admit, they are light years away from the appallingly shy 1950s girl that I was."

While there was nothing inevitable about these particular changes taking place in Irish female identity, it was nonetheless inevitable that Irish female identity would change over the years. All identities are fluid. Irish, male, white, British, Indian, working class, able-bodied—name your identity and it will be changing even as people struggle to define it. Identities change principally because they are rooted in people's lives and aspirations, which shift with the times. As such, despite the gatekeepers' desire to impose their strictures and entry requirements, they are eventually doomed to failure, because identities are living organisms that evolve in order to survive and remain relevant. These changes take place both within societies and within people.

"Cultural identities come from somewhere, have histories," writes Stuart Hall in *Cultural Identity and Diaspora*. "But, like everything which is historical, they undergo constant transformation. Far from being eternally fixed in some essentialized past, they are subject to the continuous play of history, culture and power."

This was well illustrated in my own life a few years ago when I bought my nephew and niece England football tops emblazoned with David Beckham's name for Christmas. On one level, this was an unremarkable gift for two pre-teens born and raised in West London. But in the trajectory of my family's sense of belonging—the relationship between where we have been geographically and where we have identified with culturally and politically—it was a paradigm shift.

When I was growing up in Stevenage, we would never have supported England at anything. That was in no small part because, thanks to an immigrant mother, we believed ourselves to be from somewhere else but primarily because there seemed, at the time, no easy way to claim to be British and black. People would constantly refer to these two identities as though they were mutually exclusive. And there was no good reason to disbelieve them. There were no black MPs and, with a handful of exceptions, few national black figures. If a black person came on TV you would call the rest of the family to witness the event. Moreover, as a child, English football was incredibly insular. I remember that when Tottenham signed two Argentinians in 1978 it was a national talking point. Foreign players (meaning from outside the UK and Ireland) were in single figures. The England squad would not get its first black player, Viv Anderson, until 1979. My eldest brother, who was brilliant at the game, had the nickname Pelé. Why not? For a black kid born in Dulwich and raised in Stevenage, the closest meaningful footballing reference point would be Brazil.

Then there were the things you just knew that "English" people would do with victory. That England winning would dredge up some deep-seated inferiority about the nation's place in the world which would provoke chants that would put us back in the colonies before you could say, "It ain't half hot mum." Supporting England wasn't an option. Indeed it never really occurred to us, and for a long while didn't seem to bother anyone else. But for my niece and nephew things are different. England has changed, if only by force of years. By the time their Santa list came around, few people under the age of thirty could imagine Britain as a place without black people in it, and neither my niece nor nephew saw anything to struggle with in acknowledging and embracing both of those identities. Their father was not an immigrant and laid his own claim to Englishness, and there were many prominent non-white English people in most fields. Moreover, English football had become an incredibly cosmopolitan affair. Black players wearing the England jersey had become a banal fact of life, as had foreign managers of the England team. Meanwhile, the Premier league had become a globalized venture—almost half of its players were foreign in the 2004–5 season. Indeed, if my nephew and niece were going to find one way to identify as English, in all likelihood football would be it, given that it was one national pursuit that they could easily see themselves as part of. "The imagined community of millions," wrote Eric Hobsbawm in *Nations and Nationalism*, "seems more real as a team of eleven named people."

Precisely when and how these shifts in people and societies happen is often difficult to fathom. They may, as with gender in Ireland or race in Britain, take place over a generation. But, occasionally, a single event, such as a terrorist attack, riot, election, murder or judicial ruling, might appear to transform people's sense of themselves instantaneously. In 1994 I was in Johannesburg covering the first democratic elections in South Africa. I celebrated my twenty-fifth birthday in the garden of the *Guardian*'s Johannesburg correspondent, playing chess and discussing Arsenal's fortunes with Ronnie Kasrils, the former head of the ANC's military wing, Umkhonto we Sizwe. Five years later, I returned for the next election to find that almost everybody I knew there had changed both jobs and phone numbers, and often their addresses too. The day I flew back in, Kasrils was at the *Guardian* correspondent's house again, watching Arsenal in the FA Cup final. Only this time, there was a car and bodyguard outside and I was sharing a beer with the deputy defense minister.

Such—for a favored few—was the power of that particular transition from apartheid to democracy that some individuals ceased to live in real time. Human journeys which under normal circumstances take decades, if not generations, were completed in a few years, if not months. So the prisoner became president; law-breakers became lawmakers; and armed guerrillas became arms dealers. The person who slept on your floor only ten years ago after a wild party was now a government minister with an entourage.

"It is interesting to see who still carries their own briefcase," one former ANC activist told me. "These are people I've known for years when we were in the field. Some of them are still great but some of them have become very pompous. When you have a car and a driver and you're travelling first class, some people change."

But even these single events do not appear out of a clear blue sky. More often than not, when identities change, it is the product of organic processes that shift the plates of ingrained prejudice, institutional power, popular presumption, orthodoxy and common sense over time, at such a glacial pace that we barely notice them until they have changed form entirely.

"When we reflect on nature or the history of mankind or our own intellectual activity, at first we see the picture of an endless maze of connections and interactions, in which nothing remains what, where, and as it was, but everything moves, changes, comes into being and passes away," writes Friedrich Engels in *Socialism: Utopian and Scientific*. "Every organic being is every moment both the same and not the same; every moment it assimilates matter supplied from without and gets rid of other matter; every moment some cells of its body die and others build themselves anew; in a longer or shorter time the matter of its body is completely renewed and is replaced by other molecules of matter, so that every organic being is always itself and yet something other than itself."

Time itself may be one of the prime factors in the change. In 1971, a judge on Minnesota's Supreme Court turned his chair around and refused to look at Michael Wetherbee of the American Civil Liberties Union as Wetherbee argued for a gay couple's right to be married. The court rejected the claim out of hand and cited the book of Genesis to support its unanimous decision. Since 1998, forty-one out of fifty US states have passed statutes refusing to recognize gay marriage; twenty-six of them have amended their constitutions to cement the change. Since 2003, seven states have legalized gay marriage (two later revoked it in referenda), and the proportion of the public strongly opposed to it has fallen to 28 percent. The tide seems to be turning irrevocably, and it is young people who are turning it. Those under twenty-nine are nearly twice as likely to be in favor of same-sex marriage as those over sixty-five (43 percent as compared to 24 percent). Public opinion, like identities, is no static thing. The growing number of more tolerant youngsters has in turn created the space for young gay people to grow up with different expectations than those who came before. In a more open-minded atmosphere, what it means to be gay becomes a less clandestine, less embattled affair.

A similar trend was noticeable during Obama's election campaign, when young white people proved themselves far more receptive to the idea of voting for a black candidate than their parents and grandparents. In North Carolina, white voters between the ages of eighteen and twenty-nine were almost twice as likely to vote for Barack Obama as white voters over the age of sixty-five. Nationally, the gap between young and old for Obama averaged fourteen points.

However, identities and the world that gives them meaning do not change by themselves. The rights of the Roma in Eastern Europe, of women in Saudi Arabia or rural laborers in areas of the developing world are not necessarily very different now from what they were several decades ago. By itself, all time does is renew populations and render what was new familiar. Identities are changed primarily as a result of power struggles within a group, between groups or, usually, both. Undoubtedly, one of the reasons why it is easier for younger gay people in the US is because older gay people have been fighting for their rights. In Springfield, Missouri, Randy Doennig, the head of the gay rights group Promo, described the exhilaration he felt as he fought against a state-wide referendum to ban gay marriage. "We went door to door campaigning," he said. "That's the first time we had gone door to door about anything; the first time we were engaged on a local level, and we had to talk about gay marriage . . . Our neighbors and people that we talked to voted for us. If we all run away and go somewhere else, then who changes this place? It just needs a shove."

Gay marriage was still banned in Missouri. Nonetheless, openly struggling to prevent the ban gave the campaigners some heart. Springfield is a conservative town (home to the headquarters of the Assemblies of God Church)—and there is a huge religious college nearby. It doesn't hold a Gay Pride parade: back in 2004 when I was there it was still legal to discriminate against gay people in the workplace and people didn't want to get fired. In 1989, when a university put on *The Normal Heart*, a gay-themed play about AIDS, one of the men who promoted it had his house burned down. "It's changed a lot since I came out in the seventies," says Mark Gideon, a drag queen who went to the local Evangelical college and grew up in the town. "Back then, it was just bars and the park. Now we're better organized."

And so it was that, in the week I was there, Mr Gideon's alter ego, Cleo Toris, hauled me on stage during the Black Tie Affair (a lesbian and gay fundraiser attended by more than a hundred people) and a local theater in the center of town showed *Bent*, a play about the Nazi persecution of gays. It may take time for attitudes to change. But that does not mean that time is necessarily the driving force in changing them.

Similarly, women in Ireland had long been struggling for equality. They got the vote in 1918—before women in Sweden, France and the USA—and Ireland produced the first woman to be elected to the British House of Commons and the first female cabinet minister in Europe, both in the form of Countess Constance Markiewicz. "Involvement in pre-suffrage, nationalist, labor and cultural organizations before independence had an enduring effect on a core cadre of feminist women who continued their activism in smaller numbers from the 1920s on, in organizations such as the Irish Women Workers' Union, Cumann na mBan (until the 1930s), the Women's Prisoners' Dependents' League, the Women's Social and Progressive League, the Suffrage and Local Government Association, the Joint Committee of Women's Societies and Social Workers and the founding of the Irish Housewives Association in the 1940s," writes Linda Connolly. "During the 1920s and 1930s especially, they campaigned on issues such as jury service for women, sex and marriage barriers in the civil service and imposed limitations on women's employment."

Campaigns in these areas would continue with varying degrees of intensity until the late sixties and early seventies, when issues surrounding fertility rights, divorce and equal pay came to the fore. These changes did not take place in a vacuum but in the midst of different developments, many of which were either only loosely related or completely unrelated to gender and the Irish situation but were nonetheless relevant.

Connolly quotes a founding member of the Irish Women's Liberation Movement recalling the early seventies, when Irish feminism enjoyed a resurgence: "It was at a time when we were taking a lot of our political ideas from America. The Vietnam war was at its height and the Civil Rights movement. I was a member of the anti-Vietnam and anti-Apartheid movement. So when the women's liberation movement was started in America it just seemed like an extension of other things we had been at—housing action, all that sort of thing was going on at the time."

The end of the last millennium was a similarly turbulent time in Ireland, for different reasons. The significant shifts in the power of the Catholic Church both at home and throughout the West, the role of women and men, attitudes towards sexual orientation, international migration, the free movement of capital and Ireland's relationship with the UK and Europe were all in flux. Underpinning it all was an intense, protracted and unprecedented economic boom.

Trying to explain how it felt to experience those changes as a young Irish woman, the 1999 winner of the Rose of Tralee, Geraldine O'Grady, struggled for words. "In my generation it all changed so fast it's a blur," she says. "It's hard to make sense of it in my lifetime. It's a bit surreal."

A great deal had changed in Tralee in the six years since I first visited the town in 2002. What then had the feel of a small monoracial seaside town (I recall seeing one black face in the few days I was there) now seemed quite diverse. On or adjacent to Castle Street, the main drag, there were two Polish grocery stores (one next to the local Sinn Féin office) and an African-Caribbean variety store. If you were looking for food, Castle Street offered pizza, kebabs, Indian, Chinese and Halal cuisine. These differences are reflected in the work at the Tralee Women's Resource Centre. "The most significant change has been the immigrant women using the centre," said Mary Dowling. "The profile of the town has changed massively in the last ten years. So we offer English language classes and support and advice on immigration cases, which we rarely did before."

Until the early nineties, Ireland, broadly speaking, had thought of itself as a relatively poor, conservative nation which people had to leave in order to succeed; as a country that was locked into a mutually dependent and antagonistic relationship with its former colonial neighbor, Britain, by the Troubles in the North. The nation's electoral politics were dominated by events that had taken place several generations before, when the British were forced to sign a treaty agreeing to retreat from twenty-six counties and keep just six where there was a pro-British majority. Depending on your politics, those twenty-six counties became known as the Republic of Ireland, Eire, the South, the Free State or just "the twenty-six counties"; the remaining six became known as Northern Ireland, Ulster, the North or simply "the six counties." This partial victory against the British gave rise to a political culture that was simultaneously victorious and thwarted, revolutionary and conservative, antagonistic and conciliatory. For the rest of the century and well into this one, the two main parties in the South were Fianna Fáil and Fine Gael. While the former was more socially conservative than the latter, the central distinction between them was that Fianna Fáil had opposed signing the treaty with the British whereas Fine Gael had supported it. The North, meanwhile, was riven by the unfinished business of the remaining six counties, as some Republican opponents of the treaty adopted armed struggle in a bid to repel the British.

Like many post-colonial nations, Ireland spent most of the last century struggling to find its way. "Every country ranked above Ireland in the early twentieth century pulled much further ahead," argued historian J. J. Lee. "Every [European] country below Ireland either overtook her, or significantly narrowed the gap. The result was that Ireland slid from being a reasonably representative western European economy, in terms of income per head, at the time of independence, to a position far below the western European average in 1970. No other European country, east or west, north or south, for which remotely reliable evidence exists, has recorded so slow a rate of growth of national income in the twentieth century." The notion that the Irish were second-class citizens in Europe was deeply entrenched. "The Irish are the niggers of Europe," Jimmy Rabbitte Jr tells his fledgling band in Roddy Doyle's *The Commitments*. "An' Dubliners are the niggers of Ireland. An' the northside Dubliners are the niggers o' Dublin."

Throughout this time, the Catholic Church dominated public life and shaped public conversation. Compared to other Western countries, Ireland's level of religiosity was unusually high. According to Eurobarometer, in 1975, 89.1 percent of Irish people attended church at least once a week, compared to an EC average of just over 20 percent. With poverty and religion central to daily life and political culture, suffering became embedded in the national consciousness. "It was, of course, a miserable childhood," writes Frank McCourt at the beginning of *Angela's Ashes*. "The happy childhood is hardly worth your while. Worse than the ordinary miserable childhood is the miserable Irish childhood, and worse yet is the miserable Irish Catholic childhood. People everywhere brag and whimper about the woes of their early years, but nothing can compare with the Irish version: the poverty; the shiftless, loquacious alcoholic father; the pious defeated mother moaning by the fire; pompous priests; bullying schoolmasters; the English and the terrible things they did to us for eight hundred years."

So, like McCourt himself, people left in their droves for England, America, New Zealand, Australia—anywhere. In 1984 a poster in Dublin Airport put up by the Irish Development Agency showed the graduation class of University College Dublin with the headline: "We are the Young Europeans." A year later, it turned out that every person in the picture had left to work abroad.

But then things started to change. As a well-educated, English-speaking country within the European Union, with low corporate taxes, Ireland became a magnet for international capital. Thanks to the Eurozone's low interest rates, property prices rose stratospheric-ally. Wages soon followed. At times during the early part of this century, the property section of the *Irish Times* was actually bigger than the news section. Between 1987 and 2007, the number of passengers using Dublin Airport increased almost sevenfold; during the same period, the number using British airports did not quite double.

In 1999, the Organization of Economic Cooperation and Development noted "five straight years of stunning economic performance. No other OECD member country has been able to match its out-standing outcomes in a variety of dimensions." Unemployment went from 17.4 percent in 1986 to 3.9 percent in 2000. "All of this is especially remarkable because it happened so quickly. There is a sense in which the Irish economy became global before it became national," explains Fintan O'Toole in *After the Ball*. "The staple of many national economies—small and medium-sized indigenous businesses—is a muted presence in Ireland."

Even more miraculous in many ways was the speed with which the whole trend reversed. By the end of the last decade, the global recession had hammered Ireland hard, transforming it from a poster child for globalized success to one of a handful of European nations at risk of default. A government bail-out saved its banking system from full-scale collapse only to have the government itself rescued from collapse by a bail-out by the EU and the IMF. GDP nosedived, its debt soared; in four years unemployment trebled, house prices fell by a third and the country boasted the highest emigration rate in the EU (double the second-highest, which was in Lithuania). These things happened in other countries too but, once again, nowhere near as dramatically. In just two years, house prices fell by a third from their 2007 peak and unemployment almost trebled.

"It is possible that places like Zimbabwe have bigger contractions," said Alan Barrett of Ireland's Economic and Social Research Institute. "But you know you're in trouble when you're saying at least we're not Zimbabwe. You're talking about the biggest contraction in an industrialized country since the Great Depression."

The enduring effects of this downturn are, as of yet, unclear, although the fall will, in all likelihood, be all the harder because of the significant shift in the national psyche brought about by the boom times. No longer thinking of itself as the hapless poor stepchild of Europe, a mood of self-respect approaching preening self-regard took hold. Both the shift and the uneven way in which it was understood and experienced were evident in almost every aspect of national life. Halfway through the 2002 football World Cup, Ireland captain Roy Keane abandoned the squad after an altercation with manager Mick McCarthy, who is English. McCarthy had dressed down Keane before the rest of his teammates after Keane gave an interview complaining about the standard of training facilities and the team's level of preparedness.

"Mick, you're a liar," replied Keane, who was also captain of Manchester United. "You're a fucking wanker. I didn't rate you as a player, I don't rate you as a manager, and I don't rate you as a person. You're a fucking wanker and you can stick your World Cup up your arse. The only reason I have any dealings with you is that somehow you are the manager of my country and you're not even Irish, you English cunt. You can stick it up your bollocks."

In a column in the *Irish Times* explaining the outburst, O'Toole wrote: "Like the new Ireland, [Keane] is rich, upwardly mobile and driven by a ruthless work ethic. He doesn't recognize the concept of heroic failure. He despises mediocrity and laziness. He believes that nothing less than excellence is good enough, whether in a Champions League final or a five-a-side kickabout after training. This Ireland, however, is a recent and still rather raw phenomenon. Around it there is the lingering legacy of a relatively poor society in which it made sense to be grateful for small mercies . . . This, of course, is why the Irish enjoyed their two previous World Cups so much. Low expectations are the ultimate guarantee of pleasure. If we got beaten, we were proud and happy to have been there at all."

Back home, a nation of emigrants became a nation of immigrants. Tens of thousands poured in from Eastern Europe and both the developing and overdeveloped world in search of work. In 2005, the *Evening Herald* started publishing a "Polish Weekly" supplement; in 2005, Irish language was removed as a necessary qualification to serve in the Gardai (police) in place of any second language. In terms of everyday usage, Polish replaced Irish as the second language. When my own brother arrived in Ireland in the early nineties, rice was in the ethnic-food section in the supermarket and in rural areas people would buy him drinks in bars just so they could say they had bought "a black fella" a pint. Within a decade, people assumed he was a Nigerian asylum seeker, and yam flour and non-flammable hair extensions were on sale on Dublin's Moore Street.

So Jimmy Rabbitte Jr's assumed black identity was put to the test by the arrival of actual black people who started to populate most Irish cities and villages. "Twenty years on, there are thousands of Africans living in Ireland and, if I was writing that book today, I wouldn't use that line," writes Doyle in a later book, *The Deportees and Other Stories*. "It wouldn't actually occur to me, because Ireland has become one of the wealthiest countries in Europe and the line would make no sense."

A nation which once prided itself on being welcoming, and where children would routinely be called upon to give money for black babies in the developing world, suddenly had to deal with the prospect of the adults those babies had become arriving en masse to seek a better life. The Irish responded with an antipathy that was familiar in Europe but a shock to their sense of selves. The "traditional Irish welcome," it turned out, was neither universal in its application nor intrinsic to the psyche. A 2002 report by a government advisory body showed that black pregnant women had become targets of abuse in the street and in hospitals because people thought they were only having babies in Ireland so they could gain citizenship. In 2004, a referendum to revoke the automatic right to citizenship for any person born in Ireland was held in a scarcely veiled bid to prevent black people from settling there. And Jimmy Rabbitte's northsiders did not vote much differently to anywhere else in the country.

These developments posed a challenge for the inevitable diversity that comes with diasporic competitions such as the Rose of Tralee. In 2010 the crown was won by Clare Kambamettu, whose Indian father, Ravi, met her Irish mother, Breda, in Leeds, and then both moved to Kildare when Clare was 8. Even though six of the previous ten roses represented cities, states or countries outside of Ireland (New York [twice], Italy, Queensland, Perth and London), Clare's victory was regarded by a few as somehow inauthentic.

"If I were traveling over to Tralee for the festivities I would have been disappointed at this outcome," wrote a second-generation Irish American on the website Irishcentral.com. "If she wanted to do a pageant then she should have done Miss Universe because it comprises all countries. And leave the Rose of Tralee to a born & raised 'Irish' lass." "The main charm of Ireland was its people," claimed another. "If people from everywhere are 'Irish' then that particular charm no longer exists. Pity." But others countered with a more flexible understanding of what it meant to be Irish. "How do we define Irish?" asked one. "To me, this UCG (University College Galway) graduate from Athy is surely more Irish than green beer-swilling 'Kiss Me I'm Irish' fools. This well-educated, beautiful woman was chosen above others because of her beauty and the fact that she is an outstanding example of a modern Irish woman." Another insisted. "Not quite the look???? What should the look be, red hair and freckles???? Come on let's get with the times here....This young lady seems like a woman other young girls can look up to and aspire to."

Meanwhile, tensions with Britain eased. A peace process brokered by the US made partners of Dublin and London, thereby neutraliz-ing Ireland's longstanding adversary and allowing space for self-interrogation. Fine Fail and Fine Gael's stranglehold on political culture, that owed more to Republican history than modern political reality, loosened. Their joint share of the vote slumped from 84 percent in November 1982 to just 53 percent in 2011. Traveling to Belfast from

Dublin by train, the only indication I had that we were crossing the border was the ubiquitous pinging of cell phones as everyone's providers changed. "Britain had the particularly important function in Irish identity of not being 'us,'" says O'Toole. "Now we have to decide who we are." And with wealth, that decision could be made from a position of considerable power and confidence. The Irish went from being routinely excluded from housing in England, where signs stated "No cats, no dogs, no blacks, no Irish," to being the biggest foreign investors in property in the UK. With the Troubles unwinding, even the most loathed institutions with the most sectarian reputations in the North became permissible as career opportunities. One in seven of the applicants drawn by a campaign to join the revamped RUC in the North in 2002 came from the Republic.

Such changes are both invigorating and unsettling. Generally, they involve winners and losers, thereby forcing a realignment in status that pushes people to grapple with the unfamiliar. Invariably, they entail the abandonment of certainty. Where the dramatic developments in Irish female identity were concerned, this was no different.

"There's a general feeling of confusion in what are you about," says Geraldine O'Grady, explaining how the relationship between Irish men and women has changed in recent times and what the result has been. "I can say that people are wanting more community life. I think the men are a bit baffled by it. There's a sense of growing power for women and so there's a sense of insecurity . . . The men think, what's our role in all of this?"

The fact that these changes are experienced distinctly unevenly— with attitudes often leap-frogging practice, and legislation occasionally out of kilter with public opinion—hardly helps. Women's lives may have improved considerably in Ireland in some ways, but in others the changes just shifted the location of their struggles for equality.

As the boom continued, women were far more likely to work outside the home but also more likely to be less well paid. "How Unequal," a study published in 2000, revealed a 15 percent pay gap between Irish men and women for the same work. And the gap was widening. In 1996, the difference was I£2.16; by 2001, it was I£2.47. With 13.3 percent of parliament comprising women, Ireland stands below Djibouti and just above Malawi in the world rankings for female political representation. The cost of childcare is 20 percent of the average industrial wage in Ireland, compared to 8 percent in the EU.

The initial indications from the bust seem to suggest that gender relations will be in a considerable state of flux for some time. The recession hit men and women very differently. Because the downturn adversely affected male-dominated sectors such as construction and finance, men have been more likely to be made unemployed. By the end of 2009, men outnumbered women in the unemployment line by more than two to one. But women, who are more concentrated in part-time work and the public sector, stood a far higher chance of having their hours or wages cut—or both.

Meanwhile, many of the support systems that made sense during the boom are being rethought. "Childcare costs have not decreased at all even though prices in other areas have fallen," Orla O'Connor, the head of policy at the National Women's Council of Ireland, told the *Sunday Times*. "This is putting even greater pressure on women now. We're hearing from women trying to put together alternative childcare arrangements, such as with family members, because they are desperately trying to get childcare a lot cheaper."

From her Tralee office in the Women's Resource Centre, Mary Dowling adds that many of the tasks that were never particularly valued, such as taking care of the elderly or childcare, are now missed. "So long as women were doing them, they were never particularly appreciated. But now more women are working outside of the home, you have to put a price on them, and people are finding that in a financial sense it's very expensive and in a human sense they are priceless. Some people want to blame women for that, but it's a community responsibility that women have shouldered alone."

While specific changes have to be assessed on their merits, there is some opposition to the very idea of change itself. Opposition to change per se rests on the notion of a fixed, essential sense of self which remains constant over time. Therein lies the comfort zone of the crude majoritarians, protectors of heritage and promoters of the past as the only possible future; the "bluebloods," the "*français de souche*" and the immigration laws based on "*droit du sang*" or bloodlines. That is how gatekeepers gain their legitimacy: by offering the false promise that they can not only control the way things evolve but stop them evolving altogether. It is also why they ultimately fail.

But while the Right seems like the natural home for those who guard the notion of the never-changing identity, it can just as easily find its home among the liberal Left—the peddlers of purity and authenticity who will point to the matriot's nurturing impulses or the rhythms of Africa that run through the black diaspora's soul. Nor is it just the Right that is wont to frame change as undesirable per se. The Left will often approach issues such as gentrification with similarly problematic arguments. A familiar charge, particularly in poor black areas, is that wealthy white people are moving in and changing the character of the neighborhood. While this is often true, it is not, in itself, a particularly strong argument against gentrification. There is no principle one could advance as to why an area should remain black and poor. Indeed, many of the areas that are black and poor today were rich and white yesterday and may well be black and poor again. Over the centuries, for example, Harlem has been settled by Dutch immigrants, then by other wealthy Europeans, then specifically by Jews, and then blacks. As I write, more wealthy white people are moving back in. Taken at face value, complaints about white people moving into an area and changing its character are not essentially different in their logic from complaints about African-Americans moving into and changing an area's character—even if the motivations for and consequences of those fears are quite different.

That does not mean that gentrification is a good thing or an un-important trend. But the issue is not whether an area looks different demographically and is changing economically but the extent to which the people who live in that area feel ownership over the changes that are taking place as opposed to being marginalized in their own communities or, worse still, forced out of them.

Given that identities are always in flux, those who insist that they are in fact static—impervious to human development and invulnerable to time, tide, struggle and transformation—must perform three interconnected solipsistic maneuvers. First, they must distort their history—for if something is essentially unchanging, then it must be the same now as it ever was. Second, they must quash all speculation about their future—for if it doesn't change, then it can never be different.

Both of these stances come together in arguments against gay marriage. As Andrew Sullivan argued in *The New Republic*, "If marriage were the same today as it has been for 2,000 years, it would be possible to marry a 12-year-old you had never met, to own a wife as property and dispose of her at will or to imprison a person who married someone of a different race. And it would be impossible to get a divorce." Once marriage is understood as an evolving institution, it changes the conversation. That's not an argument for gay marriage— but it is an illustration of why the argument that marriage cannot be altered is baseless. Deny a history of evolution and you also deny the possibility of progress and innovation.

The third maneuver is to ignore all the other changes that happen. One of the reasons that opinions about gay lifestyles have changed is because views on straight lifestyles have undergone a radical shift also. Between the fifties and today, divorce rates have more than doubled in the US, and the age at which people marry has climbed nearer thirty than twenty. Meanwhile, between the sixties and 2005, the percentage of births to unmarried women increased sevenfold. In circumstances where the nuclear family was imploding and the most orthodox family set-ups were becoming an option rather than the rule, it follows that views on gay lifestyles would become less censorious. In a world where people do not stay married, or feel the need to marry in order to have children, the link between marriage, procreation, sanctity and fidelity are at least attenuated and, for the most part, completely broken.

Yet these are the defenses made for the preservation of heterosexual marriage as an exclusive institution—appeals to a sense of non-negotiable, non-evolving identity; a heritage to be preserved in a glass case rather than a culture that is lived. Falling back on established custom and practice is generally a more palatable way of supporting the status quo and the power relations inherent in it. "The justification of 'tradition' does not explain the classification," pointed out Judge

Judith Katy on the New York Court of Appeals in a case involving same-sex marriage. "It merely repeats it."

Nonetheless, so heavily are some invested in precisely that justification that they will create worlds out of whole cloth where they no longer exist—and in all likelihood never did exist—in a bid to freeze time and bury all evidence of pluralism and progress under its dead weight. Nationalism provides a potent example. For in order to rally people around flag and anthem, the nationalist must convince people not only that their nation has endowed them with specific and exclusive human qualities but that those qualities are also eternal. Oftentimes, the younger the nation, the greater the effort. "Many of the new nationalisms are busy trying, often on the basis of extremely dubious myths of origin and other spurious claims, to produce a purified 'folk' and to play the highly dangerous game of 'ethnic cleansing,'" argued Stuart Hall in "Our Mongrel Selves," the Raymond Williams Memorial Lecture in 1992. "Here real dislocated histories and hybridized ethnicities of Europe, which have been made and remade across the tortured and violent history of Europe's march to modernity, are subsumed by some essentialist conception of national identity, by surreptitious return to 'tradition' often of the invented kind . . . that recasts cultural identity as an unfolding essence moving apparently without change from past to future."

Not only can new "traditions" come into being but old "traditions" can be recast or reinvented. So what looks like change can often just be continuity in a new suit. This was clearly demonstrated following the break-up of Yugoslavia, when the Croats attempted to change their language in an effort to suggest that the previous century and a half had not happened. In 1850, Serbs and Croats signed an agreement in Vienna to develop a common language, Serbo-Croatian. Linguists then did their best to draw the traditions of the two languages together, resulting in "almost identical pronunciation (except for one particularity), spelling, morphology, syntax, almost all of vernacular vocabulary, and a large portion of the scholarly lexicon," according to Paul Garde in "Unity and Plurality in the Serbo-Croatian Linguistic Sphere." Three differences remained. Croats used Latin script, whereas Serbs used Cyrillic—although one transliterates effortlessly into the other; the specific pronunciation of one sound remained distinct; and a number of words were created for particular cultural traditions.

This apparently unproblematic blend of the two dialects continued for almost a century and a half without much incident. But when Yugoslavia disintegrated, the Croats tried to obliterate this history. The 1990 Croat constitution mentions only "Croatian language written in the Latin alphabet." There were widespread efforts to eliminate certain commonly used words of Serbian origin and replace them with thoroughbred Croatian words that are either antiquated or completely made up. The result was gibberish. "Texts that systematically use this type of vocabulary are generally not understood by the ordinary person, and are frequently ridiculed," writes Garde. "In a normal conversation, for example, authors wouldn't dare use them." Not surprisingly, such cultural tampering met considerable resistance both from linguists and the general public: "When one abruptly demands the elimination of words that are commonly used," argued Croat linguist Radoslav Katičić in 1997, "and proceeds to introduce a massive number of new and unknown words—obviously created at the last minute—an enormous error is being committed towards the Croatian language and its place throughout the world. It is stripped of its dignity."

What often masquerades as a return to ancient roots is little more than the invention of tradition, marking a desperate and contradictory bid to prove that an identity is unchanging by, in fact, changing it. As often as not, the thing people are trying to change it "back" to either never went away or never really existed. "The past isn't dead," wrote William Faulkner. "It isn't even past."

On 14 April 1984, not far from Tralee, a young farmer from Cahirciveen was out for a walk one evening when he saw something that looked like a child's doll on the beach. When he took a closer look he found the mutilated corpse of a day-old baby that had been stabbed twenty-eight times. Notwithstanding the remote surrounding countryside, it did not seem that finding the mother would be a difficult task. Pregnancies are tricky things to hide, particularly in tight-knit communities.

Sure enough, within a few days, the local Gardai found their woman. Joanne Hayes, twenty-five, had already had one baby out of wedlock and was known to have been involved in a longstanding affair with Jeremiah Locke, a married man who worked at the sports center in Tralee. Joanne lived on a sixty-acre farm with her mother, three siblings and an aunt and had been treated at the Tralee General Hospital for post-natal hemorrhaging.

The police descended on the farm and by the end of the day had a graphic confession, complete with a display of knives responsible for the deed and a description of how Joanne's elder brother had taken the corpse and thrown it into the water. Joanne was charged with murder. The next day, she made another confession. She had indeed left her newborn baby to die, but in an open field in her farm. Everything she had told the police, she said, was lies—statements given under harsh duress. Despite fervent police denials, one of their number was sent to verify her tale, only to return with the corpse of another baby, whose blood type matched that of Joanne and Jeremiah. Moreover, a pathologist's report on the first baby proved that they could not have been the parents of the child found mutilated on the beach.

Almost anywhere else in Europe, Joanne's predicament would have been generally regarded as pathetic rather than pathological. Jeremiah kept telling her he was going to leave his wife but clearly wasn't. In a country where unmarried people struggled for access to contraception, let alone had a right to abortion, it was only a matter of time before Joanne became pregnant—or, more accurately, three times. She miscarried once, had a daughter called Yvonne and then became pregnant again. Third time around, she went into denial. When she began to show, nobody in her family said anything. "I know how odd that seems," she told the *Guardian*'s Polly Toynbee. "I can't explain to myself how it could have happened. We talk too little. Maybe they too hoped it wouldn't happen at all. I ask myself over and over."

Joanne claimed she gave birth alone, standing up, in a field behind the farmhouse and left the baby there. The next day, she went back, put the dead baby in a fertilizer bag and dumped it in a shallow pool in the field. Then she went to hospital, where she claimed she had had a miscarriage, and stayed there for a week because the doctors thought she might commit suicide.

But this was Ireland. Desperate to defend their integrity and her fallen honor, the Gardai claimed Joanne must have given birth to twins conceived by two different men with whom she had intercourse around the same time: one was buried in the farm, the other thrown out to sea. Needless to say, they couldn't prove that. The murder charge was eventually dropped. And so it was that, in the shadow of Tralee, home to the performance of perpetual Irish womanhood, the full extent of Ireland's sexual and state repression, not to mention the impact it has on women, was forced out into the open in the inquiry that followed.

Martin Kennedy, solicitor for the police, sought to portray Joanne as a "profligate fornicator" who "indulge[d] in carnal intercourse" in a field or in her lover's red Mini. Any confusion about the intimacy of the relationship between Church and state, meanwhile, was erased when Kennedy attacked Joanne's mother: "Suppose you died having committed perjury, you would be condemned for eternity, having committed a mortal sin."

Joanne's mother started to cry. "God, good God, all glory to Him, He knows that this is the truth," she said. "If I have to go before Him this minute, I am telling the truth." When the 274-page report was published, it was far easier on the police than it was on the Hayes family in general and Joanne in particular, even though it cleared her of stabbing the baby found on the beach in Cahirciveen. Neither the mother nor the murderer of that baby has ever been found.

One fact to emerge from the tribunal was the relative banality of out-of-wedlock births in Ireland at that time and the absolute silence that shrouded them. Justice Kevin Lynch, who conducted the tribunal, pointed out that the idea that two babies might be born and murdered so close in time in County Kerry was not as much of a coincidence as people thought, since two babies were born out of wedlock in Kerry every week.

The findings of the report into the Kerry babies suggested that, far from being a rare occurrence in Ireland in years past, having children out of wedlock—and therefore extra-marital or pre-marital sex—was a relatively common but hidden occurrence. It's just one example of the extent to which this new Ireland may have, in many ways, been different to the old Ireland more in the telling than in the reality.

Inevitably, all these social and economic changes, both real and perceived, had a significant impact on the Rose of Tralee competition. As the economy boomed, the event itself became far more showy. One year, both James Brown and The Beautiful South performed at the event.

Based in what had become Europe's fastest-growing economy, ambitions for the competition, which could bring in as much as £20 million, grew with those for the country. When support for the festival waned during the mid-nineties, the organizers decided to "upgrade and repackage." Drawing in famous people attracts sponsors. But it also costs a lot of money. So, in 2002, they turned to the centers around the world which select the Roses and asked them each to provide £1,500—half of what it costs to accommodate and entertain each finalist when they come to Ireland for the final. For the newly wealthy Irish at home and those of the relatively well-off diaspora, this did not present a problem—with one significant exception: the Irish in Britain, who tend to be concentrated in poorer communities and who had experienced little by way of a boom. "Some refused and others couldn't pay," said Norah Casey, editor-in-chief of the *Irish Post*, a British-based newspaper for the Irish community, at the time. "The people who run the British selection centers are volunteers . . . In Britain it is about more than just picking a nice girl to go to Tralee. It's a way of keeping second- and third-generation ties with Ireland alive. It encapsulates a piece of their identity parents can pass on and through it encourage kids to take pride in their Irish ancestry."

"We can't get the kind of sponsorship they get in Ireland because the Rose of Tralee is not a big thing over here," says Debbie Hendry, a former Rose winner herself. "Nobody's heard of it here. I think they are turning it into something very different to the much more personal touch it used to have."

A feud ensued which ended with the Rose of Tralee committee expelling the British contingent, which, at the competition's founding, had contributed half of the original Roses. The *Irish Post* decided to set up a separate event for the Irish community in Britain called the Irish Rose and held it in London. While it shared many similarities with the event in Tralee, the attributes they sought in an Irish Rose were different. "We created a package for a modern, forward-thinking, career-minded woman," says Casey. "Some kind of alumni for second- or third-generation Irish women."

The prizes included a week shadowing an MP, and an iMac computer. The first Irish Rose, Marie Cleary, was a teacher and Gaelic footballer from Birmingham. "Even though I was born here, I've always felt my Irish identity was very important to me," says Cleary. "I've been involved in an Irish social scene, I used to spend all my holidays in Ireland. I play GAA (Gaelic) football. When my cousins come over to visit, they always say, 'You're more Irish than we are.'"

The Irish Rose competition did not last long. With time, the British and the Irish Rose of Tralee committees managed to settle their differences. But, needless to say, the competition kept evolving in a bid to try to keep up with the changes in Irish women's lives. With women marrying late or not marrying at all, the organizers put up the age limit to twenty-seven. The ban on unmarried mothers competing was contested. "This means unmarried mothers are treated as second-class citizens by the Rose of Tralee," argued Janice Ransom, of the One Parent Exchange Network group. "It's discrimination in its highest form. What do they plan next? Virginity tests?" The Rose of Tralee committee would not budge, insisting that it was defending tradition and the rights of the married.

"The Rose of Tralee is based on the legend of local woman Mary O'Connor, a single woman who did not have any children," said then contest chief executive Liam Twomey. "The record shows she was young and single. From the inception of our event, we have based it on that criterion and we are following on the model portrayed in the Rose of Tralee song. Until now, it has never been an issue of controversy. We still don't see it as a controversy. If unmarried mothers were allowed to take part, married mothers could claim they were being discriminated against. You have to draw a line somewhere. The rules are there, they have been successful, and we see no reason to change them. The matter is not even up for discussion."

In 2008, they relented. There were no complaints from married mothers. "We try to balance tradition with the modern world, which is sometimes a difficult balancing act," said Anthony O'Gara, the festival's managing director. "I know some people who say they're bad role models, but we don't think a woman is any less of a person because she happens to have a child. The young women who come to us bring the modern world to our door, and through them we are a renewed organization every year."

At the Tralee Women's Resource Centre, Mary Dowling says she has seen a shift in the caliber of the Irish women who enter the competition compared to those from the rest of the diaspora, particularly the United States. "The American women were always more accomplished," she recalls. "It was a bit embarrassing. They would always have been going on to further studies, whereas the Irish women were always going to get married or do something less impressive. But that difference has really tailed off now. The Irish women have a sense of confidence now that they didn't have before and are going on to do different things too."

Geraldine O'Grady was one of those women. In 1999, her mother entered her for a regional heat of the Rose while she was completing her history degree at University College Cork. "My impression of it was that it was like the parody of *Father Ted*'s Lovely Girls competition," she recalls. "All hats and pastel suits. When I used to watch it as a child, I thought the rose was this smiley person—an affable sort of girl. There was a lot of conflict in me. But my friends thought it would be quite fun and I didn't think of it as a beauty competition. I thought it was about what you are about, with an emphasis on your education and what you have to say rather than whether you would be a fantastic homemaker."

Nowadays, when she judges at local selections, she sees a difference in the kind of things contestants will say. "You'll hear people tell stories about their boyfriend where it's clear that they're living together. In the past that would have been regarded as a little bit shady, and people would definitely have sat in judgment. There are people involved in it who are really progressive. But I felt there were also people who were rooted in a very old-fashioned way. I was diplomatic enough, but I was quite honest that I wanted to reconcile who I was with the title, and there were one or two people who did take exception to what I was saying."

She says she took her participation with a "pinch of salt," sang the "Tennessee Waltz" on stage and was bemused every time her escort got up when she went to the bathroom. And she won; she put her plans to become an actress on hold for a year so she could fulfill the traveling and ceremonial obligations that came with the title. It was, she says, a fantastic year. But the conflict she felt on entering never quite went away and when the year was over she resumed her education. Four decades after the competition had been set up, the global representative of demure Irish womanhood packed up her tiara and went off to do an MA in women's studies.

6. The Many in One

We each have several identities that can be compared but not ranked

I'm already discredited, I'm already politicized, before I get out
of the gate. I can accept the labels because being a black
woman writer is not a shallow place but a rich place to write from.
It doesn't limit my imagination; it expands it.

— Toni Morrison, *The New Yorker*, 27 October 2003

To the soundtrack of Black Entertainment Television, the Ultra
Beauty salon in Charleston works its magic on its clientele. This
home, converted into a beauty parlor, unfolds into a rabbit warren
of small rooms where deft fingers straighten, twist, pluck and weave.
Today there is a sense of urgency. It's late on Saturday afternoon on
Martin Luther King holiday weekend and the proprietor, Viola
Heyward, is busy. Anyone who doesn't get seen today won't be seen
until Tuesday—and for some, three days measured in bad hair is an
eternity. A few tilt back paralyzed, their necks wedged into ceramic
headrests while their eyes look up at notices calling for God's blessing
and for the customers to pay attention to their children. Others sit
upright while scissors and dryers snip and hum.

Ultra Beauty sits amid a small row of townhouses; you would
barely notice it unless you were looking for it. And in mid-January
2008, journalists from around the world were doing just that. As I
walked in, a Canadian journalist was just walking out. A few days
earlier, a man from *The Times* had paid a visit. Indeed, during those
few weeks, it was little short of incredible that any black women
managed to get their hair or nails done in South Carolina at all, given
the intense interest paid to them by the media. Not since Ronald

Reagan scapegoated "Cadillac-driving welfare queens" (code for poor black women) had anyone taken so much interest in black females—the most loyal section of the Democratic electorate—during presidential elections.

This lack of interest had been made abundantly clear in 2004 when a black woman, Gwen Ifill, moderated the vice-presidential debate. "I want to talk to you about AIDS, and not about AIDS in China or Africa, but AIDS right here in this country, where black women between the ages of twenty-five and forty-four are thirteen times more likely to die of the disease than their counterparts," Ifill told the candidates. "What should the government's role be in helping to end the growth of this epidemic?" Dick Cheney said it was "a great tragedy" of which he "was not aware." John Edwards didn't refer to black women once but said, "We need to do much more," than whatever it was Dick Cheney wanted to do.

But 2008 was different. Coming at the beginning of the primary season, after contests in Iowa, Nevada and New Hampshire, South Carolina was the first state where large numbers of African-Americans would get to vote. Black women made up around 30 percent of the state's Democratic electorate and in this Democratic primary the two frontrunners were a black man, Barack Obama, and a white woman, Hillary Clinton. Obama had won Iowa, Clinton won New Hampshire, and Nevada was effectively a draw. In South Carolina it was game on.

In the minds of some commentators, this placed black women at the very apex of a battle royal between two identities: race and gender. "The United States has never elected a president who looks like Gladys Pressley Morgan," began a piece by the *Richmond Times Dispatch*. "This year, though, she has a choice between one candidate of her race—Barack Obama—and another of her gender—Sen. Hillary Rodham Clinton, D-N.Y." It is a reasonable guess that Ms Morgan looked nothing like Obama or Clinton either.

But in American presidential politics, perceptions are everything. Back in 1978, a hard-drinking young Republican businessman from Midland, Texas, called George W. Bush lost an election against a Democrat, Kent Hance. Hance (who later converted to the Republicans) played up Bush's preppy upbringing and Yale education, telling voters that his opponent "was not a real Texan." Bush lost heavily and vowed that he wasn't going "to be out-Christianed or out-good-old-boyed again." Twenty years later, the privileged son of a former president was sold to the country as an Everyman. Having abandoned the bottle for the Bible, Bush was now teetotal. But polls showed he was still the candidate most voters said they would like to have a drink with.

So the issue of whom voters thought they could relate to on some primal level was important, even if the media framing was crude. In a special report, CNN took the race and gender theme even further. "For these women, a unique and most unexpected dilemma presents itself. Should they vote their race, or should they vote their gender? No other voting bloc this year faces this choice." This was self-evidently not true. Even by its own crass, box-ticking yardstick, this "dilemma" was by no means unique. Clinton also has a race; Obama also has a gender. Following CNN's logic, white men voting Democratic also had to choose between their race—Clinton—and their gender—Obama. But that weekend, they managed to have their hair cut in peace.

Moreover, by its own limited reasoning, the question had been proven redundant at almost every election. In 2006, Michael Steele, a black Republican, stood for the Senate in Maryland. He received his biggest vote in Garrett County, which is 98.8 percent white. His vote was weakest in St George's County, which is 63 percent black. Only 22 percent of non-white women backed him. In Ohio that same year, black Republican gubernatorial candidate Kenneth Blackwell received just 19 percent of the votes of non-white women. And during the same election cycle, just 42 percent of non-white women supported Republican Jodi Rell (a white woman) for Connecticut governor, with a majority preferring John DeStefano (a white man) instead. In each of these cases, non-white women were the least likely of any demographic broken down by race and gender to support the black man or white woman running for office.

This is not rocket science. People don't just vote for people who look like them. They vote for people they think will represent their interests. Oftentimes, these two things coincide. Of the twenty-eight majority black congressional districts (including the District of Columbia), twenty-seven are represented by black people. They are all Democrats.

In South Carolina, what you look like will have a major impact on your life chances and your priorities and therefore, in all likelihood, on your politics. In this Deep Southern state—the first to secede from the United States before the civil war and the last to fly the confederate flag on its capitol lawn—racial division is a reality. On average, African-Americans here earn less than half as much as whites and are twice as likely to live in poverty. It's not therefore surprising that black American women would be drawn to the Democratic Party—which is associated with supporting the poor— or that the congressman of the state's only majority black district would be a black man, Jim Clyburn. Indeed the electoral map was rigged that way, with many of the districts gerrymandered to ensure that black voters would be the majority in a bid to boost black representation. It doesn't follow from that, however, that black voters only backed Clyburn because he is black, that they would not have voted for a white male Democrat (Tennessee's 9th district is 63 percent black and has a white congressman) or that they would necessarily vote for a black Republican, male or female.

Yet most of the traffic in and out of the beauty parlors during those weeks was guided by the notion that black women's loyalties would not be to their families, their health or their education but instead divided, exclusively and explicitly, between race and gender, as though these two particular identities were binary and contradictory. The implication, inherent but never openly voiced, was that being a black woman is not a condition in itself but just an interlocking of two identities—womanhood (which is basically white) and blackness (which is basically male)—and that somehow black women do not live their lives as whole human beings but as divided selves. Sometimes they're black. Sometimes they're women. Somehow they never seem to get to be both at the same time: a "dilemma," we were led to believe, that was "unique" to their condition.

Such misconceptions are not new. In fact, they are perennial. When Sojourner Truth took to the dais as the only black delegate at the women's convention in Akron, Ohio, in 1851, she strove to hammer home that it was not up to those present to pick and choose whom they understood to be women. In a now famous speech, she drove a wedge through the racist put-downs of the white women and the sexist buffoonery of the men of either race:

That man over there says that women need to be helped into carriages, and lifted over ditches, and to have the best place everywhere. Nobody ever helps me into carriages, or over mud-puddles, or gives me any best place! And ain't I a woman? Look at me! Look at my arm! I have ploughed and planted, and gathered into barns, and no man could head me! And ain't I a woman? I could work as much and eat as much as a man—when I could get it—and bear the lash as well! And ain't I a woman? I have borne thirteen children, and seen most all sold off to slavery, and when I cried out with my mother's grief, none but Jesus heard me! And ain't I a woman?

Half a century later, in 1900, black educator and activist Fannie Barrier Williams wrote, "If within 35 years [black women] have become sufficiently important to be studied apart from the general race problem that fact is gratifying evidence of real progress." More than eighty years after that, former presidential hopeful Shirley Chisholm lamented, "We've always found ourselves in a sense at the tail end. Neither the Black movement as such nor the women's movement as such in this country has addressed the political problems of blacks who are female." Now, a quarter of a century on, commentators were still stuck in the same conceptual rut. "For all the passion Mr. Obama may be generating on the trail," wrote Adam Nagourney in *The New York Times*, "the Clinton Democratic Party is the party of women, older voters, Hispanics and also some white men." Well, actually, no. Clinton's was predominantly the party of white and Latino women, among other things. Black women went for Obama by huge margins. This is no small distinction. In states where there were large black populations—Georgia, Alabama, South Carolina and Mississippi—Obama won the women's vote handily. Indeed, in all four of those states, black women voters outnumbered white women voters by a huge margin. So if "women" was shorthand for anything in South Carolina, it was black women.

We all have multiple identities. We are many things at once and at all times we are also the same thing—ourselves. "A Hutu laborer from Kigali must be pressured to see himself only as a Hutu and incited to kill Tutsis," writes Amartya Sen in *Identity and Violence: The Illusion of Destiny*. "And yet he is not only a Hutu, but also a Kigalian, a Rwandan, an African, a laborer, and a human being." Any form of identity politics that seeks to diminish that multiplicity, or rank identities into some pre-ordained hierarchy, will inevitably end in distortion.

The full extent of this distortion was exemplified in an episode of the US version of the comedy show *The Office*, where Michael (played by Steve Carell) welcomes back a gay, Latino colleague, Oscar (played by Oscar Nuñez) with a celebration:

MICHAEL: Of course we are going to have a party. A celebration of Oscar. Oscar night. And I want it to be Oscar-specific.
OSCAR: Michael, I—
MICHAEL: No, no. I mean, not—not because you are gay. Your gayness does not define you. Your Mexicanness is what defines you, to me, and I think we should celebrate Oscar's Mexicanity.

The fact that we have a multitude of affiliations does not mean that certain identities may not come to the fore at certain moments. Far from being neutral, they are rooted in material conditions that confer power and privilege in relation to one another. I'm sure whenever Oscar returns to the US from Mexico, he feels his "Mexicanity" quite keenly at the border. But if he went to try and get a marriage license in Scranton, Pennsylvania (where the show is set), with his partner, I daresay his "gayness" would become far more relevant.

But the fact that at any given moment one identity may be stressed more than others does not mean that the others cease to exist. We also have choices. "We do belong to many different groups, in one way or another, and each of these collectivities can give a person a potentially important identity," argues Sen. "We may have to decide whether a particular group to which we belong is—or is not—important for us."

Michael's theme night for Oscar also raises another issue about our multiple identities. The decisions as to which ones we assert, when we want to assert them and what we want to do with them are ours. But identities are fluid in character, dynamic by nature and, therefore, complex in practice. Decisions about which ones we prioritize do not take place in a vacuum. They are shaped by circumstance and sharpened by crisis. We have a choice about which identities to give the floor to; but at specific moments they may also choose us.

In 2004, a Muslim *Guardian* reader in Britain, with a wife and three daughters, wrote to me to say that two of his girls voluntarily wear the hijab, whereas his wife and third daughter do not. "This is imposed from outside as much as inside," he wrote. "The girls used to consider themselves Pakistani, until they visited Pakistan. [This change was] internal. [But] they could not consider themselves British because the external world told them they weren't. So their identity became 'British Muslim.' Not a religious revival, but an establishment of identity. Since 9/11 however, they will not relinquish the 'headgear.' It would be a sign of defeat. Whilst worn, it symbolizes resistance."

Failing to understand the existence and importance of our multiple identities is not just a philosophical problem. Sen points to European nations' attempts to combat religious extremism among Muslims as an example. In Britain, 40 percent of Bangladeshis under the age of twenty-five are unemployed, while almost two thirds of Bangladeshis and more than half the Pakistanis in Britain live in poverty. Rather than the British government addressing them as Muslims, calling on them to embrace more moderate forms of Islam, perhaps it would have been more successful if it had addressed them as poor people who could be assisted economically. "The confusion between the plural identities of Muslims and their Islamic identity is not only a descriptive mistake, it has serious implications for policies for peace in the precarious world in which we live," writes Sen. "The effect of this religion-centered political approach, and of the institutional policies it has generated (to cite only one of frequent examples: 'the government is meeting Muslim leaders in the next vital stage designed to cement a united front') has been to bolster and strengthen the voice of religious authorities while downgrading the importance of non-religious institutions and movements."

"We are the sum of the things we pretend to be," wrote the late Kurt Vonnegut, "so we must be careful what we pretend to be."

Back in Charleston, commentators pretended that black women were conflicted between their race and their gender. The trouble was, black women weren't having any of it. "A lot of the people I deal with are single parents," says Juanita, who runs the Blessed and Beautiful hair studio in North Charleston. "And the ones who are married, the health care is an issue. The loss of our young black guys on the street is an issue. To each his own, but I think we should take this a lot more serious than just a black and a woman."

On the back wall of the studio, which is about the size of a bedsit, a sign says: "Great people talk about ideas. Average people talk about things. Small people talk about other people." These were clearly great people. Their ideas about the role of identity in the election were far more nuanced than that of the media. When asked if Obama's race or Clinton's gender would make a difference to their vote, they would say no. Nobody was going to make their decision on the basis of that alone. Asked if it would be a factor in how they voted, they would say yes. How could it not—in this country, in this state, at this time?

"You want to run for president?" asks Frank Bruni in *Ambling Into History*. "Here's what you need to do: Have someone write you a lovely speech that stakes out popular positions in unwavering language and less popular positions in fuzzier terms. Better yet if it bows to God and country at every turn—that's called uplift. Make it rife with optimism, a trumpet blast not just about morning in America but about a perpetual dazzling dawn. Avoid talk of hard choices and daunting challenges; nobody wants those. Nod to people on all points of the political spectrum . . . Add a soupçon of alliteration. Sprinkle with a few personal observations or stories—it humanizes you. Stir with enthusiasm."

For a white, male, straight, married candidate with access to several million dollars, this advice would work well. The overwhelming majority of Americans, however, would need to do a bit more. This wasn't the first time that a white woman or a black man had stood for the presidency. But it was the first time either was seriously regarded as having a chance from the outset.

This was made possible in no small part by a change in attitudes brought about by the civil rights movement, anti-racist struggles and feminism. In 1958, 53 percent of white voters in the US said they would not vote for a black presidential candidate; in 1984, it was 16 percent; by 2003, it was just 6 percent. In 2007, Gallup found that 88 percent of Americans polled said they would vote for a well-qualified woman for president, compared to just 53 percent who would have done so in 1969. This didn't necessarily mean a black or female candidate could win; only that it was now feasible for them to participate.

According to a *Washington Post* poll, other candidates had bigger obstacles to climb. The public, it seemed, was far more concerned about a potential president being over the age of seventy-two (John McCain), a Mormon (Mitt Romney) or twice divorced (Rudy Giuliani), than they were about race or gender. The fact that Obama smoked was a bigger handicap than the fact that he was black, according to the polls.

None of this was a problem for John Edwards, the only other viable Democratic candidate, and a white man. Up until then, the only demographic given a credible chance of running for the presidency was white men. Comedian Chris Rock joked that George Bush had "fucked up so bad that it's hard for a white man to run for president." Some took him seriously. In June 2007, *Esquire* ran a cover of Edwards with the question: "Can a white man still be elected president?" It is a testament to the assumptions about who qualified for the job that the question could seriously be put. Of the fifteen presidential candidates in both main parties in 2008, twelve were white men; Bill Richardson, a Hispanic Democrat, also ran. Thirty-six percent of the population, 80 percent of the candidates, 100 percent of past presidents. And for white men, this was a lean year.

While the talk at the beauty parlors was that black women would be voting on the issues, the trouble was that, whatever else the campaign between Clinton and Obama was about, it was not about issues. Their debates were personally rancorous but politically cordial. Over the previous four years, they had voted the same way in the Senate 90 percent of the time. There was no suggestion, even from the candidates, that Obama would be any worse on gender issues than Clinton or that Clinton would perform any worse on racial issues than Obama, if either one were elected. She did not stand on a feminist platform any more than he pushed a pro-black agenda. But in a political culture where personality and policy, style and substance, are so tightly interwoven, it was impossible to unpick where Obama and Clinton started and race and gender stopped without watching the whole thing unravel. A candidate's cultural presentation and biography are not simply adjuncts to their platforms; in most cases, they are central to them.

There is McCain the former prisoner-of-war; John Kerry the Purple-Heart-winning war hero soon-to-be Swiftboated; and Bill Clinton the boy from Hope. During the 2000 election, the then MSNBC anchor Brian Williams mentioned Al Gore's choice of polo shirts five times in eight days; in 2004, Kerry was slammed because his hairstyle made him look "too French."

In a country where, on current projections, one in three black boys born in 2001 are destined to go to jail and women earn 77 cents for every dollar a man makes for the same work, how people perceive race and gender is no incidental matter. Gore can change his shirts; Kerry can get a hair cut. But without drastic surgery Obama can never be white and Hillary Clinton can never be a man. Each had to project both their biographies and themselves favorably to a public that would not reject their race or gender out of hand but had no experience of imagining their race or gender in this huge and symbolic role.

Neither of them were victims at this game. Indeed each, in their own way, was a master at it. And both had a lot to project. By the age of thirty-five, Obama had already written a memoir, *Dreams of My Father*, which won him a Grammy Award for best spoken-word album for the audio book edition in 2006. In his second, bestselling book, *The Audacity of Hope*, he has a whole chapter on family, much of which is about his own. His speech to the 2004 Democratic Convention, which launched him onto the national stage, was based primarily on his personal story.

It is a compelling tale. His mother was white and from Kansas. His father was black and from Kenya. They met in Hawaii, where he was born. When he was still a young boy, his father left his mother, who later married an Indonesian man. The three of them went to Jakarta, where Obama attended school for a few years, before returning to Hawaii, where he was raised by his maternal grandparents. After two years at Occidental College in California, he went to Columbia University in New York, and from there to Chicago's overwhelmingly black South Side to work as a community organizer. He was then admitted to Harvard Law School, where he first made national headlines as the *Harvard Law Review*'s first black president in its 104-year history. Returning to Chicago, he became a state senator and then, in 2004, he delivered his barnstorming speech at the Democratic Convention, where he introduced the presidential candidate, John Kerry, and then went on to be elected an Illinois senator that same year.

To many, the atypical nature of Obama's upbringing was the most potent aspect of his appeal. Almost every strand of the American experience is there: the immigrant, the Midwest, the black childhood, the white parents, the Christian educated in a Muslim country, the Ivy League and the working class. "With his multi-ethnic family and his globe-spanning childhood, there is a little piece of everything in Obama," gushed the conservative *New York Times* columnist David Brooks. It was as though Obama embodied healing qualities for a divided nation, at war with the world, in his very DNA.

To others, his "foreignness" was cause for suspicion or at the very least for encouraging suspicion. Fox News claimed Obama had been educated in an Islamist madrassa in Indonesia (which was untrue). Rumors persisted that he remained a Muslim and had actually been born in Kenya and was therefore ineligible for the presidency. There were elements within the Clinton campaign, not least her chief strategist Mark Penn, who believed this xenophobia should be exploited. "All of these articles about his boyhood in Indonesia and his life in Hawaii are geared towards showing his background is diverse, multicultural and putting that in a new light," wrote Penn in an internal memo for the Clinton team in March 2007. "Save it for 2050. It also exposes a very strong weakness for him—his roots to basic American values and culture are at best limited. I cannot imagine America electing a president during a time of war who is not at his center fundamentally American in his thinking and in his values ...

"How could we give some life to this contrast without turning negative?" he asked Clinton rhetorically. "Every speech should contain the line you were born in the middle of America to the middle class in the middle of the last century ... Let's explicitly own 'American' in our programs, the speeches and the values. He doesn't. Make this a new American Century, the American Strategic Energy Fund. Let's use our logo to make some flags we can give out. Let's add flag symbols to the backgrounds."

Clinton rejected Penn's advice but nonetheless vacillated between regarding such attacks as off limits and flirting with them. She chided Obama because his "support among working, hard-working Americans, *white* Americans, is weakening again," and when asked if he was Muslim, responded that he was not "as far as I know."

After the 9/11 terrorist attacks and the subsequent invasions of Iraq and Afghanistan, it was intriguing to see how the accusation of being Muslim had now become such a slur that Obama's campaign team saw the need to defend themselves from it—so much so, in fact, that they themselves started to act in an exclusionary fashion. At one point, volunteers asked two Muslim women to move from behind a podium where Obama was due to speak because they feared the headscarves they were wearing would give the wrong impression. (Obama later called the women to apologize.)

Meanwhile, Obama's biracial parentage and Kenyan father also raised questions about his racial authenticity. In Obama, everyone was seeing the same thing and simultaneously understanding different things. One Zogby poll showed that, after being told his parents' race and nationality, more than half (55 percent) of whites and 61 percent of Hispanics classified Obama as biracial, while two thirds (66 percent) of blacks regarded him as black. Shortly before he declared his candidacy, he was interviewed by Steve Kroft for CBS on *Sixty Minutes*:

KROFT: Your mother was white. Your father was African.

OBAMA: Right.

KROFT: You spent most of your life in a white household.

OBAMA: Yeah.

KROFT: I mean, you grew up white.

OBAMA: I'm not sure that would be true. I think what would be true is that I don't have the typical background of African-Americans . . .

KROFT: You were raised in a white household?

OBAMA: Right.

KROFT: Yet at some point, you decided that you were black?

For some white people, the fact that Obama was atypical made him more palatable. His fellow presidential hopeful, senator Joe Biden, described Obama as "the first mainstream African-American who is articulate and bright and clean and a nice-looking guy." The host of MSNBC's *Hardball*, Chris Matthews, said, "I don't think you can find a better opening-gate, starting-gate personality than Obama as a black candidate . . . No history of Jim Crow, no history of anger, no history of slavery. All the bad stuff in our history ain't there with this guy."

It wasn't difficult to see what Matthews was driving at. Here was a black candidate who didn't scare white people. Or at least, as it would later transpire, not too many and not that much. But Matthews' statement told us far more about how America's racial history is misunderstood than it did about Obama's racial identity. His mother is a white American. Research would later show, unsurprisingly, that he does have a history of Jim Crow in his family. Her ancestors owned slaves.

But when it came to reclassifying Obama's identity, these racially illiterate white pundits found common cause with some highly racially literate black commentators. "When black Americans refer to Obama as 'one of us' I do not know what they are talking about," wrote African-American columnist Stanley Crouch in November

2006. "He has not lived the life of a black American . . . If we end up with him as our first black president, he will have come into the White House through a side door—which might at this point be the only one open." Former congressman, United Nations ambassador and civil rights leader Andrew Young said, "Bill [Clinton] is every bit as black as Barack." His reasoning? "[Clinton has] probably gone with more black women than Barack."

The full absurdity of the notion that Obama was not "really" black was illustrated in the following exchange between Salon.com columnist Debra Dickerson and the satirical host of the *Colbert Report*, Stephen Colbert:

COLBERT: Settle something for me, okay: is Barack Obama black?

DICKERSON: No, he's not. In the American political context, black means the descendant of West African slaves brought here to labor in the United States. It's not a put-down. It's not to say that he hasn't suffered. It's not to say that he doesn't have a glorious lineage of his own. It's just to say that he and I, the descendant of West African slaves brought to America, we are not the same.

COLBERT: Okay, so if he's not black, why doesn't he just run as a white guy? We know that black people will vote for white people. We know white people will vote for white people. But we're not sure that white people will vote for black people.

DICKERSON: Well, he's not white either. He's an African African-American.

COLBERT: Do we need a new name for what he is?

DICKERSON: We do.

COLBERT: How about nouveau black?

Ridiculous as this all was, the confusion surrounding Obama's authenticity had real political implications. From the outset, African-Americans were wary of him. Unlike many leaders in the past, he had not been produced by the black community but presented to them. For most of 2007, he trailed heavily among black voters, not least in South Carolina. To try and reverse the trend, his campaign team sent his wife, Michelle, an African-American woman born and raised on the South Side of Chicago, to soften up black audiences.

The fact that Michelle could even play that role was due, in no small part, to Obama's opponent, Hillary Clinton. Clinton had first become a national figure on 26 January 1992 during an interview with Steve Kroft (yes, him again). Straight after the Superbowl, she sat next to her husband, then Democratic presidential hopeful Bill, as he was grilled over persistent rumors about his insatiable sexual appetite which were blighting his chances in the primary race.

KROFT: I think most Americans would agree that it's very admirable that you've stayed together—that you've worked your problems out and that you've seemed to reach some sort of understanding and arrangement.

BILL CLINTON: Wait a minute, wait a minute, wait a minute. You're looking at two people who love each other. This is not an arrangement or an understanding. This is a marriage. That's a very different thing.

HILLARY CLINTON: You know, I'm not sitting here—some little woman standing by my man like Tammy Wynette. I'm sitting here because I love him, and I respect him, and I honor what he's been through and what we've been through together. And you know, if that's not enough for people, then heck, don't vote for him.

This interview set the stage for the next sixteen years. On the one hand, we saw an opinionated and accomplished woman. Smart and determined, Clinton came of age as feminism and counterculture were in full bloom. She graduated valedictorian at the all-women Wellesley College the same year as Woodstock and was the first woman there to deliver a commencement speech. She graduated from Yale Law School, then 90 percent male, the same year Roe *vs* Wade, the landmark Supreme Court judgment that legalized abortion, was passed. In 1979, she became the first woman at the Rose law firm in Arkansas. Throughout this time she kept her maiden name, Hillary Rodham.

These achievements were her own, but they do illustrate the advancement of a generation of educated, professional, middle-class women. "While Bill talked about social change," she wrote in her autobiography, *Living History*, "I embodied it. I had my own opinions, interests and profession. I was outspoken." Less than two months after the *60 Minutes* interview, she was questioned about possible conflicts of interest between her legal work and her husband's gubernatorial responsibilities. "I suppose I could have stayed home and baked cookies and had teas, but what I decided to do was to fulfill my profession which I entered before my husband was in public life." Feminist author Susan Faludi wrote in *The New York Times* that Hillary Clinton would bring "the joy of female independence" to the White House.

On the other hand, however, from that *Sixty Minutes* interview on, she would always be understood not just individually but as part of a two-person package—a political and marital unit alongside her husband, Bill. In many ways, this was a very modern relationship. They clearly considered each other intellectual equals. In 1992, he said that by voting for him, you would "buy one get one free." In Arkansas, he appointed her chair of the rural health advisory committee. In the White House, he entrusted one of his most important pieces of legislation—health care—to her.

This was a double-edged sword. Her husband's philandering caused Clinton constant humiliation. His enemies became hers. And being so closely associated with your husband in the capacity of the first lady of Arkansas or the nation is not the status feminist dreams are made of. Meanwhile, the characteristics that would have been regarded as essential in a man at her level—ambition, leadership, determination— were instead perceived as pushy, bossy and calculating. *The American Spectator* branded her the "Lady Macbeth of Arkansas," the beginning of a cottage industry of misogynistic Hillary hatred that would spawn countless books, websites and conspiracy theories.

All she had to do to be controversial was exist, work and think. "Meet the new political wife," said Ted Koppel in 1992. "She has a career, she has opinions. A partner in every way . . . Never in a presidential campaign has the candidate's wife become such a strong symbol of the campaign's strength and weakness."

For reasons of political strategy, she felt the need to compromise. When her husband was defeated in his re-election bid for Arkansas governor in 1980, she was told that some voters did not like the fact that she kept her maiden name. When Bill Clinton stood for re-election for governor 1982, she changed it to Hillary Rodham Clinton. In 1992, she actually entered a bake-off against other presidential candidates' wives in *Family Circle* with a recipe for chocolate-chip cookies. (She won.) By the time she was ready to stand for president, the transition was complete. Her name was Hillary Clinton and she baked cookies.

It was almost an identity unto itself. Everyone thought they knew what "Hillary Clinton" stood for and few seemed ambivalent. Asked to pick out words that best described her, members of the public chose "intelligent" and "smart." The third word they used to describe her, pollsters at the Pew Research Center said, was a pejorative term that "rhymes with rich."

Back on her own campaign trail, no second name was now necessary. Having just been re-elected New York senator—a seat she had originally won in 2000—with a whopping majority, she was a national institution. Her placards just said "Hillary." She ran on her thirty-five years of experience in public life. Once again, her husband became an issue. Since she had been first lady for eight of those thirty-five years, some felt she was trading on his achievements. "It's not that Mrs Clinton hasn't paid her dues," wrote Judith Thurman in her contribution to *Thirty Ways of Looking at Hillary*, "but rather that she hasn't paid most of them from her own account. Her official credit history in national politics starts in 2000." Her husband's aggressive campaigning on her behalf appeared to be counterproductive. According to a *New York Times*/CBS poll in December 2007, 44 percent said they were more likely to vote for her because of him, while only 7 percent said they were less likely. By February 2008, only 22 percent of respondents said they thought Bill Clinton was an asset, while an equal number said they were less likely to support her because of him.

During the campaign, nobody questioned whether Clinton was authentically female or not—but her femininity was constantly under scrutiny. An opinion article in the *Oklahoman* referred to her "frequent wearing of dark pants suits to conceal her bottom-heavy figure." The Style section of the *Washington Post* concentrated on the fact that she exposed a minute amount of cleavage while addressing the Senate.

"The neckline sat low on her chest and had a subtle V-shape," wrote Robin Givhan in July 2007. "There wasn't an unseemly amount of cleavage showing, but there it was. Undeniable." Shortly before the primaries in New Hampshire, her voice cracked, as though she were about to cry. With little to distract the media by way of policy, this almost-event dominated the news cycle the day before the vote. With few exceptions, the moment was viewed not through the lens of campaign fatigue but of gender. When she won, many credited her eye-welling moment with having "softened" her image and "humanized" her sufficiently that she scored an unexpected victory. Some claimed it was little more than a cynical ploy. Had she lost, an entirely contrary analysis pertaining to feminine weakness in the heat of battle had undoubtedly already been prepared.

The coverage frequently overstepped the mark. Chris Matthews at MSNBC was forced to apologize for his relentless attacks. His colleague David Shuster was suspended after he questioned the fact that Chelsea Clinton had been asked to lobby superdelegates and celebrities. "Doesn't it seem as though Chelsea's being pimped out in some weird sort of way?" he asked. Men turned up to Clinton's rallies with banners saying, "Iron my shirt" and one T-shirt that said, "If only Hillary had married O.J. instead!" At one meeting, an elderly woman asked John McCain, "How do we beat the bitch?" McCain laughed and replied, "That's an excellent question."

The multiple identities of Clinton (woman, politician, wife, professional, cuckold) and Obama (black, biracial, son of immigrant, Ivy League, orator) made their candidacies both possible and problematic. Such were the dynamics of race and gender as they related to their biographies that much of the debate about their candidacies was driven by them. But while the clients in Charleston's beauty parlors were anxious to break away from narrow definitions of race and gender, others handcuffed themselves to the crudest forms of identity politics and threw away the key.

While the media portrayed blackness and womanhood as two binary and bifurcated identities, a few white feminists attempted to position them as inherently in conflict and contradiction. The result was to reduce the competition between the two to a sordid trade-off between Obama's race and Clinton's gender, as though the two were vying for a medal in who was the most oppressed.

Most shocking, given her lifetime of thoughtful and impassioned activism, was Gloria Steinem. Steinem argued in an article in *The New York Times* on 8 January 2008 (the morning of the New Hampshire primary) that "Gender is probably the most restricting force in American life, whether the question is who must be in the kitchen or who could be in the White House. Black men were given the vote a half-century before women of any race were allowed to mark a ballot, and generally have ascended to positions of power, from the military to the boardroom, before any women (with the possible exception of obedient family members in the latter)."

Without acknowledging that black men in America were being lynched for attempting to exercise their vote almost fifty years after white women went freely to the polls, or the fact that black men have descended to the lowest positions of penury and penal servitude in America today, Steinem's argument was both fatuous and dangerous. She would later claim she was misunderstood, but given that this was the central thrust of her piece, it is difficult to see how. "I'm not advocating a competition for who has it toughest," she claimed. Sadly, that was precisely what she *was* doing.

In a radio debate, African-American Princeton academic Melissa Harris-Lacewell excoriated Steinem:

I just feel we have got to get clear about the fact that race and gender are not these clear dichotomies in which, you know, you're a woman or you're black. I'm sitting here in my black womanhood body, knowing that it is more complicated than that. African-American men have been complicit in the oppression of African-American women. White women have been complicit in the oppression of black men and black women . . . For a second-wave feminist with an understanding of the complexity of American race and gender to take this kind of position in *The New York Times* struck me as, again, the very worst of what that feminism can offer—in other words, division.

Meanwhile, Robin Morgan, author of 1970 feminist essay "Goodbye to All That," decided to revive her thirty-year-old refrain for modern times. "A few non-racist countries may exist—but sexism is everywhere," she wrote. "So why should all women not be as justly proud of our womanhood and the centuries, even millennia, of struggle that got us this far, as black Americans, women and men, are justly proud of their struggles?"

Just before the biggest day of the primary season, Chelsea Clinton, Hillary's daughter, circulated Morgan's essay with the following note to her friends: "Please forward this to all the men you know too—voting in the election tomorrow, voting next week, already voted. I don't agree with all the points Robin Morgan makes but I do believe her thesis is important for us all to confront—I confess that I didn't entirely get 'it' until not only guys stood up and shouted 'iron my shirts' but the media reacted with amusement, not outrage."

A month later, former vice-presidential candidate Geraldine Ferraro went so far as to claim that Obama was only doing as well as he was *because* he was black. "If Obama was a white man, he would not be in this position," she said. "And if he was a woman of any color, he would not be in this position. He happens to be very lucky to be who he is. And the country is caught up in the concept." This is a stunning claim, given that, in the US, black men make up 6 percent of the population, almost 50 percent of prison inmates in 2000, and just 1 percent of the Senate—in the form of then-Senator Barack Obama.

This attempt to play race off against gender, as though they were bargaining chips, is as old as it is corrosive. In the wake of the American civil war, a fierce debate raged over the 15th amendment to the US constitution, which would give the vote to black men but not to women of any race. What might have been a strategic consideration weighing pragmatism and principle became a sordid scrap over which group was most deserving of the franchise, white women or black men.

Elizabeth Cady Stanton, one of the nation's leading suffragettes throughout the nineteenth century, believed that giving the franchise to black men was a license for an explosion of sexual violence. After a black man in Tennessee was lynched for allegedly raping a white woman, Stanton wrote not of the horrors of the lynching but of the prospect of further rapes if black men got the vote: "The Republican cry of 'Manhood Suffrage' creates an antagonism between black men and all women that will culminate in fearful outrages on womanhood, especially in the southern states." In the feminist paper *The Revolution*, she wrote that, forced to choose, "We prefer Bridget and Dinah at the ballot box to Patrick and Sambo."

During the same period, Frederick Douglass insisted that the situation of black men required more urgent attention than that of white women: "When women, because they are women, are hunted down through the cities of New York and New Orleans, when they are dragged from their houses and hung upon lamp posts . . . then they will have an urgency to obtain the ballot equal to our own."

When pressed on whether everything he said could not just as easily apply to black women, he said, "Yes, yes, yes. It is true for the Black woman but not because she is a woman but because she is Black." These kind of zero-sum arguments are entirely wrongheaded on both sides, for three reasons. First, they treat identities as monolithic and interchangeable. They're not. Sexism and racism, for example, have different histories and operate in different ways. There are certainly some things black men can do in the US that white women cannot do. At the most banal daily level, white women will generally wait longer in the queue for the bathroom, but they will find it much easier to get a taxi in most large cities than men. Once they get in the taxi, they will be far more vulnerable to sexual assault; once they get out of the bathroom, they will be far less likely to be stopped by the police while driving home. Thankfully, it is not a competition, and there is enough misery to go round.

To try simply to exchange one for the other—even for rhetorical purposes—really won't teach you much about either. Class, gender, race, sexual orientation—you name the identity and it will have its own roots, dynamics and dimensions. Some are visible, some are not. Some are physical, some are not. Some are chosen, some are not. "The difference between being black and being gay," Quentin Crisp once said, "is that you don't have to come downstairs one day and say: 'Mum, Dad, I'm black.'"

Second, there is a presupposition of a definitive league table whereby the "equality" of some is subordinated to the "equality" of others. In short, one person's experience and pain is privileged over another's. To compare and contrast the qualitative differences between how certain identities function can be instructive, but to rank them quantitatively as though one inherently takes precedence over the other, as Steinem and Morgan did, is not only flawed but potentially dangerous.

Third, pitting under-represented groups against each other undermines any potential for building the kind of coalitions necessary to eradicate the discrimination that gives these very identities progressive potential in the first place.

More often than not, these beggar-thy-neighbor arguments are just a way of people avoiding responsibility for their own actions or words by changing the subject and attempting to silence others by pulling rank. The result is cheap point-scoring that helps nobody and alienates almost everyone.

When the former UK secretary of state for international development Clare Short rejected a request from Zimbabwe for additional aid to buy back land occupied by settlers under colonialism, she said, "We are a new government from diverse backgrounds, without links to former colonial interests. My own origins are Irish and, as you know, we were colonized, not colonizers."

Short's claim that her Irish origins trumped her government position and effectively neutralized Zimbabwe's request was little short of ludicrous. Quite who authorized her unilaterally to sever links to former colonial interests is not clear. But a change of government does not mean an eradication of history or responsibility. In any case, she was not representing the Irish government. She was elected by British voters to serve in a British government—the one-time colonizers of Zimbabwe and still colonizers of part of the island of Ireland.

Such attempts at identity-based one-downmanship are doubly flawed. Not only are they irrelevant to the question at hand—Short's Irish origins have nothing to do with the question of aid to Zimbabwe—but they also have little bearing on the identity that has been invoked. Her apparent refusal to give aid, on the grounds that she is of Irish heritage, is of no benefit to the people of Ireland.

This is precisely what happens with discussions about homophobia in Jamaica. Jamaica is, among other things, an impoverished nation racked by violence and economic inequality. In 2005, 1,674 murders were committed there, more than double the UK murder rate in a population less than one third the size of London's. The sources for this violence are many. Both the US and the Eastern Bloc armed rival political parties during the Cold War; the guns were then used by gangs to run the drugs trade and enforce mafia-style control of certain "garrison" communities. At the same time, Jamaica spends far more servicing debt—much of it foreign—than it does on health, education or policing. Unemployment stands at around 15 percent; inflation at 12 percent. In global poverty rankings, Jamaica sits between Syria and Kazakhstan, but it also has one of the most unequal distributions of wealth in the world.

Homophobia there, both political and popular, has taken on a particularly vicious expression. "Violent acts against men who have sex with men are commonplace in Jamaica," concluded Rebecca Schleifer in a Human Rights Watch report "Hated to Death: Homophobia, Violence and Jamaica's HIV/AIDS Epidemic" published in November 2004. "Verbal and physical violence, ranging from beatings to brutal armed attacks to murder, are widespread . . . [These] abuses take place in a climate of impunity fostered by Jamaica's sodomy laws and are promoted at the highest levels of government." Those who seek to downplay the issue do not simply place homophobic violence in the context of Jamaica's overall situation. They try to bury it there and hope no one will ever find it.

"The victimization of homosexuals is part of a continuum of violence in Jamaican culture in much the same way that predial larceny [stealing crops] is often punished illegally by angry mobs who take the law into their own hands and lynch the apparently guilty," argues Carolyn Cooper in *Sound Clash: Jamaican Dancehall Culture at Large*. "Homosexual behaviors, or even the suspicion of intent, do put the individual at risk." Cooper, chair of the reggae studies department, University of the West Indies, went on to explain to me that, "Compared to a big city like New York, you could say Jamaica is homophobic. But not compared to, say, Kansas or smalltown USA. Buju Banton, a dancehall singer notorious for his anti-gay lyrics, is no less homophobic than George Bush."

Jamaican gay activists find such talk at best irritating and at worst unforgivable. "Whether Jamaica is as homophobic as Kansas or Uzbekistan is irrelevant," says Thomas Glave, a professor of English at the State University of New York in Binghamton who was born in the US and raised for much of his childhood in Jamaica. "We're not full citizens of society."

"These questions highlight the dilemma of the nationalist project," explains Philip Dayle, the Jamaica legal officer at the International Commission of Jurors. "We must start with the universality of human rights. In Jamaica, nationalism trumps sexual orientation and race trumps sexual orientation. So when faced with nationalism and race together, issues of sexual orientation don't stand a chance."

Similarly, the argument over whether black men or white women are more oppressed than the other does not relieve the oppression of either. There is no feminism worthy of the name that does not seek to liberate all women—including black women. There can be no anti-racism that does not seek to liberate all black people—including black women. This is no mere rhetorical flourish. As we saw with Frank Ricci, the Connecticut firefighter who took the New Haven Fire Department to court after he was denied a promotion, the propensity of under-represented groups to fight amongst themselves for scarce resources is one of the central barriers to progressive advancement.

Back on the campaign trail, both Clinton and Obama understood the need to strike a delicate balance between evoking the symbolic importance of their identities and ignoring them altogether. On the one hand, it was understood that her gender and his race were central to their appeal to large and important groups of voters; on the other was a tacit understanding that those same identities had to be played down in order not to alienate other large groups of voters. Their task was to harness the historic resonance of their candidacies while claiming that the very thing they signified—that one was black and the other female—would not make a big difference.

Asked about the significance of her gender, Clinton sometimes neutralized the question: "I couldn't run as anything other than a woman"; at other times embraced it: "I'm proud to be running as a woman and I'm excited that I may be able to finally break the hardest of glass ceilings"; and occasionally denied its relevance altogether: "Obviously, I'm not running because I'm a woman; I trust the American people to make a decision not about me or my gender but about what is best for you and your families."

During his speech at the Democratic convention in 2004, Obama started by stressing his race and his mixed-race heritage, albeit in more coded fashion. "Let's face it. My presence on this stage is pretty unlikely," he began, before referring to his parents' "improbable love." He then went on to claim that "There is not a black America or a white America—there is the United States of America." His stump speeches during the primaries were littered with references to abolitionists and civil rights victories. One of his central rally-cries— "the fierce urgency of now"—was a quotation from Martin Luther King. But when he finally accepted the nomination, on the forty-fifth anniversary of King's "I have a dream" speech, he pointedly declined to mention King by name, referring to him instead merely as "the old preacher."

Beyond the symbolic issues surrounding their own candidacies, issues of race and gender rarely came up during the primary campaign. When they did, the two candidates tried to bat them away. Neither felt they could afford to be understood within the limiting confines of being a "black" or "female" candidate. This made sense for their campaigns, but it made a nonsense of the notion that their victories would signal a paradigm shift in America's gender or racial politics. There was never any suggestion that either of their platforms would benefit the lives of black people or women any more than most of their Democratic rivals, or each other.

This urge to look different while promising to behave the same has become the central thrust behind much of the push for "diversity." This use of identity as a marketing tool, as opposed to an effort to promote equality, was driven primarily by the corporate sector in the US and, to a lesser extent, the UK, particularly during the nineties. But it was in politics that it found its most blatant expression, most usually as an emblem of individual success that belies collective failure.

In 2002, the Tories appointed their first chairwoman, Theresa May. Standing for the cameras in front of a coterie of young Tory workers, many of them women, and with an Asian face at his shoulder, the Tory leader Iain Duncan Smith pointed to May's appointment as proof that the party was more inclusive. An official spokesman said it indicated that the Tories "are living in the twenty-first century, not the nineteenth." May agreed. "It's always been an open, decent and tolerant party, but this is a very upfront example of that," she said. But when May was asked what she would do about getting more women into parliament, she abandoned her support for mandating that women constitute half the candidates on shortlists in winnable seats, claiming instead that the party had already been "making good progress as we are." In gaining a woman at one of the highest levels, the Tories actually lost an advocate for greater women's representation.

Neither Obama nor Hillary's electoral success, some claimed, would change a great deal in the lives of black or female Americans. "[Obama] is being consumed as the embodiment of color-blindness," Angela Davis, renowned activist and professor of history of consciousness at the University of California, Santa Cruz, told me in November 2007. "It's the notion that we have moved beyond racism by not taking race into account. That's what makes him conceivable as a presidential candidate. He's become the model of diversity in this period, and what's interesting about his campaign is that it has not sought to invoke engagements with race other than those that have already existed."

In order to make their candidacies viable, Obama and Hillary had to eviscerate their highly politicized identities of any tangible political significance. That America would look different was central to their meaning; that it would act the same was central to their message. "The Republican administration is the most diverse in history," continued

Davis, "but when the inclusion of black people into the machine of oppression is designed to make that machine work more efficiently, then it does not represent progress at all. We have more black people in more visible and powerful positions. But then we have far more black people who have been pushed down to the bottom of the ladder. When people call for diversity and link it to justice and equality, that's fine. But there's a model of diversity as the difference that makes no difference, the change that brings about no change."

Herein lay the essential problem with the manner in which identity politics became employed during the Democratic primary. The symbolic value of Obama and Clinton's candidacies had been routinely embraced even as the substantial effect of their potential victory had been ducked.

But while symbols should not be dismissed as insubstantial, they should not be mistaken for substance either. That a black man or a white woman would be the Democratic candidate was hailed as historically significant. But what that would mean for black people or women was dismissed as irrelevant. The candidates' personal political victories promised no broader advancement for women or racial minorities: the significance of their identities had been completely decoupled from the very things that gave their identities meaning. In a time of war, recession and class calcification, their ascent helped restore the nation's self-image as the home of class fluidity, boundless opportunity and unstoppable progress. "It's the old idea that anyone can grow up to be president," wrote Michael Kinsley in *Time*. "Not just that, but that even at age 230, we are still young enough and flexible enough to be expanding our notion of who we mean by 'anyone.'"

But while these breakthroughs were significant for the US, they were by no means unique. When the US went to the polls for the presidential elections, nine women were holding elected office in countries as varied in their cultural and political histories as Bangladesh, Ireland, Finland and Liberia. Margaret Thatcher's eleven-year tenure as British prime minister had done little for women in the UK, while 2008 saw two women party leaders face off in Bangladesh during a period of growing Islamic fundamentalism.

Ethnic minorities had also been elected to heads of state around the world before, from Peruvian president Alberto Fujimori (of Japanese descent) to Jamaican president Edward Seaga (of Lebanese and Scottish descent). So too have leaders from historically oppressed ethnic or racial groups such as Bolivian president Evo Morales (the country's first fully indigenous head of state), even if there have been none from historically oppressed ethnic or racial minorities.

Many, like Davis, felt the need to dial back the rhetorical euphoria gripping the nation. "Having a woman in the White House won't necessarily do a damn thing for progressive feminism," argued *Bitch* magazine co-founder Lisa Jervis in *LiP* magazine. "Though the dearth of women in electoral politics is so dire as to make supporting a woman—any woman—an attractive proposition, even if it's just so she can serve as a role model for others who'll do the job better eventually, it's ultimately a trap. Women who do nothing to enact feminist policies will be elected and backlash will flourish. I can hear the refrain now: 'They've finally gotten a woman in the White House, so why are feminists still whining about equal pay?'"

However, on many fronts, this backlash had already begun before the lash had even been raised. Before a single vote had been cast, Stuart Taylor argued in the *National Journal* on 6 February 2007 that "Obama embodies and preaches the true and vital message that in today's America the opportunities available to black people are unlimited if they work hard, play by the rules, and get a good education." Meanwhile, a Pew survey revealed that almost half of African-Americans born to middle-income parents in the wake of the civil rights era had descended into poverty or near poverty as adults, and that black Americans are more dissatisfied with their progress than at any time in the past twenty years.

When South Carolina's votes came in, it turned out that black women were not at all divided. And nor were Democrats as a whole. In what had been anticipated as a close election, Obama took 55 percent to Clinton's 27 percent. Demographically, he swept the board, winning women and men, every age group apart from the over-65s, every region of the state, income bracket and level of education, the married and the unmarried, liberals, conservatives and moderates.

Black women voted for Obama in almost precisely the same pro-portion as black men did—around 80 percent. The only group he did not win that night was whites—the men went for Edwards, the women for Clinton. And the one group that was never interrogated about its identity was the one group that, throughout the primaries, most consistently and overwhelmingly voted for people who looked like themselves—white men.

7. The Enemy Within

Identities make no sense unless understood within the context of power

We are, above all, a European people of the white race, of
Greek and Latin culture and the Christian religion . . . the Muslims,
have you seen them . . . with their turbans and djellabas?
You can see clearly that they're not French . . . Try to mix oil and
vinegar. Shake the bottle. After a minute, they separate again.
Arabs are Arabs, French are French.

– Charles de Gaulle, 1959

The late-evening train from London's St Pancras to Luton makes it painfully clear why not everyone regards British culture as the pinnacle of human civilization. The carriages are crammed tight with people, many of whom have been out for the night and some of whom are drunk. Some are dozing off in the clothes they set out to work in some fourteen hours earlier. All look weary. A few call home to ask family members to pick them up from the station, or to whisper goodnight to their kids. Others are tucking into fast food, their lips shiny with grease, trying to stop the crumbs from falling on their laps.

However, for all its tawdriness, there is much to recommend this small scene too. The two young, drunk men opposite me keep poking each other and giggling. They have just finished a bucket of Kentucky Fried Chicken and are wolfing down their pre-packed desserts. Along with the woman sitting next to me, I tease them about their terrible diet and how this will all feel like it was a big mistake in the morning, if indeed they can even remember eating it. They joke along at their own expense. There is what Paul Gilroy has described as a convivial nature to British culture which extends to and beyond race; an ease of presence and coexistence that allows these kinds of playful, gently mocking interactions with strangers.

When I arrive in Luton town center, I look lost. A gay black man, out for the night with his two Muslim friends (a straight couple walking hand in hand), guides me to my hotel. The receptionist is Lithuanian. One of the women who serves the breakfast the next morning is Estonian; the other is English. A few days later, when I try to catch a bus out of town, I strike up a halting conversation with two Romanian gypsies. They want to know about my laptop, life in America and jobs anywhere. When the bus doesn't come, we end up sharing a cab. They insist on paying their half upfront, showing pictures of their wives and telling bad, dirty jokes.

For all the public foreboding, the England I generally experience is one of very different kinds of people rubbing along, at best, in good humor and, at least, without rancor. But in times of crisis, like during the terrorist attacks on London on July 7, 2005, such claims are rightly re-examined. Luton's railway station gained a particularly gruesome notoriety during that episode as the place from which the bombers set off on a dummy run nine days before the attacks. You can see them on grainy CCTV footage with large backpacks, buying their tickets—a dress rehearsal for suicide and carnage.

Farasat Latif, who lives and works in Luton, is dedicated to making sure something like that never happens again. He receives European Union funding to tackle violent radicalization in the Muslim community, advises young Muslims always to obey the law and helps rehabilitate people of all races and religions who come out of prison.

On paper, he would appear to be a model citizen. A British-born Muslim of Pakistani descent, he was raised in a working-class family, studied hard, went to university and today provides for his own family and is active in his community. When he is not proselytizing against violence, he reads to his six-year-old daughter every night, in the hope that she will develop a strong vocabulary and grow up to be a confident and well-educated woman.

This is all a far cry from the hell-raiser who spent most of his student life on bail. While studying at the London School of

Economics during the late eighties and early nineties, Latif was a militant left-wing activist. There doesn't seem to have been a single demonstration at which he couldn't get himself arrested, whether it was for abortion rights or against apartheid. He considered himself a Marxist and, wedded to anti-imperialism, anti-capitalism and anti-Zionism, he believed that only a massive uprising by the British working class could turn world events around.

At one stage, during the tumultuous riots against the poll tax in 1989, he was caught red-handed holding a brick in his hand by several policemen. "There was chaos everywhere and the whole thing was getting really intense. I kept thinking I'd better get rid of the brick before I got caught with it," he recalls. "But another part of me really didn't want to let it go . . . I was really into direct action and, to be honest, at that age it was a lot of fun."

And yet Latif, who now regards those days as part of his misspent youth, is considered more of a potential threat to the British state as a law-abiding Muslim than he ever was as a rioting Leftist. For, somewhere along the way, he abandoned Marx for Mohammed and insurrection for Islam. He no longer believes in democracy: "Democracy says people should decide, I say God should decide," he explains. "In civil law and criminal law, legislation is the sole prerogative of God."

The young man who once went on pro-choice demonstrations and whose closest friends were female now refuses to shake a woman's hand. He wed his second cousin from Pakistan in an arranged marriage and insists that she wear the hijab in the presence of her own relatives: "I wanted to marry someone who had not been exposed to the ills of the West . . . If I died tomorrow my wife would never take off the hijab, but she was more lax about wearing it in the presence of her cousins and I had to tell her that she had to."

He is far less concerned about resolving problems in this life than preparing himself for the next. "If you're in a hotel room for a couple of days before you move into a nice big house with your family, then you don't spend a lot of time worrying about making it look nice and doing it up," he explains. "You're focused on what's coming next."

Damascene moments are rare in real-life conversions. To make sense of these turnarounds, we expect some bolt of lightning instantaneously to shed light on a new path but, more often than not, like the change in the fortunes of Irish women, these transformations are more akin to the gradual clearing of a dense fog. Ray Hill, the former National Front candidate who joined the anti-fascist movement, told me that he fell into right-wing politics due to circumstances and fell out of it due to disillusionment. In *Blinded by the Right*, David Brock, a former right-wing hack in the US who later repented and turned Left, wrote, "As a young zealot, I disciplined myself to ignore the soft tug of my own conscience and see only what I was supposed to see." After a while, the pull became too great, and he had to turn his back on what he had known.

A similar process occurred with Latif. Raised in predominantly white towns on London's outer rim, there was never a time when he didn't know he was Muslim. He never ate pork, from the age of six he went to Islamic Sunday school, where he learned about the Koran, and when he grew older he never drank. But religion was never a particularly important part of his identity. He didn't fast or pray, even on Fridays. His experience with Muslim elders back then was hardly inspiring either. He remembers them as elderly men who spoke English as a second language and had no concise or intelligent arguments. "They were nice people but a bit dumb," he says. Most of his friends were white and Christian, and his experience growing up in Hatfield and St Albans, two commuter towns, was one of tolerance, compassion and even anti-racism. "My mum didn't speak any English and our white neighbors looked after her. They found her a job. They were good people. When the National Front came to try and have a demonstration in Hatfield, they were beaten up at the train station."

He became politicized by the Israeli bombing of Lebanon and then by apartheid. "I saw these people picketing Barclays bank and asked them what they were doing," he says, recalling his teenage years. He joined them and used to bring friends to go in and trash the bank. But he couldn't go to any of the meetings because they took place in pubs.

The first time being a Muslim became for him a political issue was during the Salman Rushdie affair. Rushdie's *Satanic Verses* had sparked outrage in sections of the Muslim community for its alleged blasphemy. Latif felt that those he once considered his comrades were now forcing him to choose sides: "I felt insulted by Rushdie and felt empathy with the demonstrations. [My left-wing friends] said I should sign this thing defending Rushdie, and I felt that would mean abandoning my community."

Did he think the book should be banned, as many demonstrators demanded? "I believe they had a right to call for it to be banned," he said. The Rushdie affair was soon eclipsed by the First Gulf War, and Latif returned to the leftist fold. Then came his arrest at the poll tax demonstration and the very real possibility that he might have to serve time in prison. His mother had recently divorced, and needed him. Aware that his imprisonment would crush her, he had already decided that, if he was incarcerated, he would tell her he was going to study in Belgium for six months. In his desperation, he had appealed to God to help him. It was the first time he can recall leaning on his religion. Thanks to a good reference from his professor—who sat in the House of Lords—he was spared a custodial sentence, but the vulnerability that this close shave exposed stayed with him.

Upon graduation, Latif went back to St Albans to live with his mother. He was still working with left-wing groups but started to visit the mosque and got into some conversations with Salafi Muslims, who occasionally visited him at home. "It started to make sense to me," he says. "They made a statement and then they would back it up with a passage from the Koran."

So began a four-year transition during which he flitted between two worlds, one militant, secular and leftist, the other pious, religious and conservative. His friends on the Left chided him. Since his political life and his social life were so closely intertwined, he stopped socializing with them so much. He started to pray five times a day. Then came the salwar kameez, the skull cap and the marriage he asked his mother to arrange. During the Bosnian War, Latif was impressed by the zeal of some in the Muslim community who sent or took aid to affected areas and even raised money to send arms in a bid to break the blockade. He had wanted to sit in on more radical Islamist groups then, but as he was a relative newcomer to the devout, they did not trust him sufficiently and spurned his advances. (He acknowledges now that, if they had let him, he might have ended up with a far more radical Islamist sect.) The Left's response to the war—particularly by those who supported the Serbs—disappointed him. By 1996, he had crossed over into another world and, for now, it seems as though he has no intention of heading back. "I used to have multiple identities," he says. "Now I really only have one. Islam."

Just as there is no silver bullet that can explain such a dramatic switch in affiliations, there are nonetheless a few strong strands of continuity between Latif's youthful years and his adult life that are worth pointing out.

When it came to politics, Latif never did things by half. He was never a liberal. Indeed, he was a fellow traveler with some of the most militant groups on the Left, which is why he found himself being arrested so often. Once he grew dispirited with the Left, there was nothing to suggest that he would move on to something moderate.

His new agenda is no more likely to succeed than his previous one. He was for revolutionary socialism through direct action during one of Britain's most reactionary periods. His plan for Britain now, he says, is to convert the entire country to Islam, not by force but through persuasion. "I see the British working class as potential Muslims," he says. "But I don't see them as enemies." The central difference is that, before, he sought material gain through political struggle; now he will tot up his victories in the afterlife. But the ultimate futility of his pursuits in this life remains constant.

Finally, notwithstanding his positive childhood experiences, he never felt British, even though it's the only country he's ever lived in. For a long time, Britain, like most countries in Europe, has struggled to provide a road map that allows people to both fully belong and be different. Unlike America, where people have the option of hyphenating their nationality and their ethnicity, European national identities are far less flexible and inclusive. There is only one way to be French. The state says you can take it or leave it. The trouble is that the pervasiveness of French racism means that even those non-white French people who choose to take it find themselves constantly knocked back. Even those who like Britain—and I would count myself among them—don't necessarily really feel fully part of it. Latif always thought of himself as Pakistani. "I know what Islam is," he says. "I have no idea what British is."

Latif stands at the epicenter of a moral panic in Europe. Thanks to acts of war abroad and terror at home, not to mention rioting and the rise of the extreme Right and religious fundamentalism, the European intelligentsia has been obsessing over Islam for at least a decade now.

With Muslims constituting sizable minorities in many European cities from Marseilles to Malmö, their presence has sparked fear among those who perceive their presence as both a potential existential and essential threat to European democracy and culture. This panic has found its most regular and raucous expression in discussions around what Muslim women wear. In the Netherlands, plans to ban the burqa, believed to be worn by just fifty women in the country (or .0003 percent of the population), were shelved by parliament only when it became clear that the ban would violate the right to religious freedom and equality.

In Britain, a government minister sparked a debate about the niqab, a veil that covers all but the eyes which is, again, worn by a tiny percentage of Muslim women who are themselves a tiny percentage of the population. Jack Straw said it made him feel uncomfortable when women came into his constituency office wearing the niqab and he wanted to start a debate about it. With novelist Martin Amis accusing Muslims of sheltering "miserable bastards" and Rushdie stating that "veils suck," the debate never reached a particularly high level. But it did further stigmatize the Muslim community as an innate and inherent problem.

"I'll go further than Jack Straw and say they need to take off their veils," a sixteen-year-old student told the *Guardian* after Straw's intervention. "You need to see people face to face. It's weird not knowing who it is you're passing in the street, especially late at night when someone might jump you." As though we didn't have enough to worry about: now, veiled Muslim women were perceived as a physical threat to white teenage boys.

In France, girls wearing headscarves to school were cast as a threat to the integrity of the Republic and a desecration of the gains of the French Revolution. While the government was occasionally anxious to frame the debate as being about all religious symbols rather than just those of Muslims, it was in reality all about the establishment's desire to tame a perceived Islamic resurgence. Since immigrant parents had been incapable of integrating their children into French secular culture, went the theory, second-generation French Muslims would become wards of the secular state. The reality, however, was far more complicated. The two sisters at the center of the controversy in 2003, Lilia and Alma Levi, were converts to Islam. Their father is an atheist, Sephardic Jew and their mother a non-practicing Catholic. The girls were expelled from school in suburban Aubervilliers after they refused to remove their headscarves or accept another scarf, provided by the school, which revealed their neck, earlobes and hairline. "I'm not in favour of the headscarf," said the father, "but I defend the right of my children to go to school. In the course of this business I've discovered the hysterical madness of certain ayatollahs of secularism who have lost all their common sense."

And this was no simple right-wing onslaught. Salma Yaqoob, an anti-war activist and councilor in Birmingham, was speaking at an anti-war meeting at the European Social Forum in France in 2003 when another woman on the platform objected to her headscarf. "How dare she be sitting on this platform dressed like that?" she said. Yaqoob replied, "How can you possibly be a feminist and ask me not to wear it?" "It takes a lot of strength and courage to wear a headscarf in this climate," Yaqoob told me in her office in Birmingham city council. "It's part of my spirituality. It's part of my own personal journey. It's a true test of pluralism."

"Removed and reassumed again and again," argued Frantz Fanon, Martinique-born philosopher, psychiatrist and revolutionary, "the veil has been manipulated, transformed into a technique of camouflage, into a means of struggle." Wherever you stand on the issue of headwear, a broad swathe of political opinion clearly believes that

Muslims are a problem that has to be dealt with. In a referendum in Switzerland, 57 percent voted to ban minarets—even though there are only four in the entire country. Mistaking Islam in Europe in the twenty-first century (the religion of a relatively small and mostly non-white, poor minority) for Christianity in the eighteenth century (the religion of the state, the ruling class and the overwhelming ethnic majority), some convinced themselves that they were doing the unfinished work of the Enlightenment.

"Ayan Hirshi Ali was no Voltaire," argues Ian Buruma in *Murder in Amsterdam*, describing a Somali-born Muslim critic of Islam who compared herself to the French secular philosopher and championed by many Western "liberals" and reactionaries alike. "For Voltaire had flung his insults at the Catholic Church, one of the two most powerful institutions of 18th-century France, while Ayan risked offending only a minority that was already feeling vulnerable in the heart of Europe."

Far from being neutral and abstract, our identities are rooted in material conditions that confer power and privilege in relation to one another. "The Malay came to know one another as such only after, and in opposition to, the arrival of the Chinese," writes Kwame Anthony Appiah in *The Ethics of Identity*. "The Hindu became Hindu only when the British created the class in the early 19th century, to take in those who weren't members of the famous monotheisms, and the identity gained salience only in opposition to the South Asian Muslims." But quite how these different identities relate to each other is entirely contingent on their context.

This was clearly illustrated during an interview I had with the former South African leader F. W. de Klerk, who tried to make apartheid sound a bit like an abortive attempt to create an early version of the European Union in Africa—a region split into various national groupings where each kept their autonomous jurisdiction but remained part of a whole. "When I was a young man, I supported the idea of building a federation that would look a little bit like Europe," he said. "The Zulus would have Zululand, like the French have France, the Xhosas would have their own country like the

Germans and the Afrikaans would have theirs, and all these different nation-states would be held together by something like the European Union."

The only trouble was that it was the Afrikaaners who were doing the slicing. They kept the best and biggest parts of the cake for themselves and crammed the stuff that was less than appetizing down the throats of the majority. Countries must at least hold a referendum before they join the EU, which follows negotiations on terms of membership. Non-white South Africans had no such choice. The "federation" of which de Klerk spoke demanded the forcible removal of people from their homes and sent them hundreds of miles away.

Given these crucial facts, de Klerk's description was utterly disingenuous. Ignoring rights, agency, authority or status makes a nonsense out of any attempt to fathom consequence, outcome, effect or ramification. In short, to try to understand the role of identities outside of their power relationships is to misunderstand them completely.

Take domestic violence. There is such a thing as domestic abuse (or Intimate Partner Violence) against men at the hands of women. Indeed, it is much more prevalent than most imagine, not least because it all too often goes under-reported. One need not be in denial about that. Where men are physically or emotionally attacked by women, that should be unequivocally condemned. There may even be a case to be made for more resources being devoted to men who suffer domestic abuse and for broadening our understanding of what domestic abuse involves. Morally speaking, women abusing men is no less reprehensible than men abusing women.

And yet to equate the two would be a mistake for several reasons. First, women are still far more likely to be the victims of IPV than men. According to the 2000 US National Violence Against Women Survey conducted by the Centers for Disease Control and the National Institute for Justice, almost two thirds of intimate partner rapes and physical assaults are committed against women. Second, since men are generally physically stronger than women, the damage they can inflict when they engage in physical abuse is far more dramatic. The survey, which interviewed a representative sample of 8,000 men and

8,000 women, found that 40 percent of women who suffer IPV are injured and 11 percent need medical attention. The correlating figures for men are 20 percent and 4 percent. In 2005, 78 percent of IPV cases ending in death were female.

Furthermore, taking in the broader context of male–female relations, women who are abused are more likely to find themselves in socially precarious situations. They are, for example, far more likely to be responsible for childcare and less likely to be financially independent. This makes it far more difficult for women to escape situations in which they are victims of domestic abuse.

Finally, men are far more at risk of being victims of IPV if their partners too are male. Approximately 15 percent of men who lived with a man as a couple, according to the survey, reported being raped, physically assaulted, and/or stalked by a male cohabitant, while 7.7 percent of men who had married or lived with a woman as a couple reported such violence by a wife or female cohabitant. Conversely, women living with women were less likely to be victims of IPV than women who lived with men.

So to equate men hitting women with women hitting men, as though the fact that one person hits another means the abuse has an equal effect and should be accorded equal weight in public consideration regardless of the sex of the perpetrator and victim, would be a mistake. "It's nothing to do with moral relativism," explains Liberty Aldrich, director of domestic violence and family programs at the Center for Court Innovation in New York. "It's about what is the impact of that hit on the victim and the answer to that lies in the power structures that exist in society."

So where do Muslims stand in the power structures that prevail in Britain in particular and Europe in general? Economically, they are struggling. According to the 2001 census, more than a third of Muslim households in Britain have no adults in employment. Almost three quarters of children of Bangladeshi and Pakistani origin (the ethnic groups with which most British Muslims identify) live in households below the poverty line. Almost a third of young British Muslims leave school without any qualifications. In each case, these statistics are at least double the national average. Little wonder then that, among Muslims in Britain, as with Muslims in France, Spain and Germany (where things are not a whole lot better), unemployment is the issue they are most concerned about. Under-represented in parliament and the press and over-represented in prison and the dole queues, Muslims feel a strong sense of alienation and exclusion.

On the street in Britain, those of Pakistani and Bangladeshi descent are eight times more likely to be victims of a racial attack than whites and, between 2000 and 2005, officially reported racist violence rose 71 percent in Denmark, 34 percent in France and 21 percent in Ireland. With few governments collecting data on the race of crime victims, it has been left to NGOs to record the sharp rise in attacks on Muslims, those believed to be Muslims and Muslim targets. Add the fallout from the "war on terror," and the objective reality is, and long has been, that for all the mainstream paranoia, Muslims have far more to fear from the West than the West has to fear from Muslims.

It is therefore not surprising that, according to a Pew survey, more than 80 percent of British Muslims think of themselves as Muslim first and citizens of their country second (considerably more than in Jordan, Egypt and Turkey) and almost half believe that there is a conflict between living in a modern society and being a Muslim (higher than every other country polled, including Pakistan and Nigeria). Indeed, by all accounts, British Muslims are a sullen lot. They are less likely than non-Muslim Britons to think that relations between the West and Muslim countries are good or that democracy can work well in Muslim countries. Of all the Muslim minorities in Europe, the British are the most likely to believe that people in Western countries are arrogant, violent and selfish, even as their non-Muslim compatriots are among the least likely to think so.

Alienation to this degree can carry terrible consequences, and there is no point in denying it. Roughly one in six Muslims in France, Spain and Britain believe that suicide bombing in defense of Islam can be justified, while less than one in five British Muslims believe that Arabs were responsible for the terrorist attacks on 9/11.

There are a handful of nihilistic young Muslims in Europe who will exploit this and who are keen to bomb and destroy, and a far larger number sufficiently disaffected that they are prepared to riot.

In the words of James Baldwin, "There is nothing so dangerous as a man who has nothing to lose. You do not need ten men, only one will do." For a relatively small community, Britain's Muslims have produced a large proportion of the world's terrorists, and this is in no small part because Britain has been able to produce so many men (and it is almost exclusively Muslim men in the West who have been attracted to violence) with so little to lose.

Refusing to acknowledge there are root causes for this particular state of affairs helps no one. For the best part of a decade, British Muslims have been fed a nightly diet of bombings and occupation in Afghanistan, Iraq, Lebanon, the Gaza Strip and the West Bank; imprisonment and torture in Guantanamo Bay, Belmarsh, Basra and Abu Ghraib; and tales of alleged wanton murder and rape in Hamdania, Haditha, Balad and Mahmudiya. It would be strange to think that you could declare war on terror, wage it in such an abhorrent and immoral manner, and seriously believe that terror would not fight back.

"There is a grievance," explains Yaqoob. "There's no reason to deny that. All you need to know that there is a grievance is a TV. These young men who want a short cut to heaven see innocent people being killed and then retaliate by going out and killing innocent people. There's a chilling logic to it. It's wrong. But it is logical."

That this response would find expression through religion is no mystery either. There is no sensible conversation you can have about Islamic identity that does not address what is happening to Muslims locally and globally. Muslims will be more likely to organize around their religious identity, both at home and abroad, so long as they feel attacked as a result of that religious identity. In this respect, Islam is no different from any other identity. When a community feels besieged, then fundamentalists—be they of religion, race, nationality or anything else—will move to center stage. Fear will polarize people and send them scuttling into crudely constructed camps, giving more power to the gatekeepers. When faced with a threat, either real or imagined, it is the fundamentalists' rhetoric, which in more ordinary times would sound simplistic and exclusionary, that will appear attractive for its apparent uncompromising clarity. In a world divided into them and us, people feel forced to pick sides. Views that were once dismissed as narrow-minded will be embraced as principled. The marginal becomes mainstream.

Whatever Latif's intentions, his fundamentalism has become the largest immovable object confronting the political injustices he is so keenly aware of, in just the same way that ultra-left politics had been—albeit rooted in a different tradition and with a different outcome.

And so it was that the more reactionary, fundamentalist currents within Britain's Muslim community began to gain influence as Muslims found themselves attacked. The only death threats Yaqoob ever received as a result of her high-profile involvement in anti-war and anti-racist politics were from other Muslims. One said, "You're going to be buried with the dogs."

"They would say, 'Why do you mix with the kaffirs?'" she explains. "We were taking them out of their comfort zone. We would say live and let live. When it came to gays, I would say to fellow Muslims: 'You're a minority and if you want rights as a minority then you have to support rights for other minorities.' So they said I was a kaffir and I promoted homosexuality."

And yet this alienation cannot simply be reduced to the responses of war and terror. For in America, the very center of these polarizing military misadventures, Muslims feel far less excluded. That is not to say that Islamophobia is not a problem there. Far from it. A 2006 Gallup poll showed that 39 percent of Americans were in support of Muslims in the US, including American citizens, being required to carry special identification. In 2005, the Council on American Islamic Relations (CAIR) recorded a 30 percent increase in the number of complaints about Islamophobic treatment.

In the immediate aftermath of the 9/11 attacks, the US government undertook the "preventative detention" of around 5,000 men on the basis of their birthplace, and later sought a further 19,000 "voluntary interviews." Over the next year, more than 170,000 men from twenty-four predominantly Muslim countries and North Korea were fingerprinted and interviewed in a program of "special registration." None of these measures produced a single terrorism conviction.

Nonetheless, American Muslims are far less likely to think of themselves as Muslim first than any European Muslim, and considerably less likely than most to think that suicide bombing can be justified. Precious few have become involved in terrorist activities, even though their opposition to the wars has been solid.

How come? Well, first, American Muslims are much better off. As more recent immigrants with better qualifications than their European cousins, they are better paid and better educated than the average American rather than being among the poorest in the country. America is far more comfortable with the notion that cultural identity can thrive within a flexible national identity. Whether churches are established or not, most Europeans are ill at ease with public expressions of religion, whereas another Pew poll shows that America views religion as very important. And in a country where every national group gets its own day, complete with a parade, flags and delicacies from the "home country," there is greater scope for understanding the difference between autonomy (a distinct cultural space from which people interact with the rest of society) and segregation (where people seek to separate themselves from the mainstream). In America, to qualify your national allegiance through ethnicity, race or religion is not necessarily regarded as diluting it.

"Everybody needs a sense of their identity," Fedwa Wazwaz, a board member of Minneapolis's Islamic Resource Center, told me. Wazwaz had just arrived at al-Amal, a private Muslim school in suburban Minneapolis, to pick up her daughter, Maryam. On the wall in an office hung a T-shirt asking "Got Islam?"—a play on a popular milk commercial—while a poster invited entrants to join the Koran competition.

On the whole, American Muslims feel less marginalized as a result of their religious identity and, since they are thriving economically, they are less likely to retreat into that identity and use it as the primary mechanism through which to confront either any discrimination they face or policies they oppose.

The one telling exception to this are African-American Muslims, most of whom are converts, who apparently have more in common with their European counterparts than their religious compatriots.

Unlike most other Muslim groups in the US, they did not arrive in America voluntarily and so, with nowhere else to go, they have far less attachment to the dream of American social mobility. But, like British Muslims, they have fewer qualifications with which to advance their careers and therefore few economic prospects; they are more economically disillusioned, alienated and extreme in their religious beliefs than those who have come from afar. African-American Muslims are more likely to think of themselves as Muslims first, then Americans than fellow Muslims who were not even born in the country, and are more likely to have favorable views of Al Qaeda too. The diversity of opinions within Islam is as wide as within any other religion and is rooted in social, national and economic context. "Hugo Chávez is the same faith as George Bush but they're very very different," points out Yaqoob. Obvious really. And yet for those who claim Islam itself is the problem, it is a decidedly inconvenient truth.

For much of Europe's political class, the notion that Islam is inherently ill equipped for the modern world is underpinned by two central distortions. First, they point to things that are problems in all communities and treat them as though they are particular to Islam. Homophobia, sexism, anti-Semitism, spousal abuse and ethnic rivalry are all cast as issues which Muslims, specifically, must grapple with in their bid for full inclusion and even at times full citizenship. Among other things, Muslims are routinely asked to commit to patriotism, peace at home, war abroad, Zionism, modernity, secularism, integration, anti-sexism, anti-homophobia, tolerance and monogamy. Some of these are excellent and should be fought for vigorously on principle. But Muslims are not being asked to sign up to them because they are good or bad in themselves but as a precondition for belonging. If other people do not abide by these ideals, they are subject to criticism; if Muslims do not, it is grounds for banishment or exclusion. In 2006, the German state of Baden-Württemberg devised a series of questions for citizenship tests that were asked only of Muslims from particular countries; they covered women's rights, religious freedom and domestic life.

In Britain, the emergence of "home-grown bombers" from the

Muslim community has been mentioned as though it were a new development, when in fact Britain has been growing its own bombers for years. Among other things, we have had a longstanding war with Northern Ireland. There is a whole evening dedicated to burning one of them; it's called Guy Fawkes night.

Second, they point to deeply problematic practices that are primarily associated with Muslims—honor killings, burqas, forced marriages, political violence—and cast them as though Islam were alone among religions in harboring extremism and dysfunction. When decades of child sexual abuse and its concealment by the hierarchy are exposed in the Catholic Church, it is put down to individuals taking advantage and an institution in denial but not to Catholicism itself. But when Muslims do bad things, it is never about individuals, their flaws, national customs, societal pressure or political and economic context. It is about Islam. It is as if Latif's fundamentalism were turned on its head: as though the secularists agree that Muslims can only have one identity.

What only a few are prepared to say but what most seem to mean is that Islam in particular, not religion in general, is the problem. Geert Wilders, a Dutch MP from the far-right Freedom Party, which boasts 9 seats out of 150 in Holland, has branded the Koran "a fascist book" on a par with *Mein Kampf* and has called for it to be banned. He insists there is no such thing as "moderate Islam" and that, if Mohammed were alive today, he would "be hunted down like a terrorist." Rhetorically, Wilders is certainly extreme; politically, his pronouncements have rapidly become a less refined version of mainstream thinking in the European political class. In Germany a book by Bundesbank board member Thilo Sarrazin, *Germany Does Away with Itself*, evoked an ostensibly apocalyptic future where Turks (currently around 5 percent of the population) compete to outnumber Germans, thereby "dumbing down" the country with their inferior gene pool.

Blaming inbreeding among Turks and Kurds for "congenital disabilities," Sarrazin claims immigrants from the Middle East are a "genetic minus" for the country.

"But the subject is usually hushed up," he writes. "Perish the thought that genetic factors could be partially responsible for the failure of parts of the Turkish populations in the German school system."

At the time of this writing, the book is its 14th edition and is Germany's best-selling book since the second world war. A poll published in the national magazine *Focus* in October showed 31 percent of respondents agreeing that Germany is "becoming dumber" because of immigrants, with 62 percent calling Sarrazin's comments "justified."

"Sarrazin didn't say anything new, didn't break any taboos and didn't contribute anything to the debate," explains Mekonnen Mesghena, head of migration and intercultural management at the Heinrich Böll Foundation. "But what was really shocking were the number of intellectuals who said: "His tone wasn't right but he has a point.""

The inevitable result of first particularizing and then pathologizing Islam in Europe is the perception that it has produced a crisis in the multicultural model that must now be addressed. This "crisis" can be most generously described as a concern that, in the name of supporting cultural and ethnic pluralism, liberal European states are neglecting their core values of equality and tolerance and in so doing sacrificing Enlightenment principles on the altar of sensitivity.

Before dealing with that, it is worthwhile reiterating once again that these conversations have mostly been taking place not only in a time of war but in a specific kind of war involving terrorism, with all the polarizing anxiety that entails. "Terror is first of all the terror of the next attack," explains Arjun Appadurai in *Fear of Small Numbers*. "Terror . . . opens the possibility that anyone may be a soldier in disguise, a sleeper among us, waiting to strike at the heart of our social slumber. The terrorist combines the qualities of the soldier and the spy, thus blurring another boundary on which modern politics has largely been based." Terror suspects in Britain who have no record and have never shown up on surveillance radar are called "clean skins." In moments of tension, every brown skin is just a clean skin waiting to happen. These are not the most propitious conditions in which to put forward nuanced arguments. But they are precisely the conditions that make such arguments more urgent and necessary.

There are three problems with the idea that to get to social peace, racial harmony and physical security we must first march over the grave of multiculturalism. First, given the high levels of racism, the resurgence of fascism, involvement in illegal wars and violations of human rights in the "war on terror," there was never much social peace to begin with. And it is particularly flawed as an argument against Islam since most of these acts of aggression have been committed *against* Muslims, either at home or abroad, rather than *by* them.

Second, the model of multiculturalism never commanded a huge amount of support to begin with. Multiculturalism is less an ethos than a simple statement of fact. Governments do not create cultures, let alone multicultures. These emerge from the lived experience of people and are by their nature untidy, vibrant, dynamic and, on occasion, difficult. Governments can certainly play a role—at certain moments even a crucial one. They can intervene to promote integrated social housing and integrated schools and to pass anti-discrimination legislation, all of which have an impact on how we live. They can choose whether to fund religious schools, how to respond to religious festivals and how to arbitrate over civil disputes about dress codes, dietary requirements and zoning laws. They can, in other words, set the tone for the conversation and help create the material conditions for meaningful discussions to take place. But they cannot put words in our mouths.

They cannot change our views about ourselves, our surroundings and our citizens by telling us what to wear, whom to marry or how to worship. Nor can they legislate for love, friendship, suspicion or kindness. The French state can tell Muslim children of Algerian extraction who are stuck in the depressed outer rims of big cities with other children who are Muslim or black, where unemployment is high, policing is brutal and academic failure accepted and expected that it sees them only as French citizens and pays no attention to their skin color or religion. But those children might be excused for not believing it. There are many factors that brought Europe to this point, including colonialism, race, class, globalization, immigration and war. Religion is not even the half of it, and culture is a product of all of it.

But finally and, in some ways, most importantly, these "multicultural conundrums" are rarely as thorny as they are made out to be.

Oftentimes, they are intellectual straw men reaching for low-hanging fruit. The principles are clear. You enforce the law, without fear or favor. You promote equality to all and for all. Forced marriages are essentially kidnapping. Honor killings are murder. Those who engage in them should be prosecuted. But, for the most part, these are not even remotely close calls. I have never heard anyone argue for kidnapping or murder on the grounds of cultural sensitivity. If I did, I would not imagine that I had struck a great blow for the Enlightenment by rebuffing them. It should go without saying that no woman should go through Immigration and Customs with her face covered. It should also be beyond question that any woman has the right to be screened by a female immigration officer.

If an imam doesn't like women walking past his mosque in a bikini, that's too bad for him. If an MP doesn't like women walking into his surgery in a niqab, that's too bad for him, too. Both have the right to say what they think—provided it doesn't promote violence or in some other way break the law—and women have the right to wear what they like. "Where women are forced to wear the headscarf, that must be fought," explains Yaqoob. "But where they are being forced not to wear it, that must be fought too." Since we are, as yet, unable to read people's minds, we cannot prevent a grown woman from wearing the burqa on the grounds that she does not know her own mind any more than we can prevent a woman from dropping charges against her abusive partner and returning to live with him.

There are noise ordinances to deal with early Muslim prayers, zoning regulations to deal with the building of mosques, and school boards and parent–teacher associations to deal with school uniforms. Like every other group, Muslims are entitled to call for those laws and ordinances to be changed to accommodate their needs. And so long as these civic bodies are democratic, accountable and subject to constitutionally enforced guarantees of equal treatment, they have the right to refuse on the basis of the merits of the case.

This does not guarantee outcomes we would always support. But it suggests that a process already exists to make a legitimate outcome possible. It does not mean that there will not be tough grey areas where the rights of the individual and collective, the religious and secular, are evenly balanced. This, after all, is what democracies and judiciaries are for. Deciding such cases is a matter of weighing principle and pragmatism, motivation and effect, minority rights and majority rule. But they are not that many and, for the most part, they are not that tough.

Take the decision in September 2005 of a Danish newspaper, *Jyllands-Posten*, to publish over twelve cartoons, some of which depicted the prophet Mohammed. The cartoons ran alongside an article entitled "Mohammed's Angst', which arose from an important debate within Danish society about the prevalence of self-censorship and the climate of fear over discussing and debating Islam. A few weeks earlier, another Danish paper, *Politiken*, ran a piece about how a children's writer, Kåre Bluitgen, had had trouble finding an illustrator to work with him on a book he was writing called *The Koran and the Life of the Prophet Mohammed*. Because of Islam's tradition of aniconism and opposition to idolatry, different sects of Islam have different views on the propriety of pictorial images of Mohammed. But all sects regard insulting the prophet as a grave transgression.

According to Bluitgen, two artists declined for fear of violent reprisal. This was, without doubt, a deplorable and unfortunate state of affairs. *Jyllands-Posten* took up the issue with a call for forty illustrators to do their own caricatures of Mohammed. In the end, twelve cartoons were printed. Some were witty, interesting and engaging. One has a clearly frightened cartoonist sketching in the half-light apparently for fear of being caught; another has a young Danish-Muslim boy called Mohammed writing in Persian on a black-board: "Jyllands-Posten's journalists are a bunch of reactionary pro-vocateurs." But some were at best crude and at worst deeply offensive. One showed Mohammed with a bomb in his turban; another had him greeting a group of suicide bombers with the words, "Stop, we've run out of virgins"; yet another had him with both a halo and a pair of horns.

For the paper, this was clearly not just an act of journalism. It was not an attempt to explore and resolve the tensions revealed by Bluitgen's attempt to find an illustrator for his book but a cause and a deliberate provocation. It was a crusade. The cartoons were published alongside the following editorial:

The modern, secular society is rejected by some Muslims. They demand a special position, insisting on special consideration of their own religious feelings. It is incompatible with contemporary democracy and freedom of speech, where you must be ready to put up with insults, mockery and ridicule. It is certainly not always attractive and nice to look at, and it does not mean that religious feelings should be made fun of at any price, but that is of minor importance in the present context. [. . .] we are on our way to a slippery slope where no one can tell how the self-censorship will end. That is why *Morgenavisen Jyllands-Posten* has invited members of the Danish editorial cartoonists union to draw Muhammad as they see him.

A group of Danish imams petitioned ambassadors from several Muslim countries to ask for a meeting with the Danish prime minister to talk about the cartoons in the light of the "on-going smear campaign in Danish public circles and media against Islam and Muslims," of which the cartoons were simply one aspect. The prime minister refused to meet them.

Some Muslim organizations then filed a complaint against the paper under a Danish law that "prohibits disturbing public order by publicly ridiculing or insulting the dogmas of worship of any lawfully existing religious community"—a relatively uncontentious law that few claimed was in contradiction to modern secular society. They got nowhere.

Then two Danish imams went to the Middle East to drum up support to take on the Danish government. By the new year, the cartoons were becoming an international incident. Consumer boycotts were launched throughout the Middle East, and Danish consulates were attacked and burned in Syria, Beirut and Tehran. Death threats were issued to those responsible for the cartoons.

Meanwhile, in Europe, newspapers throughout the continent, with the exception of the UK, reprinted the cartoons in solidarity with *Jyllands-Posten*. This was, we were told, not an issue of taste but freedom, in which fundamental European values were at stake.

"It is necessary to crush once again the infamous thing, as Voltaire liked to say," said an article in *France Soir*. "This religious intolerance that accepts no mockery, no satire, no ridicule. We citizens of secular and democratic societies are summoned to condemn a dozen caricatures judged offensive to Islam. Summoned by whom? By the Muslim Brotherhood, by Syria, the Islamic Jihad, the interior ministers of Arab countries, the Islamic Conferences—all paragons of tolerance, humanism and democracy."

The *Frankfurter Allgemeine Zeitung* argued that Europe should stand firm against the proposed boycott of Danish goods by the Muslim world. "There is now a need for a responsible, but also confident, display of European solidarity, and no more gestures of remorse." For the Danish journalists who published the cartoons, the clash of civilizations they referred to had become a self-fulfilling prophecy that served the interests of the Islamists who led the protests worldwide just as well as their own.

"This is a far bigger story than just the question of twelve cartoons in a small Danish newspaper," Flemming Rose, *Jyllands-Posten*'s culture editor, told *The New York Times*. Rose was right. But it was not the story he claimed it was. Rose explained that "this is about the question of integration and how compatible is the religion of Islam with a modern secular society." In fact, it was a tale of power, hypocrisy and a crippling lack of self-knowledge.

"The cartoonists treated Islam the same way they treat Christianity, Buddhism, Hinduism and other religions," Rose told the *Washington Post*. "And by treating Muslims in Denmark as equals they made a point: We are integrating you into the Danish tradition of satire because you are part of our society, not strangers. The cartoons are including, rather than excluding, Muslims." Nothing could have been further from the truth. For while cartoonists may have treated Christianity in the same way, *Jyllands-Posten* would not.

In April 2003, Danish illustrator Christoffer Zieler submitted a series of unsolicited cartoons offering a lighthearted take on the resurrection of Christ to the paper. Zieler received an email from the paper's Sunday editor, Jens Kaiser, saying: "I don't think *Jyllands-Posten*'s readers will enjoy the drawings. As a matter of fact, I think they will provoke an outcry. Therefore I will not use them."

Having refracted the whole conflict through a racial, ethnic and religious lens, what the European media misunderstood as an attack on its freedom by militant Islam was actually perfectly consistent with the continent's traditions of civic, legal and cultural engagement.

So the cartoons were meant as a provocation. And they worked. Around 139 people died in protests and riots from Nigeria to Afghanistan; all were Muslims, none were Danes or even Europeans. There were demonstrations against the cartoons throughout Europe. But what was posed as a dilemma over the limits of multiculturalism was in fact nothing of the kind. There was no doubt that some of the cartoons were offensive. Nor should there have been any doubt that the paper had the right to publish them without fear of violent reprisal. But the right to freedom of speech equates neither to an obligation to offend nor to a duty to be insensitive. If the American Civil Liberties Union advocates the right of the Ku Klux Klan to march in a particular area, that does not mean that it either supports the march itself or that it should show its support by marching with them.

If our commitment to free speech is important, our belief in anti-racism should be no less so. "I tend to think some things are off-limits," Stuart Hall argued in an interview with the *Observer* in response to questions about the cartoons. "Not in the sense that you should not be able to say them, but you need some care about how and when you go into them. If you wanted to make a joke about concentration camps, you should think twice. At least twice. Given the complexity of relations between Islam and the West, I would think at least twice about those cartoons. You cannot simply say it is my right to do it and then be surprised at the consequences. You have to take on the personal risk and decide whether it is worth the price."

The cartoons did not appear in a vacuum. They were published in a country engaging in an illegal invasion of Iraq, where the government was re-elected on an anti-immigrant agenda and where, according to the Danish Institute for Human Rights, racially motivated crimes had doubled between 2004 and 2005. They were displayed in a newspaper that was criticized in 2002 by the Danish Council of the

Press for its racist reporting in a journalistic culture that studies revealed was obsessed with pathologizing immigrants in general and Muslims in particular. In 2004, a report on Denmark by the European Network Against Racism (ENAR), an organization of NGOs funded partly by the European Commission, revealed that of 382 *Jyllands-Posten* articles on immigrants, 212 were negative—and this was consistent with the rest of the Danish newspapers.

Moreover, the right to offend must come with at least one consequent right and one subsequent responsibility. People must have the right to be offended, and those bold enough knowingly to cause offense should be bold enough to weather the consequences, so long as the aggrieved respond within the law. Muslims were in effect being vilified twice—once through the original cartoons and then again for having the gall to protest against them. Such logic recalls the words of the late South African black nationalist Steve Biko: "Not only are whites kicking us; they are telling us how to react to being kicked."

If the notion that freedom was under attack was contentious, the idea that Europe was the home of unfettered free speech and this was now being trashed by Muslim heathens was absurd. Without anything as explicit as a First Amendment, Europe's freedom of speech laws are far more piecemeal than those of the United States. Many were adopted as a result of the Holocaust—the most potent reminder of just how fragile and recent the continent's liberal secular tradition truly is. In 2005, *Le Monde* was found guilty of "racist defamation" against Israel and the Jewish people over an article entitled "Israel–Palestine: the Cancer." The appeal court concluded that the piece "targeted a whole nation, or a religious group in its quasi-globality."

Even as the debate over the cartoons raged, far-right historian David Irving sat in jail in Austria charged with Holocaust denial for a speech he had made seventeen years earlier; Islamist cleric Abu Hamza had just been convicted in London for incitement to murder and racial hatred; and Nation of Islam leader Louis Farrakhan was banned from Britain because his arrival "would not be conducive to the public good."

All these contradictions simply illustrate that the question has never been whether you draw a line under what is and what is not acceptable but who gets to draw the line (an issue of power) and where they draw it (a matter of ideology). Flemming Rose and others clearly believe that Muslims, by virtue of their particular religion, exist on the wrong side of the line. The newspapers weren't talking truth to power; they were slurring the powerless.

The idea that to publish these cartoons in Europe was a sign of bravery would be laughable were it not for the fact that real acts of bravery were taking place on this issue elsewhere. In Yemen and Jordan, editors responsible for republishing the cartoons were sent to prison for two months to a year. In Algeria, editors were arrested. Also in Algeria, and in Jordan, Yemen, Saudi Arabia and Malaysia, newspapers were suspended or shut down by the state. The only European nation where anything remotely comparable took place was Belarus—a country with no democratic traditions and a tiny Muslim population—where the editor of *Zgoda* was sentenced to three years in prison for incitement to racial hatred for republishing the cartoons and the paper was closed down.

Nonetheless, on February 15, 2006, while debate over the issue was still fairly intense, the president of the European Commission, José Manuel Barroso, voiced his support for *Jyllands-Posten*, insisting that Europe had to stand up for its core values."If not, we are accepting fear in our society," said Barroso, speaking in Strasbourg. "I understand that it offended many people in the Muslim world, but is it better to have a system where some excesses are allowed or be in some countries where they don't even have the right to say this? This reminds me of my own country [Portugal] up to 1974. I defend the democratic system."

On the same day, in the House of Commons, the British government voted to expand counter-terrorism laws by making "glorification" of terrorism a criminal offense. Speaking after the vote, then prime minister Tony Blair said the new law "will allow us to deal with those people and say: Look, we have free speech in this country, but don't abuse it."

The contradiction between what Barroso understands by freedom of speech as it relates to Europeans when talking about Muslims and what Blair means when he refers to what Muslims are allowed to say in Europe is instructive. For Europeans, there are no holds barred. Some excesses are allowed in "defense of the democratic system" because to do otherwise would be "accepting fear in our society." For Muslims, freedom of speech is contingent on its responsible usage. The "abuse" of those freedoms is not just frowned upon but criminalized. Those who indulge in it will have to be "dealt with."

Such is the nature of "integration" as European establishments understand it with regard to Muslims. It's not so much a call for dialogue as the imposition of an ultimatum. True, there are worse gauntlets. As far as it goes, integration is a great thing. The more contact you have with different kinds of people, the less potential there is for stereotyping and dehumanizing those different from yourself. The more one chooses a life that is voluntarily segregated from others and retreats into one's own community, the less scope there is to explore, discover and engage with those common human traits that transcend identity. It cannot be meaningfully mandated—you can't legislate friendship or criminalize enmity for their own sake. But it should be encouraged. I have had enough experience asking gay men about their girlfriends and wishing Jews a happy Christmas to know how crippling ignorance can be.

The trouble is, unless integration is coupled with the equally vigorous pursuit of equality and anti-discrimination, it doesn't go particularly far. Rwanda had plenty of inter-ethnic marriages and was socially mixed before the genocide; Jews were more integrated into German society than into any other European nation before the Holocaust; the former Yugoslavia was once a model of a multiethnic state before it collapsed into war and slaughter.

No process of integration can really have much moral meaning without some reckoning with where power lies and how it might be differently distributed. The American South is a good example. In 1948, when South Carolina senator Strom Thurmond broke with the Democrat Party and ran a segregationist campaign for president, he said, "All the laws of Washington and all the bayonets of the army cannot force the Negro race into our theaters, our swimming pools, our schools, our churches, our homes." It later turned out, to the amusement of many but the surprise of few, that no bayonets were needed to drive him into the bed of a black woman. Indeed, during that very period he was sleeping with black women and had a black daughter.

"It makes perfect sense," Edmund Ball, author of *Slaves in the Family*, told *The New York Times*. "The typical case is that the son of a master's family tested out his sexuality on a vulnerable young woman in the master's house. That is exactly what Strom did."

Under segregation, black women breastfed and raised white children, and since most slave owners were not that wealthy, many black and white families shared the same roof. The question was not whether the races could mix but what the ground-rules for them mixing were. These relationships were generally neither consensual nor mutual but coerced and one-sided. The whites-only signs kept African-Americans from many a public place; but in the most intimate parts of their lives, black and white people were as integrated as they possibly could be.

Little wonder then that, by the late nineties, the idea of integration had failed to garner a huge amount of affection among many African-Americans. "The issue for black people was never integration or segregation but white supremacy," says Charles Payne of the University of Chicago. "The paradigm of integration and segregation was a white concern. That was how they posed the issue of civil rights given their own interests, and that was how the entire issue then became understood. But the central concerns of black people were not whether they should integrate with white people or not, but how to challenge white people's hold on the power structure."

In other words, the value of integration is contingent on who you are asking to integrate, what you are asking them to integrate into and on what basis you are asking them to do so. If you look at who has the most trouble integrating in Western Europe, it is not Muslims but white people. A YouGov poll for the Commission for Racial Equality in 2004 showed that 83 percent of whites in Britain have no friends who are practicing Muslims, while only 48 percent of non-white people do. It revealed that 94 percent of whites, compared with

47 percent of people from ethnic minorities, say most or all their friends are white. Since 90 percent of Britain is white, this is not as outrageous as it sounds. But nonetheless, the statistics do tell a story. It is really very difficult to avoid white, Christian culture in Britain. Most people get Sunday, Easter and Christmas off; there is an established Christian Church and the overwhelming majority of people speak English. But if you are white and Christian, it is relatively easy to avoid non-white and non-Christian people and their cultures if that is what you want to do. Indeed, even if you don't want to avoid them, in some areas it would be difficult to come into contact with them. Few Christians in Britain know when Passover, Divali or Ramadan are.

And it seems there are many white people who do not want to know. A Mori poll for *Prospect* magazine in 2005 showed that 41 percent of whites, compared with 26 percent of ethnic minorities, want the races to live separately. Moreover, it is clearly not the presence of non-white people that invokes bigotry but their absence. According to an *Observer* investigation in 2005, Devon and Cornwall—two of the whitest counties in the country—recorded among the highest number of racial incidents in proportion to the size of their non-white population. The report revealed that it was the most isolated black communities in the rural areas who were most prone to racist abuse. In Switzerland, it was in the cities—Zurich, Basel and Geneva—where the populations are diverse, that people voted against the minaret ban.

Since white, Christian people are not being asked to integrate, what is being paraded as integration is not in fact an ever-renewing process of negotiation into a fluid, ambiguous and vibrant culture but a series of finite demands for assimilation into a fixed, agreed and therefore mythological heritage. "Whether I like it or not, Islam is the second biggest religion in France," said French president Nicolas Sarkozy. "So you've got to integrate it to make it more French." Mr Sarkozy obviously doesn't like it at all. More importantly, it clearly has not occurred to him that, if this relationship is going to work, France will also have to become more Islamic, just as the French made parts of Asia and West and Northern Africa become more Christian. Following a gun attack carried out by a 21-year-old Muslim, Kosovan, immigrant at Frankfurt airport in which two US servicemen were killed and another two injured, the German interior minister, Hans Peter-Friedrich, said Islam "did not belong to Germany." If that's the case then how, one wonders, would Muslims ever feel that Germany belonged to them? This is only a problem for those who believe Muslims have nothing to offer. Otherwise, it is up to them to explain why any self-respecting Muslim would want to integrate into a society that sees his or her faith as incapable of making a valuable contribution.

For the trouble is, as we know from Tralee, these "European" values are not fixed and, while they may have commanded consent, they have never enjoyed unanimity. To hear the charges laid at their feet, you would think Muslims are not only genetically homophobic, sexist, anti-Semitic, politically violent and socially disruptive, but that they invented these social ills and introduced them to an otherwise utopian space where everybody shared the same beliefs and culture.

One of the most comical examples of this took place in Germany in October 2007 when a promising young Iranian-German footballer, Ashkan Dejagah, refused to go to Israel to play for the German under-21 team in a European qualifier. Dejagah, who was born in Iran and came to Germany as a child, claimed that if he went to Israel he might be denied entry into Iran. His decision not to go sparked accusations of anti-Semitism from German Jewish groups, alongside calls from some politicians, who saw the situation as a litmus test for inclusion and integration, that he be dropped from the team. (After some deliberation, German officials decided to keep him in the squad.)

"Whoever represents Germany, whether a native German or an immigrant, has to identify with the history and culture of our society," said Ronald Pofalla, the general secretary of the conservative Christian Democrats. "If he does not want to do so out of personal political reasons, then that national jersey should be removed."

There are at least six million reasons why Dejagah would be better off not identifying with German history and culture when it comes to contemplating a visit to Israel, but two will suffice here. First, he will find a far less murderous recent history of anti-Semitism in his Iranian heritage than he will in his German. Second, as I pointed out earlier, if any nation exemplifies the limits of integration without a vigorous culture of anti-racism, it is Germany—the European nation where Jews were most assimilated and yet almost found themselves wiped out.

The point here is not that Germans are forbidden from accusing anyone else of anti-Semitism because of their nation's anti-Semitic history—no competition between Iranians and Germans to see who has hated Jews least can produce a winner worth hailing—but rather that anyone invoking Germany's history and culture as a blueprint for inclusion should do so with care and humility—particularly when talking about Jews.

Similarly, following rioting by black and French-Arab youth in France in 2007, Jacques Myard, a nationalist deputy, explained the disturbances thus: "The problem is not economic. The reality is not economic. The reality is that an anti-French ethno-cultural bias from a foreign society has taken root on French soil and it is feeding on basic anti-French racism even if the rioters have French nationality."

The French may need to import many things, from trashy popular films to fast food, but the one thing they have long produced themselves is a culture of riotous assembly. I have seen farmers hurl livestock at police, and ducked as students converted street furniture into missiles. There is nothing foreign about rioting in France—the country was built on a riot.

In Britain, the government has frowned upon arranged marriages to foreigners while somehow forgetting that arranged marriage forms the basis for many British literary classics and that, of the six British monarchs of the last century, five married foreigners and most of those unions were arranged.

All of which is to say that, for better and for worse, Europe's Muslims are far more European than many of their fellow Europeans care to admit. Given the colonial links, the prevalence of Western culture in the global arena and the power of the Western economy, this should really come as no surprise. For many, it is the only place they know. And yet, in Britain, each time a terror cell is found, the media gasp at the discovery that the bombers or potential bombers played cricket, worked in chip shops and supported Manchester

United. If Islam is responsible for making them, Britain is no less so.

Driving back to Luton station with Latif, I ask him, since he has always felt Pakistani rather than British, whether he would ever consider moving to Pakistan. "No," he says. "I don't like the culture over there, the way you have to bribe people to get things done. I'd much rather be here."

8. Lost in Translation

So long as the global means the erosion of democracy, the local will mean the elevation of identity

The urge to express one's identity, and to have it recognized tangibly by
others, is increasingly contagious and has to be recognized as
an elemental force even in the shrunken, apparently homogenizing,
high-tech world of the end of the twentieth century.

– David Hooson, *Geography and National Identity*

When the euro was introduced, the European Central Bank allowed
just one concession to national identity. Twelve countries would
voluntarily deprive themselves of their national currencies and their
control over interest rates to pool economic sovereignty on an unprecedented scale. From Athens to Lisbon and Sardinia to Helsinki,
all the notes would now be the same—but each country would get
to emboss coins with its own local insignia. So a one-cent piece, for
example, in Austria, bears a gentian (an Alpine flower), in Spain the
façade of the Cathedral of Santiago de Compostela, and in Portugal
the royal seal of 1134.

So in the Eurozone, the change in your pocket tells a story about
who moves where. Small purchases leave traces of human contact.
Research has shown that, in French border regions, people without
higher education are far more likely to have foreign euro coins than
those with a higher education; the situation is reversed in non-border
regions. The explanation? The further you move away from the
borders, the more contact with foreigners becomes the experience
of a social elite, whereas the closer you are, the more likely it is that
the circulation of coins will reflect contact between working people.

Rummage around in your pockets after a few days in Brussels and the extent to which you are in an intercontinental hub becomes clear. It took just a weekend for my wallet to fill up with change from Greece, Portugal, France, Germany, the Netherlands, Luxembourg and Italy.

This should come as no surprise. Brussels is home to more ambassadors and journalists than Washington, DC. It plays host to the European Commission, the Council of the European Union, the European Parliament (three quarters of the time) and the North Atlantic Treaty Organization. On top of that is the familiar post-war, post-colonial migration—in this instance bringing people from the Congo, Rwanda, Morocco, Tunisia—that is evident in most European cities. One in five of those who live in Brussels is not Belgian. In restaurants and hotels, people size you up as you approach to work out what language to address you in—English, German, French or Dutch—so they can give you an appropriate menu. You are less than three hours' train ride away from four capitals (Paris, The Hague, Luxembourg, London) and five countries (France, the Netherlands, Luxembourg, the United Kingdom and Germany). Both distinctly parochial (one of its main tourist attractions, the Mannekin Pis, is a small statue of a little boy urinating into a pool) and undeniably cosmopolitan, Brussels is the closest thing yet to a global village.

But the city is not just a physical place but a political signifier. Brussels means Europe—not Europe the continent but Europe the project: the plan to save the continent from another bloody war. Or, depending on how you view it, the bureaucracy that has accrued substantial political power but little popular affection. The euro was conceived here. It is not surprising that this is where the coins keep coming back to from the disparate corners of the region.

But you don't have to travel far from the cradle of this supranational citadel to discover that while a Europe without borders is well on its way to becoming a reality, a Europe without rancor is still a long way off. Just eleven minutes on the train sits the small town of Linkebeek (population 4,759). At first sight, there is not a whole lot to Linkebeek. It is sufficiently tiny that, when I asked directions to the town center, I was told that I was actually standing in it. I was the only one to get off the train there. Its quiet sloping streets and spacious driveways suggest the sedate comforts of suburbia.

Linkebeek sits in Flanders, the Flemish-speaking region of Belgium. The trouble is, 84 percent of its inhabitants are French-speaking. For its mayor, Damien Thiéry, this is a big problem. Flemish separatists attend his city meetings to monitor his language. If he speaks a single word of French, all the council's decisions from that session could be disqualified and he could be removed as mayor. He says these language monitors have become so disruptive he has taken to calling the police before each meeting.

"The Flemish say, 'You are on our territory, so you have no say,'" says Thiéry. "The Flemish politicians have become more and more intolerant . . . [But] I'm the mayor for all of the population and should be able to talk with all the population. I don't want to be responsible here in my commune for a pitched battle between demonstrators from the two camps."

What he describes sounds like a form of linguistic apartheid in which the majority in his town are discriminated against on the basis of the language they speak. Flemish authorities give €179 a year for school trips for each child that speaks Flemish (a Dutch dialect) and only €68 for French speakers. If the town wants subsidies for the town library, 75 percent of the books must be in Dutch, despite the fact that only 16 percent of the town speak Flemish as a first language.

It wasn't always like this. In 1922, Linkebeek was 70 percent Flemish-speaking. But as Brussels grew and became more expensive, commuting became easier, French speakers moved out of the capital and the linguistic complexion of towns such as Linkebeek changed dramatically. In 1947, the proportion of Flemish speakers went down to 60 percent; by 1960, they were in a minority with 45 percent. Today it is just one in six. Thiéry says he always talks Flemish with Flemish people. "I think the solution is that we must be bilingual."

He may be right. But that still may not be enough to assuage his most vociferous detractors. With the far-right Flemish nationalist party, Vlaams Belang, poised to march in Linkebeek a month after I spoke to him, he feared the worst. "I really don't see any way out. It's like a broken marriage. Where there is one person who really doesn't want to live with the other any more, there's no point in hanging on. If [the Flemish] want to leave, then they should go."

Thiéry puts all this tension down to a culture clash between Flemish and French political cultures. "The Flemish believe 'This is our territory and you have to speak Flemish.' The French character is 'Let's ask the population what they need and then find an answer.'"

Eddie de Block has quite a different interpretation of the differences between French-speaking and Flemish-speaking cultures. He is the mayor of the bigger (but nonetheless small) town of Merchtem (population 14,838), which is just fifteen miles from Linkebeek, on the other side of Brussels. "We have a very vibrant community here," he says. "Everybody works. Unemployment in this town is just 2.6 percent. That's typical Flemish. In Wallonia [the French-speaking part of Belgium] they are a bit more easygoing. They take a long time to get their work done. They get it done in the end. But it might take longer."

In many respects, Linkebeek represents the future nightmare de Block wishes to prevent—a once Flemish town overrun and transformed by French speakers. Given that French speakers constitute just 3 percent of Merchtem, this does not seem likely. Nonetheless, just to make sure, he passed a law that everybody in schools must not only learn Dutch but can only speak Dutch on the premises, including in the playground and during parent–teacher evenings. "When they go into the school they have to speak Dutch. It's not allowed to speak any other language on municipal property. If they don't like that there are other [private] schools."

At de Block's behest, the council also passed a law that all signs in the town's Wednesday-morning market had to be in Dutch. This occurred after a meat seller displayed a sign in Arabic. "We don't know what they are selling and so we said they have to write it in Dutch," explains de Block. The law was struck down for infringing freedom of speech but is nonetheless adhered to, he says.

De Block may be trying to run a monolingual town but he lives a multilingual life. As well as being mayor, he is a doctor who speaks excellent English and fluent French. Practicing in Brussels, where 80 percent of his patients are French-speaking, he treats his patients in their mother tongue. "As a doctor, I have to speak the language of my patient wherever possible."

The measures he has implemented in Merchtem, he argues, are designed to encourage not discrimination but integration. "This way when people come to stay in this community they have no problems. They can go to the sports clubs, cafés and pubs and integrate with everybody and communicate with everybody."

De Block protests too much. I spent an afternoon in Merchtem. When I went into a pub and it was clear I did not speak Dutch, a fellow drinker started chatting to me in French. When I asked directions to de Block's office in incomprehensible Dutch, another man asked me if I spoke French and then guided me quite happily and fluently. It didn't feel as if it would be difficult to integrate into Merchtem at all if you only spoke French, since most people here, like de Block himself, are bilingual. You just wouldn't be able to integrate on his terms. "People have to speak Dutch. I think that we must defend the Flemish culture. It's really necessary because the other influences are very strong."

At first sight, the presence of these local feuds erupting within commuting distance of one of the most audacious, supranational projects of the twentieth century seems paradoxical. On the one hand, there is Brussels, home to the EU, whose stated aim is to promote international comity, trade and travel, with all those coins illustrating all that multinational contact. Encircling the city are petty, rancorous regional linguistic and economic feuds within small towns. Just as traditional borders are coming down, the Flemish are seeking to throw up new ones. Polls show that between 40 percent and 50 percent of the Flemish want independence from Belgium. In 2010 The New Flemish Alliance, which supports the peaceful, gradual secession of Flanders from Belgium, became the largest party in both Flanders and Belgium. And for what? You can already travel from Belgium to the Netherlands, France, Germany and Luxembourg without a passport and without changing currency.

But the truth is that, when it comes to identity, the global and the parochial have a symbiotic relationship. The smaller the world seems and the less control we have over it, the more likely we are to retreat into the local spheres where we might have influence. Analysis of the

World Values Survey by Professor Pippa Norris of Harvard's Kennedy School reveals that, notwithstanding the explosion in both global trade and communication, the primary territorial identity that most people choose is local or regional, as opposed to national, continental or cosmopolitan. Only 2 percent identified as cosmopolitan, meaning an exclusively continental or world identity; 15 percent identified primarily with their continent; 38 percent with their nation state; while 47 percent chose their region or local area. Meanwhile, voter turnout is falling across the globe (the 2008 US election being a notable exception) and confidence in national parliaments is eroding, with majorities on every continent believing that governments do not represent the will of the people, according to a Gallup International Millennium Survey conducted in 2002.

The reason is that globalization, in the neo-liberal form that has been aggressively pursued for a generation, undermines democracy and the sovereignty of the nation state. "By many measures, corporations are more central players in global affairs than nations," writes Benjamin Barber in *Jihad vs McWorld*. "We call them multinational but they are more accurately understood as postnational, transnational or even anti-national. For they abjure the very idea of nations or any other parochialism that limits them in time or space. Their customers are not citizens of a particular nation or members of a parochial clan: they belong to the universal tribe of consumers defined by needs and wants that are ubiquitous, if not by nature then by the cunning of advertising."

The result is a dislocation between politics and power, because you don't get to vote for corporations. So people may vote for a party with a certain economic program. But if that program isn't sufficiently kind to capital, investors can move their money to a place where labor is cheaper, unions are weaker or interest rates are higher, rendering democratic demands moot when pitted against the pursuit of profit. Take Brazil. In 2002, Luiz Inácio Lula da Silva was elected president at the head of the left-wing Workers' Party on a platform of fighting poverty and redistributing wealth—the first time a Left government had been elected in the country's history. But on the way to his inauguration, the invisible hand of the market took him by the scruff of the neck and shook what was left of the socialism out of him. In the three months between his winning the vote and being sworn in, the nation's currency plummeted by 30 percent, $6 billion in hot money left the country and some agencies had given Brazil the highest debt-risk ratings in the world. Lula's initial task became not serving the needs of those who voted for him but the needs of the markets. "We are in government but not in power," said Lula's close aide, Dominican friar Frei Betto. "Power today is global power, the power of the big companies, the power of financial capital."

So we are economically interdependent as both consumers and producers, but isolated and impotent as citizens. Our ability to control our political destiny seems to be increasingly impeded as our hands are prized from the traditional democratic levers.

Never has this been clearer than during the crisis that sent the world's economy into freefall in 2008. Imagine you are a young, middle-class Hungarian couple who are trying to buy a house that year. Prices are skyrocketing because people are getting mortgages in euros (the interest rate is low in the Eurozone) rather than in the Hungarian forint (which has much higher interest rates). Given that Hungary is set to join the Eurozone soon, taking out a mortgage in euros seems like a good bet and, even if it weren't, the interest rates on a forint mortgage would be too expensive. So, like many of your fellow citizens, in a country where more than half the national debt is in a foreign currency, you buy a house quickly before the prices are so high you can never enter the market and you get a mortgage in euros.

Meanwhile, half a continent and an ocean away in Florida and beyond, a housing bubble has already burst as people who bought homes they could never afford start to foreclose. The banks that have lent them money find themselves broke and stop lending. Unable to get loans, Americans stop buying goods. German factory orders, which are more dependent on exports than most, slump nearly 40 percent, which means that Hungary's exports to Germany collapse too. Traders flee small currencies for safer ones, sending the forint tumbling as people fear that Hungary will default on its debt. When our young couple bought their house, there were 240 forints to the euro; nine months later there are almost 300. The couple's euro-based mortgage is going through the roof they can barely afford. Meanwhile, their parents have been told that their pension entitlements will be scaled down because of a deal the government had to sign with the International Monetary Fund just in order to stay afloat.

The couple, along with many others, blames the Hungarian government. The prime minister is forced to resign, but the opposition is reluctant to take over because it has no plan or ability to resolve the crisis either. They look around for someone who can rectify the situation and realize that there is no viable democratic response to the process that is ruining their lives. No Hungarian politician or party offers much by way of a solution, and they don't belong to any other entity which they could influence to make the kind of changes they need to see to protect their livelihoods. If they went to the polling booths, there would be no one they could vote for or against that could make any difference. If they took to the streets, it is difficult to work out to whom they should make their demands or at which symbolic building they should wave their placards.

Such are the democratic deficits of neo-liberal globalization. Feeling under threat from a large world whose politics and economics we are unable to control, many resort instead to the defense of "culture," the one thing people think they have a grip on. In short, they retreat into identities—often reinvented as the local, the known and, above all, the traditional—as a protective mechanism against the encroaching outside world, which is often experienced as chaotic, cosmopolitan and evolving. Quite what that identity might be— language, nation, race, region—is down to context. More often than not, such retreats are reactionary. "Minorities are the flash point for a series of uncertainties that mediate between everyday life and its fast-shifting global backdrop," writes Arjun Appadurai. "This uncertainty, exacerbated by an inability of states to secure economic sovereignty in the era of globalization, may translate into a lack of tolerance of any sort of collective stranger." (In Hungary, the economic downturn coincided with a huge spike in attacks on the Roma and support for fascism.) These people seek not to redirect change but to halt it; not to reshape a meaningful future but to revert to a mythical past.

This is by no means inevitable. There are groups, such as the

Zapatistas (which organizes the Mexican Indian poor in the state of Chiapas, Mexico) or the Narmada Bachao Andolan (which has mobilized environmentalists, ethnic groups and farmers against the Sardar Sarovar dam in India), who locate their particular struggles within the broader context of anti-globalization and seek to create common cause across continents and ethnicities. But such examples are sadly rare. More common, particularly in the West, are those who cast around not for allies with which to challenge the process but for scapegoats on whom to blame it.

But since those responsible for these insecurities are so elusive— who can get their hands on a hedge-fund manager, currency trader or EU commissioner?—people will often target those who are more visible, vulnerable and available. What masquerades as the purist protection of tradition is usually in fact a far more strategic attack against a known and accessible stand-in for the enemy that cannot be reached. "Globalization, being a force without a face, cannot be the object of ethnocide," argues Appadurai. "But minorities can."

In the US, there have long been spates of violent and some-times fatal attacks against Latino day laborers who gather at certain locations around suburbs and cities in the early morning waiting for contractors and others to pick them up. "People see day laborers and they see a proxy for illegal immigration," explains Amy Seymour, a lawyer with the Immigrant and Non-standard Worker Project. "If they have an anxiety about globalization or outsourcing and the precariousness in their working lives, they may look at day laborers and see them as embodying all the things that are making them anxious."

In other words, as the US government opens its borders to goods and services through the North American Free Trade Agreement, some Americans feel threatened in their livelihoods. Finding no way to combat that politically (both main parties supported NAFTA), they fall back on their nativist "American" ethnicity. The person responsible for outsourcing their jobs may be remote, but they can see the "other" in Latinos; they can hear it in their language; they think they can feel it in their pay packet. The fact that these Latinos may too be American is irrelevant. The day laborers act as a

convenient substitute for the real source of the economic insecurity—
the multinationals who are exporting their jobs.

In some respects, the very proximity breeds contempt. Dublin's
Croke Park, for example, is the largest sporting stadium in Ireland—a
country where sports are no neutral matter. There are Irish sports,
such as hurling and Gaelic football, and then there are sports imported
from England, such as cricket, soccer and rugby. In periods of political
tension, such differences can easily be politicized, and nowhere more
so than in Croke Park, home of the first Bloody Sunday. On November
21, 1920, British paramilitaries entered the stadium (where they were
certain to find Catholics) during a Gaelic Athletic Association (GAA)
match between Dublin and Tipperary and littered it with gunfire,
killing fourteen in retaliation for fourteen British intelligence officers
who had been killed in a terrorist attack earlier that day.

Until 1973, article 27 of the GAA's constitution stipulated that a
member could be banned from playing its games if found to be also
playing "English games." Meanwhile, article 42 prohibited GAA
facilities from being used for sports whose interests were in conflict
with those of the GAA—in other words, rugby and soccer. Given
the popularity of the Irish World Cup soccer squad in the 1990, 1994
and 2002 World Cup finals (managed each time by Englishmen),
broader Irish society had clearly long since moved on. And Croke
Park had long hosted American football matches, a sport few in
Ireland follow closely. But it was not until 2005 that the GAA voted
to relax article 42 so that Croke Park could be leased to other sporting
bodies to pave the way for the stadium to be used for international
rugby while the traditional national rugby venue of Lansdowne Road
was being refurbished. When England played Ireland at rugby there
in February 2007, grown men wept in the stands.

"In some respects, the more Irish culture has become global, the
stronger the importance of maintaining Irish difference has become,"
writes Tom Inglis in *Global Ireland*. "The greater the level of contact
with other people, the greater the need to develop a different sense
of identity and belonging."

Such apparent contradictions are not new and can produce delicious
ironies. In her autobiography, the black radical Angela Davis recalls

going into a shoe store in downtown Birmingham, Alabama, with her sister Fania and trying on the goods. It was the early sixties in the Deep South and, ordinarily, two black teenagers would have been shown to the back of the store where a black clerk would have dealt with them. But Angela and Fania pretended they were from Martinique and spoke French to each other. "At the sight of two young Black women speaking a foreign language, the clerks in the store raced to help us," writes Davis. "Their delight with the exotic was enough to completely, if temporarily, dispel their normal disdain for Black people."

But with the rise in neo-liberal globalization, such contradictions have become particularly acute. On the one hand, we all have more in common than we used to. We drink Coke, wear Nikes and eat at McDonald's, and many of those who cannot, generally speaking, would like to. Thanks to Facebook, email and Skype, we have never communicated more with more people in more places. As consumers, we have never had more in common. In India, call-center workers learn to flatten their vowels, take Western names and learn the plotlines of American sitcoms to make customers in a continent they have never visited feel more at home.

On the other hand, however, we have become fearful of the outside world and do everything we can to establish and enhance our "difference." The period when Indian call centers were taking off coincided with the rise of Hindu fundamentalism as a potent and lethal political force. "I am afraid that the celebrated cultural identities are being erased by modernization, by Americanization, by television, by a whole process of making modes of life uniform," writes Pierre Hassner in *La Violence et la paix*. "Yet at the same time, within this universality, the need to distinguish oneself is becoming stronger. People used to say that the Fifth Republic became Americanized while remaining anti-American; today we are Americanizing ourselves while at the same time inventing an exaggerated cultural identity in order to distinguish ourselves from others."

But the real issue is not America (a place) but neo-liberal capitalism (a system). The nature of the globalized threat and the localized scapegoat is a tale of democracy eroded, sovereignty diminished, insecurity inflicted and alienation enhanced. The fact that all this should be so clearly illustrated so close to a supranational center such as Brussels is no coincidence. There are few places where this tension has been clearer than during the rapid growth in size and power of the European Union and the response within national political cultures. Over half a century, the EU has gone from being a body designed to protect the continent from itself to an effort to challenge American economic hegemony. It started as the European Coal and Steel Community, a tariff-free area including just France, Germany, Italy, Belgium, the Netherlands and Luxembourg. Just over fifty years later, it is a 27-member-strong political and economic union, boasting a common currency (for most of its inhabitants), a court of human rights and a central bank.

"If one wants a shorthand explanation for the renewed momentum of European integration in the mid-1980s," argue Wolfgang Streeck and Philippe Schmitter in *From National Corporatism to Transnational Pluralism,* "one would probably account for it as the result of an alignment between two broad interests—that of large European firms struggling to be perceived to have competitive advantages in relation to Japanese and US capital and that of state elites seeking to restore at least part of the political sovereignty they had gradually lost at the national level as a result of growing international interdependence." (With its social fund to assist poor areas and its social chapter to secure basic workers' rights, European integration has at times embraced social democratic impulses also. But, by the end of the last century, the difference between social democracy and neo-liberalism on inter-national trade's effect on democracy was minimal.)

On a cultural level, some of these developments were wonderful. Having left England in 2003, I saw these transformations each time I returned as London changed from a post-colonial city to a truly global one. The presence of EU migrants, mostly from Eastern Europe, had an effect on the high streets, on soap-opera plotlines and on our culinary culture. So pervasive was the demographic shift that, after a while, I stopped assuming white people in London spoke English.

The only thing more staggering than the pace of European

integration over the past fifteen years has been the lack of account-
ability that has gone with it. Neither the president of the European
Commission nor any of the commissioners who wield most power in
the EU are elected. They are selected in rounds of horse trading by
national governments on the basis of political patronage. Indeed, the
European Parliament, the only directly elected component of the EU,
cannot initiate legislation. This explains why turnout for EU elections
has been in steep decline since their inception. For the first elections,
62 percent showed up; by 2009, numbers were down to 43 percent.
The European Central Bank, in particular, has almost completely
unfettered power. It sets its own inflation target, publishes neither the
minutes nor the voting record of its rate-setting meetings and, while
its president appears at hearings before the European Parliament, the
parliament has absolutely no power over him or her.

"What democratic control do European citizens possess?" asks Sue
Wright in *Community and Communications*. "Voting out the European
Parliament changes nothing because it has little power. Voting out
national parliaments would have a secondary effect on the EU, but
the European voters could not coordinate their action on this, and at
the present time are unlikely to censure national governments for
such a purpose. For populations able to remove their own governments when they are dissatisfied with them, this lack of control is
experienced as undemocratic." When countries within the EU vote
against measures that would require unanimity, they are usually asked
to vote again and get it right the second time around. When they
vote *for* them, there is no second chance.

So even as Europe has pooled sovereignty, broken down borders
and extinguished one of the central tropes of national identity—
currency—nationalism has been on the rise. In Belgium, Denmark,
France, Austria and Italy, hard-right nationalist and anti-immigrant
parties regularly receive more than 10 percent of the vote. In the latter
two countries, they have been in government. In France, the Front
National came second in the presidential elections of 2002. In 1993,
the election of a single councilor for the far-right British National
Party prompted outrage from the Archbishop of Canterbury and the
Metropolitan Police Commissioner; sixteen years later, the party

won two seats in the European elections. All this marks a sharp increase in the size, influence and geographical reach of nationalism since the EU became a single market. The link between the two is not direct and causal: too many other variables—from Islamophobia, terror threats and immigration prompted by the desperation of the global South—exist to claim that. But given the anti-EU platforms of the far Right and their strong presence in successful anti-EU referenda, a connection clearly exists.

The likelihood that these parties would ever seize power, let alone know what to do with it, is slim. "Xenophobia, readily shading into racism, a more general phenomenon in Europe and North America in the 1990s even than it was in the days of fascism, provides even less of an historic program than Mazzinian nationalism," argues Eric Hobsbawm in *Nations and Nationalism since 1780*. "Indeed, it rarely even pretends to be more than a cry of anguish or fury."

True enough. And yet that cry is a piercing one. It speaks of white disadvantage, regional implosions and economic insecurity. The end of post-war guarantees such as decent pensions and affordable housing, the collapse of the unions that might have defended those guarantees and the industries which made these economies viable, has all been integral to the global neo-liberal agenda. But so too has the massive movement of people from the developing world and Eastern Europe who came, either legally or illegally, seeking work. The simultaneous arrival of "others" who are unknown with the disappearance of much that is known is not difficult either to exploit or manipulate. And in the absence of a substantive response of their own, mainstream parties generally condemn the messengers and co-opt the message. Even as almost every European nation has liberated capital to roam freely around the globe, they have severely restricted immigration from outside the EU. Like arsenic in the water supply of their political cultures, the bigotry of these nationalist parties has infected most areas of domestic policy-making, from policing to the warped efforts at integration recounted earlier.

So nationalism has emerged as one of the two most powerful immovable objects against extending the powers of the EU in particular and globalization in general, positing the most reactionary expression of national identity—the ethos of the culturally and racially pure *Volk*—against the impure encroachment of cosmopolitans and foreigners and the threats they pose to an ossified sense of patriotism. The other anti-EU force, particularly during referenda, comes from the polar opposite wing of the political spectrum: Trotskyists, Communists, environmentalists and anti-globalization protesters calling for greater democracy and participation and talking in terms of democratic sovereignty. Notwithstanding their profound disagreements on almost everything, at key moments both anti-EU forces find themselves on the same side. Similarly odd bedfellows emerged in the US against NAFTA, in India against rapid export-led economic growth and in other countries over various trade deals.

"It seems clear that, despite the over-rationalized expectations favoured by the internationalist perspectives of the left, nationalism is not only not a spent force," argued Stuart Hall in "Our Mongrel Selves." "It isn't necessarily either a reactionary or a progressive force, politically." In Europe, this has contributed to three consistent trends over the last fifteen years: the rise of the far Right, the rise of the hard Left or Greens (and sometimes both), and a significant slump in voter turnout. The margins have grown, the mainstream has floundered and the whole is increasingly less than the sum of its fragmented parts. Yet it is the Right that has done a far better job at incorporating identity-based groups into its fold than the Left.

Not only is nationalism on the increase, so too is the number of "nations" seeking to be recognized. The bigger the EU becomes, the smaller the areas where a strong sense of national identity may take hold. In Europe, they are finding their most fertile soil in regions aspiring to be nation states, such as Scotland, Catalonia, the Lombardy region or Flanders, the cases for which have gained a new sense of legitimacy in recent years.

In the past, the notion that such areas could become nations was undermined by their relatively small size. "A nation restricted in the number of its population and in territory, especially if it has a separate language, can only possess a crippled literature, crippled institutions for promoting art and science," argued Friedrich List in *The National*

System of Political Economy, echoing a view common in the mid- to late nineteenth century. "A small state can never bring to complete perfection within its territory the various branches of production."

In 1843, the *Dictionnaire politique* of Garnier-Pagès deemed it "ridiculous" that Belgium or Portugal would be independent, purely on the basis of their size. But the EU has created a whole new landscape in which nation states can be understood. "The smallness of a country is much less of a problem than it was in the past," Brussels economist André Sapir told *Newsweek* in September 2007. Matters such as defense, printing your own currency and economies of scale suddenly became redundant. If sovereignty were to be pooled anyway, why not pool it in smaller units? "All the advantages of being within the nation state are either already on offer from the European Union or being developed," writes Sue Wright. "To some analysts 'a Europe of the Regions' has opened up the spectre of the redundancy of the nation state."

To others, it is merely a form of nationalism-lite, a protected space in which local impulses can act out in the knowledge that the consequences will never be too grave. "When separatist small-nation movements see their best hope in establishing themselves as sub-units of a larger politico-economic entity (in this case the European Community), they are in practice abandoning the classical aim of such movements, which is to establish independent and sovereign nation-states," claims Hobsbawm in *Nations and Nationalism*. "Or perhaps it is simply a bald recognition that the days when sovereignty held any meaning beyond the ceremonial are over and every nation-state is now in essence and in reality part of 'a larger politico-economic entity.'"

Which brings us back to Belgium. From the outset, Belgium has always been a precarious idea. The country was founded in 1830, and its vulnerability to schism was not an accident of history but a deliberate consequence of it. Britain was keen to keep the Dutch in their place and maintain a buffer between France and Prussia while ensuring that at least one Channel port did not go to either, and Belgium was created primarily at her bidding. Queen Victoria's uncle, Leopold, was put on the throne, and Britain pledged military support in case of attack. This new state contained a Dutch-speaking north (Flanders) and a French-speaking south. The vulnerability of the country to fracture provokes shrugs now, but it was Germany's invasion of Belgium in 1914 that triggered Britain's entry into the First World War.

At its inception, Belgium was dominated by the French. The constitution was drafted in French only and the new political class comprised almost exclusively the French upper classes. Gradually, over the next century, Flanders began to assert its political and linguistic rights, establishing Dutch in schools, extending its use to courts and gaining a Flemish university in Ghent.

But what has grown into a linguistic rift was actually born in economic imbalance. Thanks primarily to the textile, steel and coal industries, Wallonia was, for a long time, Belgium's economic powerhouse. With the decline of heavy industry, the collapse of agriculture and the rise of information technology, the fortunes of the two regions reversed. The demise of Wallonia was far more precipitous than the advances in Flanders. In 1917, Belgium was the second wealthiest nation in the world per capita and Wallonia was the wealthiest part of it. By 2002, Wallonia was the fifty-sixth wealthiest region in Europe. On its way down during the sixties, Wallonia passed Flanders edging up. In 1952, productivity in Wallonia was 15 percent higher than in Flanders; by 2002, it was 35 percent lower. At 10 percent, unemployment in Wallonia is twice that of Flanders. As de Block made clear, the Flemish regard themselves as having a very strong work ethic when compared to the more laid-back Walloons.

"I don't mind that we subsidize them," he says, insisting that the issue is Wallonia's profligate ways, not their language. "We send money to Ethiopia and the Congo so why shouldn't we send money to Wallonia? But they should properly account for it." Wallonia, then, to de Block, is comparable to Ethiopia and the Congo, only closer. Much, much closer.

With greater parity between Wallonia and Flanders came the demand from an increasingly assertive Flemish nationalist movement for greater autonomy. The outcome has been a cumbersome, porous and inherently unstable edifice on which the entire state has teetered. Belgium has one federal parliament, three regional parliaments (there is a small German-speaking community too), and three community parliaments, which are based entirely around language, as opposed to territory. And then there is Brussels, which is its own thing: an overwhelmingly French-speaking city which happens to be bang in the middle of Flanders. It has its own administrative area, known as BHV (Brussels-Halle-Vilvoorde). (The latter two are Flemish towns on the outskirts of the capital.)

The upshot of all this is that, as a lived experience, Belgium barely exists at all. Political parties, trade unions, television stations, environmental groups, universities and boy-scout groups—to mention just a handful—are all divided on linguistic grounds, so the institutions one can truly describe as Belgian are few and far between: there is the monarchy (which is constitutional), the soccer team, the army (which has not fought a war under its own flag for decades), the diplomatic service and the national courts. "Now there's a new generation on each side, and they don't know each other," Pierre Vercauteren, a political scientist at the Catholic University of Mons, told the *Washington Post*. "It has complicated negotiations because they don't have a common knowledge and can't reach a compromise."

"Many people, if not most people, never think about their language at all and never attach any emotional significance to it," avers Paul Brass in *Elite Competition and Nation Formation*. "Many illiterate rural persons, far from being attached emotionally to their mother tongue, do not even know its proper name."

It is precisely this unconscious attachment, however, that can make language such a potent force. For many nationalists, it marks the essential starting point for their patriotic appeal: the claim to a natural, instinctive common characteristic. "Those who speak the same language are joined to each other by a multitude of invisible bonds by nature herself, long before any human art begins," wrote German philosopher Johann Fichte in his 1806 *Address to the German Nation*. "They understand each other, and have the power of continuing to make themselves understood more and more clearly; they belong together and are by nature one and an inseparable whole."

Limping into the twenty-first century, some still make this case. "At the core of the [Québécois] personality is the fact that we speak French," said René Lévesque, the founder of Parti Québécois, which supports independence from Canada. "Everything else depends on this one essential element and follows from it or leads us infallibly back to it."

Yet as Belgium (and indeed Quebec) illustrate, the fact that language has found itself on the frontline of national and international disputes suggests that what we speak and why is no accident, but the product of power struggles for economic, political and cultural supremacy or resistance. The Soweto uprising in South Africa was sparked by the insistence of the apartheid regime that Afrikaans, the language of the Boer white minority, had to be used for mathematics, arithmetic and social studies from the second year in black secondary schools. Desmond Tutu branded Afrikaans "the language of the oppressor."

In Estonia, language rights were not a result of the country's battle for independence from the Soviet Union but the precursor to and harbinger of it. Under Soviet rule Estonians were forced to speak Russian. As the campaign to secede from the USSR gathered force, the Republic passed a swathe of language laws making Estonian the state language and demanding that official and sales personnel be able to use it within four years. The popular support these measures received and the inability of the USSR to counter them signaled the beginning of the end of Soviet domination in the Republic. During the Second World War, German-Americans were arrested for speaking German. Before the arrival there of Christopher Columbus, more than 300 languages were spoken in North America; today there are only around 175, 90 percent of which are effectively moribund. "Between a half and two thirds of the world's population is bilingual to some degree," says the Council of Europe Language Policy Division. "And a significant number are plurilingual. Plurilingualism is much more the normal human condition than monolingualism."

"National languages are . . . almost always semi-artificial constructs and occasionally . . . virtually invented," writes Hobsbawm in *Nations and Nationalism*. "They are the opposite of what nationalist mythology supposes them to be, namely the primordial foundations of national culture and the matrices of the national mind. They are usually attempts to devise a standardized idiom out of a multiplicity of actually spoken idioms, which are thereafter downgraded to dialects, the main problem in their construction being usually which dialect to choose as the base of the standardizing and homogenized language."

The best example of this is Hebrew, which by the end of the eighteenth century had been reduced to a classical language, a religious tongue reserved for liturgies and the synagogue; it was almost never spoken socially. Reviving it was regarded as crucial to the Zionist project that created the state of Israel. "Once a collectivity living on a particular territory speaks a specific language," argued Eliezer Ben-Yehuda, one of the central architects of the Hebrew revival, in Medina Yehudit, "this collectivity constitutes a people of its own and the land on which they have established themselves becomes the nation-state of this people."

And so Hebrew was resurrected from a written language to a spoken one with the specific purpose of helping to create a country. Yehuda sought to make Hebrew a language used by "both important and less important people, women and children, young men and women, in the realm of all subjects of daily life, at any hour of day or night, all as all nations do, each in their own language." It was a mother tongue that children literally taught their mothers.

"It is always a mistake to treat languages in the way that certain nationalist ideologues treat them—as emblems of nation-ness, like flags, costumes, folk-dances, and the rest," writes Benedict Anderson in *Imagined Communities*. "Much the most important thing about language is its capacity for generating imagined communities, building in effect particular solidarities."

In few places has this been truer than the US and Europe, where language has been used as a proxy for national belonging and, in recent times, to culturally police new immigrants. Since the early eighties, more than thirty American states have made English the official language, including six of the ten states where people are least likely to speak English at home.

Meanwhile, in Europe, several countries, including England, have introduced language tests for new immigrants, on the basis that full citizenship rights cannot be exercised without a certain level of linguistic competence. The issue here is not whether speaking the language of the majority where you live is a good idea. It is difficult to play a full role in a society if most people living in it cannot understand you and you cannot understand them.

But it does not follow that language is necessarily the primary obstacle to participation in that society, or that mastering a language will facilitate such a role. If it did, then people of European descent in Africa who do not speak local languages—which is most of them— would be economically and politically marginalized. But they are not, because in the continent they once colonized and where they still control many resources, Europeans are sufficiently powerful that local people are forced to speak their language.

So the introduction of language tests has less to do with participation than it does with social control. In response to rioting by those primarily of Pakistani descent in Britain's northern towns in 2001, the then British home secretary David Blunkett called for citizenship tests and language lessons to force the integration of these communities. There were many problems with this, but the most obvious was that most of the people that took to the streets were English-speaking people who were already citizens. They were, for the most part, young men who had been born in England. The root of their discontent was arguably economic, racial and religious in nature, but whatever else it was, it was not linguistic. It was their parents, who stayed at home, who were less likely to speak English.

The push to tie language to citizenship and inclusion has become almost unstoppable in most of Europe. As neo-liberal globalization forced millions in the south to seek a livelihood through economic migration in the north, European countries in particular sought to insist on certain cultural qualifications. "Language is our cultural identity and the basis of our mental existence," Christian Democratic legislator Anette Hübinger said in defense of a resolution to "anchor" the German language into the national constitution. "Consequently, learning and mastering a national language is the key to successful and sustainable integration." According to a Harris poll in 2007, 86 percent of Germans, 83 percent of Britons, 61 percent of French and Italians and 50 percent of Spaniards believe that citizenship and language tests are necessary for new immigrants.

This is particularly ironic given how loose a historical attachment there is between many of these nations and their own "national" languages. The notion that a British monarch would speak English as their native tongue, if indeed at all, is a relatively recent one, and the barons responsible for the Magna Carta, who are today hailed as among the first patriots, did not speak English. Hobsbawm estimates that only 2.5 percent of Italians spoke the national language at the time of unification. "We have made Italy. Now we must make Italians," said Massimo d'Azeglio at the first meeting of the newly united Italy's infant parliament. At the time of the French Revolution, half of France didn't speak French and only 12–13 percent spoke it correctly. A national survey of 486 French primary-school teachers revealed that, as recently as the interwar years, a local language was still spoken in the region where 85 percent of the respondents lived, and that almost one instructor in two spoke that local language fluently. In Spain, the issue is far from resolved. The official language is Castilian, but roughly a quarter of the country also speaks one of the three main co-official regional languages: Catalan, Basque or Galician.

In the Basque country, defense of the local language has been central to a nationalist agenda that has, at times, become violent. In 2008, the authorities on the Balearic island of Majorca planned to set up a "language police" to impose the local Catalan language in restaurants. In August of that year, a group of high-powered Spaniards, including a soccer player, an opera diva, authors and philosophers, wrote a manifesto for a common language, claiming that, "In the last few years, there are more and more reasons to be concerned in our country about the institutional situation of the Castilian language."

Wary of the political implications of such a sensitive matter,

Spanish prime minister José Zapatero said, "The Spain which exists as we know it for hundreds and hundreds of years is one which speaks in one language and in several." But which, one wonders, should the immigrants embrace? While half of Spaniards believe language tests should be used for new immigrants, a significant number cannot agree on which language they themselves should be speaking.

"The nineteenth century in Europe marked a historical turning point in the construction of modern nationalism," write Tony Judt and Denis Lacorne in "The Politics of Language" in *Language, Nation and State*. "No one any longer said 'The nation exists because it has a language,' but rather 'The nation exists, therefore it must be given a language.'"

In this regard, Belgium differs from most other European nations only to the extent that it has waited far longer to resolve this dialectic and finds its crisis more acute. So, on the one hand, the nation's unraveling is clearly no joke. The small town of Liedekerke decreed that all town business and education must take place in Flemish, with children who cannot speak the language being banned from school trips such as hikes or swimming classes. In another Flemish town, Vilvoorde, Flemish-speaking families were given priority in social housing. Meanwhile, Miss Belgium was heckled at her coronation when she proved unable to answer questions in Flemish as well as English.

A poll by the private Field Research Institute released in September 2007 showed that 66 percent of the inhabitants of Flanders believe Belgium will be split up "sooner or later," while 46 percent support a split. Another poll in September showed 39 percent of the Flemish supporting independence against just 12 percent of the Walloons. A year later, another poll showed that the majority of Walloons wanted to secede from Belgium and join France. There was serious talk of creating a corridor linking the mostly French-speaking Brussels to the rest of Wallonia in the same way that West Berlin had been connected to the rest of West Germany before the Wall came down.

Yet, on the other hand, it was difficult to take it all seriously. In December 2007, a French-language station, RTBF, broadcast a mock break-up of the country. The two-hour report had crowds of Flemish nationalists waving flags and cheering as French speakers prepared to leave the country. Panicked viewers called the station, prompting the prime minister's office to berate the program makers for being irresponsible and tasteless. "Our intention was to show Belgian viewers the intensity of the issue and the real possibility of Belgium no longer being a country," Yves Thiran, the head of news programming, said at the time. By then, there had been no government for five months as a result of the language crisis.

Yves Leterme, the Flemish prime minister whose nationalist rhetoric had, in no small part, contributed to the most recent crisis, is himself the son of a Walloon. A third of the supporters of Wallonia's main soccer team, Standard Liège, are Flemish. The town-hall decrees which attracted so much press attention owed more to positioning and posturing than to actual policy. I could not find any French speakers who had been directly affected by them beyond being made to feel uncomfortable. The presence or absence of a government did not seem to panic Belgians on either side of the linguistic divide unduly.

With a per capita income of more than $40,000, Belgium has one of the wealthiest populations in the world, with some of the best-educated children. The German paper *Die Tageszeitung* described it as the "most successful 'failed state' of all time." A Flemish journalist put the nation up for auction on eBay, offering "a kingdom in three parts." The purchaser would have to shoulder "300 billion euros in debt," he pointed out. The item was pulled off the site—but not before someone had offered $13.9 million for it.

In any case, the notion that French posed the biggest threat to Flemish is absurd. The fact is that new technologies, economies of scale and globalization will soon render such strictly local linguistic feuds if not obsolete then as having no more symbolic value than the British determination to keep Gibraltar or the Moldovan debate about the use of Cyrillic or Latin script. Those who are seriously interested in preserving Dutch as opposed to bashing the French have far bigger fish to fry.

The primary threat to a language such as Dutch, which has fewer native speakers than the population of Texas, is the commodification of new technology. "We are presently witnessing a massive transfer of all the world cultures to numerical support systems," argues Quebec-based academic Jean-Claude Guédon, "to the point where in twenty or thirty years at most, anything that has not been coded as 0 or 1 will be completely marginalized to the point of being forgotten, as are medieval manuscripts, which in our time are the unique domain of a few learned specialists." It cost the Basque regional government an immense amount of money to get Microsoft to produce Windows and Office in the Basque language. Iceland had to fight with Microsoft over the same thing. "The danger for minority languages—and for all small languages—is to be excluded from a select circle of languages, for which it is commercially viable to develop systems of voice recognition or of translation by computer," claims Ned Thomas, editor of *Contact*, the bulletin of the European Bureau for Lesser-used Languages.

While French is one of those languages and may be geographically the closest it is neither the biggest nor the best poised to undermine Dutch. In 2007, the top ten most popular films in Belgium were as follows:

1. *Pirates of the Caribbean: At World's End*
2. *Harry Potter and the Order of the Phoenix*
3. *Ratatouille*
4. *Shrek the Third*
5. *Spider-Man 3*
6. *The Simpsons Movie*
7. *I Am Legend*
8. *The Golden Compass*
9. *Night at the Museum*
10. *Live Free or Die Hard*

The most popular local film, *Ben X* (which was in Dutch), came in nineteenth, grossing less than *Alvin and the Chipmunks* and *Mr. Bean's Holiday*. I speak fluent French, but a local journalist I spoke to suggested I make calls to local mayors in English to avoid hostility. I put it to Mr de Block that, while he was busy trying to thwart the spread of French, English was actually dominating everything. He did not disagree. "But we like the English," he said with a smile. "We consider them our allies." French-speaking Belgians, on the other hand, are simply his fellow citizens.

Under such circumstances, the difference between protecting a language because of chauvinism and making a stand against cultural extinction is a fine but crucial one. The issue rests firstly with the circumstances of its impending doom. Is it perishing from "natural" causes or is it being willfully slaughtered? Of the Welsh language, the Revd Henry Griffiths of the Dissenting College, Brecknock, once said, "Let it die fairly, peacefully and reputably. Attached to it as we are, few would wish to postpone its euthanasy. But no sacrifice would be deemed too great to prevent its being murdered."

Secondly, it depends on the nature of the defense. Protecting English, French, Spanish or German against non-native-speaking immigrants is less about defending language than excluding others, because none of those languages is seriously under threat from Bengali, Arabic, Turkish or Basque.

Back in Merchtem, Mr de Block was showing his lenient side. "Of course, if an immigrant from Congo or Ethiopia comes into the town hall and speaks in English or French, I take them aside and explain to them in English or French that they have to speak Dutch and tell them where they can go to learn. For the first time, that's okay. But then they have to make an effort on their own. We're in Flanders. On municipal property you must speak Dutch." De Block tells me this in his office, in the town hall . . . in English. When I point this out to him, he shrugs.

Keeping the Wolf from the Door

For it is not true that the work of man is done
That there is nothing more for us to do in the world
That we leech off the world
That we should be content to be brought to heel by the world
For the work of man is only just beginning
And it falls to man to conquer every latent restraint entrenched in the recess of his passion
And no race has a monopoly on beauty, on intelligence and on strength
And there is room for us all at the rendezvous of history.

— Aimé Césaire, *Cahier d'un retour au pays natal* (translation author's own)

The thing we forget about the story of the boy who cried wolf is that, when all is said and done, there is actually a wolf. So when people claim an impending or existing clash of civilizations, there is, of course, always a chance they may be right.

When it comes to identity, there is always a wolf lurking somewhere. There has never been a time in human history when someone hasn't been trying to rally one group against another on the basis of their differences.

That's not the fault of difference itself. The problem is not that diversity exists, it is what we choose to make of it. In short, do we understand our various identities as being an integral part of our common humanity or as something separate, above and beyond it?

The other thing often forgotten about that fable is that the villagers' instinct is to band together and protect the boy and his flock—and they don't stop immediately they discover he is lying but keep trying. There has also never been a time in human history when some have not defied attempts to divide them on the basis of their difference and have not instead united to defend or expand human rights. All too often, those people have been all too few. But that simply makes their achievements all the more impressive. Challenges such as combating climate change—which could literally sink all our constructs and take us with them—make the task of first recognizing our commonalities and then mobilizing them for the common good all the more urgent.

If you look at the broad trajectory of equality and human rights, then women, gays, black people, religious and national minorities and the disabled—the majority of humanity—are all doing better than they were a century ago. Feminism, anti-racism, gay rights and national liberation have been among the most liberating forces of recent times, and their work is not yet done—it is no wonder that reactionaries attack their legacy. "The arc of history is long, but it bends towards justice," insisted Martin Luther King in a speech in 1967. But it doesn't bend of its own accord and the curve is anything but smooth. If you look at the atrocities of the last hundred years— the genocides, famines, expulsions, violence (domestic and social)— we have barely emerged from the Dark Ages. People are right to be wary when identity instills itself front and center in politics.

There are no straightforward answers and few basic, universal truths as to when the politics of identity may be elevated to great and worthy purpose and why it may descend into venal, vile bigotry. This is not the stuff of broad brushes.

But there are some general principles. First and foremost, this is not simply about understanding people better. It's all very well creating dialogue, but when people come to the table they have to have something to talk about. Identities are about how we think about ourselves in relation to others. But those thoughts do not come out of a clear blue sky. Identities are rooted in material circumstances. In certain circumstances, whether you are British, black, gay, Iraqi, Hindu or female can be the difference between life and death, poverty and wealth, citizenship and statelessness. Power, resources and opportunity are in play in how we choose to understand (or misunderstand) the value of ourselves and others.

It is difficult to talk seriously about our common humanity when large sections of the planet live in sub-human conditions. With almost half the world's population living on less than $2 a day, in the West, issues such as immigration, trade, foreign policy, asylum, aid and development become questions of whether you think a large proportion of the South is worthy of clean drinking water, basic education, health care and basic human rights and what should happen if they come to your door looking for them.

There is nothing necessarily altruistic in this. It is poverty, despair, destitution and exclusion that provide the breeding ground for some of the most intense and reactionary identity politics. The hungrier people are, the more likely they are to rally around whatever agenda they think may get them food. These are the foot soldiers of nationalism, religious zealotry and ethnic conflict; not people who want a greater share of the pie, just people who need to eat something, anything, and who are not even getting the crumbs.

Eradicating these imbalances is as much in the interests of the West as in those of the global South, not to mention the increasing pockets of relative desperation that live within the West. Through inequities in trade abroad and iniquities of social policy at home, we are creating a local and international underclass with little or no stake in a system that has little or no interest in them. "The socially excluded are exiles from the industrial age," says Geoff Mulgan, co-founder of the think tank Demos, "people who can't swim with the tide of globalization."

It is these people whom, through our immigration legislation and enhanced security networks, we seek to contain, and, through our criminal justice system and foreign policies, we seek to police. From gated communities, we move inexorably to gated countries and continents. Our prisons are full, our borders fortified, our embassies armed, and global summits take place behind cordons of riot police. It is the private affluence and public squalor of the eighties gone global.

Such a state of affairs does not rectify itself through good will and respectful exchange about identity and difference. Humanism must be fought for, not least because there are so many vested interests in fighting against it. "If there is no struggle, there is no progress," said the African-American abolitionist Frederick Douglass. "Those who profess to favor freedom and yet depreciate agitation are men who want crops without ploughing up the ground; they want rain without thunder and lightning. They want the ocean without the awful roar of its many waters . . . Power concedes nothing without a demand. It never did and it never will." The issue is how we make that progress come about, what concessions we are after and what methods of struggle are employed.

It is in the resolution of these strategic questions that greater understanding and constructive dialogue are of great use. How we talk about these things demands sensitivity. This works both ways. Insensitivity never achieved much. Baiting, ridiculing and humiliating are poor substitutes for satire, irony and humor, although they often masquerade as such. When these are employed by the powerful against the powerless, it is not clever but cowardly. Freedom of speech is an important right and value, but it coexists with other values which are no less important.

However, oversensitivity never achieved much either. Not every nuance, challenge, wordplay or display of ignorance is a slight; not every slight is worthy of being escalated into an incident; not every provocation need be indulged. Just because someone claims victimhood does not mean they have to be believed or that they cannot also be a perpetrator of victimization. We all have a duty to help create the "safe spaces" for people to both engage in self-criticism and accept criticism from others. But we have no less a duty to engage in an honest and open manner that makes such difficult discussions possible.

"Our worst side has been so shamelessly emphasized that we are denying that we ever had a worst side," wrote African-American intellectual W. E. B. Du Bois. "In all sorts of ways, we are being hemmed in."

The more democracy there is, the greater is the chance that such discussions will actually lead somewhere. And by democracy I mean not just voting and holding elections—even the most crude dictator has got the hang of that by now—but an actual connection between citizens and their institutions whereby ordinary people can influence and change the world around them.

This would not eliminate even the most vile expressions of divisiveness, but it would give people the opportunity to organize meaningfully to further their interests and make the alliances necessary to defend and expand common ground. This does not guarantee progressive outcomes, particularly for minorities. But it does ensure the ability to mobilize public opinion towards better outcomes.

However, with the frame we have been using for the past century or so—the nation state—barely viable as a democratic entity, the scope for engagement has become more limited. In the absence of any true control over their own lives, people cling to identity as to a life raft—desperately, instinctively, driven by the impulse to save self, kith and kin rather than with regard or respect for the whole. Life rafts are useful, particularly in emergencies, but they will never be as good as a functioning boat.

It is precisely in these moments that those who would like to deny the complexity, fluidity and multilayered nature of identity thrive, by flattening out the landscape into "us and them." In times of crisis, there is little opportunity for nuance or reflection. People don't talk, they scream. And nobody really listens.

That is why it is precisely in these moments that solidarity is most crucial. For when the gentile condemns anti-Semitism, the white challenges racism or the citizen takes on xenophobia, they lift the sense of siege on "the other," creating possibilities for the Jew, black or foreigner to denounce the dupe and the demagogue in their own community.

Identity is not seeking a role in politics. It is already there. Nor is it seeking a role in our lives. It is there too. For better, for worse and usually for both, it is an integral part of how we relate to people as individuals and as groups. The choice is whether we want to succumb to its perils amidst moral panic and division or leverage its potential through solidarity in search of common, and higher, ground.

Bibliography

Adhikari, Mohamed, *Not White Enough, Not Black Enough, Racial Identity in the South African Colored Community*, Ohio University Press, 2005

Aernoudt, Rudy, *Wallonie Flandre, Je t'aime moi non plus*, Roularta, 2006

Anderson, Benedict, *Imagined Communities, Reflections on the Origin and Spread of Nationalism*, Verso, 2006

Appadurai, Arjun, *Fear of Small Numbers, An Essay on the Geography of Anger*, Duke University Press, 2006

Appiah, Kwame Anthony, *The Ethics of Identity*, Princeton University Press, 2007

Arendt, Hannah, *Eichmann and the Holocaust*, Penguin, 2005

Barber, Benjamin R., *Jihad vs McWorld, Terrorism's Challenge to Democracy*, Ballantine, 2001

Bayart, Jean-François, *The Illusion of Cultural Identity*, C. Hurst & Co., 2005

Berger, John and Mohr, Jean, *A Seventh Man, Migrant Workers in Europe*, Viking, 1975

Branford, Sue and Kucinski, Bernardo, *Lula and the Workers Party in Brazil*, The New Press, 2003

Brock, David, *Blinded by the Right, The Conscience of an Ex-Conservative*, Three Rivers Press, 2002

Broyard, Bliss, *One Drop, My Father's Hidden Life—A Story of Race and Family Secrets*, Little, Brown, 2007

Bruni, Frank, *Ambling into History, The Unlikely Odyssey of George W. Bush*, HarperCollins, 2003

Buruma, Ian, *Murder in Amsterdam, Liberal Europe, Islam and the Limits of Tolerance*, Penguin, 2006

Cable, Daniel and Judge, Timothy, "The Effect of Physical Height on Workplace Success and Income. Preliminary Test of a Theoretical

Mode," *Journal of Applied Psychology*, 2004, vol. 89

Carr, E. H., *What is History? The George Macaulay Trevelyan Lectures*, Penguin, 1990

Castells, Manuel, *The Power of Identity*, Blackwell Publishing, 2004

Connolly, Linda, *The Irish Women's Movement, From Revolution to Devolution*, The Lilliput Press, 2003

Cooper, Carolyn, *Sound Clash, Jamaican Dancehall Culture at Large*, Palgrave Macmillan, 2004

Council on Black Internal Affairs, *The American Directory of Certified Uncle Toms, Being a Review of the History, Antics and Attitudes of Handkerchief Heads, Aunt Jemimas, Head Negroes in Charge, and House Negroes Against the Freedom Aims of the Black Race*, 1st Millennial Edition, CBIA & DFS Publishing 2002.

Davis, Angela Y., *Angela Davis, An Autobiography*, Random House, 1974

Doyle, Roddy, *The Deportees and Other Stories*, Jonathan Cape, 2007
—*The Commitments*, Minerva, 1991

Engels, Friedrich, *Socialism: Utopian and Scientific*, Foreign Languages Press, Peking, 1975

Erasmus, Zimitri (ed.), *Colored by History, Shaped by Place, New Perspectives on Colored Identities in Cape Town*, Kwela Books, 2001

Fanning, Bryan (ed.), *Immigration and Social Change in the Republic of Ireland*, Manchester University Press, 2007

Fitzmaurice, John, *The Politics of Belgium, A Unique Federalism*, Hurst and Co., 1996

Garde, Paul, "Unity and Plurality in the Serbo-Croation Linguistic Sphere" in Judt, Tony and Lacorne, Denis (eds.), *Language, Nation and State*, Palgrave Macmillan, 2004

Giddings, Paula, *When and Where I Enter, The Impact of Black Women on Race and Sex in America*, Bantam Books, 1988

Gitlin, Todd, *The Twilight of Common Dreams, Why America is Wracked by Culture Wars*, Owl Books, 1996

Gross, Ariela J., *What Blood Won't Tell, A History of Race on Trial in America*, Harvard University Press, 2008

Hatzfeld, Jean, *A Time for Machetes, The Rwandan Genocide: The Killers Speak*, Picador, 2006

—*Into the Quick of Life, The Rwandan Genocide: The Survivors Speak*, Transatlantic Publications, 2005

Hobsbawm, Eric, *Nations and Nationalism since 1780, Programme, Myth, Reality*, Cambridge University Press, 1992

Hobsbawm, Eric and Ranger, Terence (eds.), *The Invention of Tradition*, Cambridge University Press, 2008

Inglis, Tom, *Global Ireland, Same Difference*, Taylor & Francis, 2008

—*Ireland*, University College Dublin Press, 1998

—*Moral Monopoly, The Rise and Fall of the Catholic Church in Modern Ireland*, Gill & Macmillan Ltd, 1987

Johnson, Eric A. and Reuband, Karl-Heinz, *What We Knew, Terror, Mass Murder and Everyday Life in Nazi Germany, An Oral History*, Basic Books, 2006

Judt, Tony, *Postwar, A History of Europe since 1945*, Penguin, 2005

Judt, Tony and Lacorne, Denis (eds.) *Language, Nation and State, Identity Politics in a Multilingual Age*, Palgrave Macmillan, 2004

Keohane, Kieran and Kuhling, Carmen, *Collision Culture, Transformations in Everyday Life in Ireland*, The Liffey Press, 2005

Levy, Andrea, *Small Island*, Headline Review, 2004

Macey, David, *Frantz Fanon, A Life*, Granta, 2000

MacIntyre, Alasdair, *After Virtue*, Duckworth, 2007

Mamdani, Mahmood, *When Victims Become Killers, Colonialism, Nativism and Genocide in Rwanda*, Princeton University Press, 2002

Marx, K., *The Eighteenth Brumaire of Louis Bonaparte*, Foreign Language Press, Peking, 1978

McCourt, Frank, *Angela's Ashes, A Memoir of a Childhood*, Flamingo, 1997

McWilliams, David, *The Pope's Children, Ireland's New Elite*, Gill and Macmillan, 2006

Morrison, Susan, *Thirty Ways of Looking at Hillary, Reflections by Women Writers*, Harper, 2008

O'Connell, Michael, *Changed Utterly, Ireland and the New Irish Psyche*, The Liffey Press, 2001

O'Toole, Fintan, *After the Ball*, New Island, 2003

Scott, Joan Wallach, *The Politics of the Veil*, Princeton University Press, 2007

Sen, Amartya, *Identity and Violence, The Illusion of Destiny*, W. W. Norton & Co., 2006

Shatz, Adam (ed.), *Prophets Outcast, A Century of Dissident Jewish Writing about Zionism and Israel*, with an Introduction by Adam Shatz, Nation Books, 2004

Sheehan, Cindy, *Not One More Mother's Child*, Koa Books, 2005

Stone, Judith, *When She Was White, The True Story of a Family Divided by Race*, Miramax Books, 2007

Tomasky, Michael, *Left For Dead, The Life, Death and Possible Resurrection of Progressive Politics in America*, The Free Press, 1996

Wilson, John K., *The Myth of Political Correctness, The Conservative Attack on Higher Education*, Duke University Press, 1998

Wright, Sue, *Community and Communication, The Role of Language in Nation State Building and European Integration*, Multilingual Matters, 2000

Acknowledgments

There are too many friends and colleagues whose conversations and insights have helped me write this book to mention them all. I'm fortunate enough to know a lot of wise people, and they are smart enough to know who they are.

But there are some to whom I owe particular gratitude for the help they gave me with this book. First and foremost, I'd like to thank Mary Mount, who's as great an editor as any writer could hope for and who has been both encouraging and engaged from the outset. The same is true for Colin Robinson, who supported the project and continued to give all the support I needed and wanted even after he had moved on to pastures new. Jonny Geller, my agent, has had my back throughout. And Sara Abbas, who did the lion's share of the research, was both tireless and timely in her pursuit of the facts I sought. Those who say you should never work with friends haven't met these people. Sarah Day also did a forensic job of copyediting.

Others were a great source of knowledge, advice and support at crucial moments, making the most valuable contributions: Alain Franco, Andrea D'Cruz, Arun Kundnani, Ben Carrington, Bénédicte Ledent, Erich Dietrich, Fintan O'Toole, Glynnis Crook, Jonathan Freedland, Laura McEnaney and Mary Gilmartin.

Institutionally, I am indebted to the *Guardian*, which funded much of the reporting that has ultimately ended up in this book. Intellectually, I am grateful to the work of Eric Hobsbawm, Stuart Hall, Paula Giddings, Benjamin Barber, Tom Inglis and Gershom Gorenberg, whose research and analysis—both specific and general—provided a foundation for many parts of this book.

Finally, I must thank Tara and Osceola, who arrived halfway through this endeavor, for their patience and understanding.

Index

Gary Younge is a *Guardian* columnist and feature writer based in the US. In 2009 he was awarded the James Cameron prize for journalism for his reporting of the 2008 US presidential election. His books include *Stranger in a Strange Land: Encounters in the Disunited States* and *No Place Like Home*, shortlisted for the Guardian First Book Award. He lives with his family in New York City.